OCCASIONAL PAPERS
OF
T. R. MALTHUS

OCCASIONAL PAPERS

OF

T. R. MALTHUS

ON IRELAND, POPULATION, AND POLITICAL ECONOMY

from Contemporary Journals,
written anonymously and hitherto uncollected

Edited and with an Introductory Essay

by

BERNARD SEMMEL

Burt Franklin Essays in History & Social Science #1.

BURT FRANKLIN, *Publisher*
New York (25), 1963

Published by Burt Franklin
514 West 113 Street
NYC (25)

First published:
New York 1963

Printed in U.S.A.

330.153 M299p

c - 1

TABLE OF CONTENTS

(continued)

PART I

INTRODUCTORY ESSAY
MALTHUS
and the Reviews

MALTHUS AND THE REVIEWS

By Bernard Semmel

I. The new science of political economy and the *Edinburgh Review*. II. The relations between T. R. Malthus and the *Edinburgh*: Orthodoxy vs. Heresy. III. Malthus' articles for the *Edinburgh*; their relation to the emergent classicism. IV. The *Quarterly Review* and political economy; Malthus' articles for the *Quarterly*. V. Concluding Remarks: Mill and Empson on Malthus.

The articles in this volume—both by and about Malthus —although well-known to contemporaries, have, probably because of their publication in periodical journals, been largely forgotten today, though certain among them are landmarks in the history of social and economic thought. It was John Maynard Keynes, the great advocate of Malthus in our day, who, in a well-known essay, regretted "the almost total obliteration of Malthus' line of approach and the complete domination of Ricardo's for a period of a hundred years" as "a disaster to the progress of economics." [1] Today, there are many who would agree. This volume brings together seven hitherto inaccessible essays, originally published anonymously, which T. R. Malthus prepared for the *Edinburgh Review* and for the *Quarterly Review* between 1808 and 1824, essays of substantial interest to those concerned with the development of the ideas of one of the great thinkers of our times. In addition, the present collection incorporates

---

[1] J. M. Keynes, "Robert Malthus," in *Essays in Biography* (London: Macmillan, 1933), pp. 140f.

3

an article concerning Malthus and his doctrine by William Empson, Malthus' colleague at Haileybury, written for the *Edinburgh Review,* in 1837, and a slashing critique of Malthusian economics which John Stuart Mill prepared for the Benthamite *Westminster Review,* in 1825. In this essay, we hope to describe Malthus' relations with the leading reviews of the time, his role in some of the controversies of of the day, and the meaning of the papers in this volume for the evolution of Malthusian doctrine and of economic science generally.

I.

The French physiocrats, and the Scottish philosopher Adam Smith, inspired by the works of a notable group of English, French and Italian predecessors and contemporaries, sought in Newton's Nature the solution to economic problems, just as contemporary political scientists, philosophers, and theologians had attempted to find Nature's way in their special spheres. Not too surprisingly, they discovered that the natural laws of economics could be embodied in an abstract, deductive system—for was not Newton's God a geometer?—whose axioms and propositions led to a final and inescapable conclusion. The disappointments of the French revolution were to spur the nineteenth century to reject most of the products of the enlightenment—deism, the social contract, rationalism, natural rights—but not the science of political economy, whose grand conclusion—laissez-faire and Free Trade, general government non-intervention in economic life—seemed most appropriate for the needs of the new century.

During the last decades of the eighteenth century and the first few decades of the nineteenth, the writings of the political economists—even the more difficult writings of the physiocrats —were widely read throughout Europe and America. The great popularizer of the new economic school was the Glasgow professor, Adam Smith, whose *Wealth of Nations* proceeded through dozens of translations and editions. In cultivated circles, nearly everyone read and discussed the new

4

economics, and the literature of the first half of the nineteenth century—Peacock's *Crotchet Castle* or Dickens' *Hard Times* are instances—is replete with references to the subject. In faraway Russia—a mirror for Western fashion—Pushkin, as early as 1833, presented a Eugene Onegin to whom Latin was "not worth attention," and whom "Theocritus and Homer bored," but

> If true delight you would afford him
> You'd give him Adam Smith to read.
> A deep economist, indeed . . .
> This subject filled his conversations.

Not only Smith, but Pushkin also related that "some lady may find matter, / In Say and Bentham for her chatter." Nowhere, of course, did political economy find itself so much at home as in England, the home of Smith and Bentham, and of Malthus, Ricardo, and the Mills, and also of the new industrialism which was transforming politics and society, and which, inevitably, provided a stimulus for the development of economic science, and for its growing acceptance by large sections of the public. Indeed, in the houses of parliament, just as the common law and the Bible had formed the staples of reference and quotation in the debates of the seventeenth century, and the classics in the eighteenth, so were the political economists the authorities to which the members of the British legislative referred with great frequency during the first two-thirds of the nineteenth century.

Yet the writings of the leading English economists were frequently lengthy, and made for hard going at times, and it would be difficult to account for the widespread—and frequently detailed—knowledge of the doctrines of political economy by so many members of all classes of the public, if the original works were the sole means for the dissemination of economic doctrine. The first half of the nineteenth century saw many talented popularizers—Mrs. Marcet and Harriet Martineau were perhaps the best known of these—who endeavored to make the conclusions of political economy

5

known to the lower middle and working-classes. But it was the great *Reviews* which brought the ideas of the economists to the professional men, merchants, factory-owners, and country-gentlemen—the most influential part of the "public." The first and the greatest of these quarterlies was the *Edinburgh Review*, founded in 1802, and, from the beginning a leading proponent of the views of the political economists. (The *Quarterly Review*, founded under Tory auspices in 1809, was, as we shall see, at first openly hostile to the doctrines of political economy, but subsequently relented.) The *Edinburgh* reviewed works in all fields—in theology, literature, history, science, and economics—for a public which came to rely upon it to be kept informed upon the thinking of the day. The gentleman of the time with even a pretense to cultivation maintained a file of the *Edinburgh* in his library, and the first volumes of the *Review* had to be reprinted to fill the shelves of those who had happened to miss early numbers. By 1814, over 12,000 copies of the *Edinburgh Review* were published each quarter-year, and the editors maintained that each copy was probably seen by three or four readers.

Although the *Review* took, like Bacon, all knowledge for its province, it stressed the importance of the new political economy, and devoted much of its space to the subject. Fetter has called it, "for its day and generation, a 'Reader's Digest' of economic literature." [2] This is not surprising given the presence of the economist Francis Horner among the talented group of Scotsmen who founded the journal. In the early days of the *Review,* the economic articles of Horner were joined by those of another brilliant Scotsman, Henry Brougham, whose impressive work on the economics of colonies was published in 1803. Both Horner and Brougham —as well as two other founders of the review, Sydney Smith and Francis Jeffrey—had attended lectures on political economy given at Edinburgh University by Adam Smith's disciple and biographer, Dugald Stewart. All were influenced by Stewart—especially Horner and Jeffrey, who also turned his

[2] F. W. Fetter, "The Authorship of Economic Articles in the *Edinburgh Review*, 1802-47," in *Journal of Political Economy*, June 1953, Vol. LXI, No. 3, p. 234.

hand, on occasion, to economic articles. Clive, a recent historian of these young journalists, has suggested that "the *Edinburgh* reviewers, banished to a desert island with only a proverbial favourite volume, would undoubtedly have chosen *The Wealth of Nations,* certainly in preference to either Testament."[3] This is not far of the mark as testimony to the faith of the reviewers in a political economy still in a fairly rudimentary stage of development, and which had only begun to understand itself.

II.

Thomas Robert Malthus was born in 1766, near Guildford, Surrey, the son of Daniel Malthus, a correspondent of Voltaire and an executor of Rousseau. Young Malthus' education was begun by his father in the pattern of Rousseau's *Emile,* but was continued under more conventional auspices by the noted Gilbert Wakefield, and at Jesus College, Cambridge, from which Malthus emerged with a variety of honors, including that of ninth wrangler in the mathematical tripos of 1788, and a fellowship at Jesus in 1793. In 1798, he took orders as a clergyman of the Church of England, and was curate at Albury, Surrey, for a period. In 1798, as well, there appeared Malthus' *Essay on Population,* proclaiming that the increase of population was outrunning the resources for food production, a tract which was to become the most widely read economic work of the time, always excepting Adam Smith, and was to proceed through several editions. Up until the publication of Ricardo's *Principles* in 1817, Malthus held the field as England's foremost living political economist. In 1805, he was appointed to the chair of political economy—the only existing one at the time— at Haileybury, the East India Company's college, where future officials of the Company were trained before assuming duties in India. He remained at Haileybury until his death in 1834.

[3] John Clive, *Scottish Reviewers* (Cambridge, Mass.: Harvard University Press, 1957), p. 127.

The *Edinburgh Review*, from its earliest numbers, supported the Malthusian principle of population, and, in the years immediately following, readily accepted Malthus' other opinions upon economic subjects. It was Horner who had recruited Malthus for the *Edinburgh*, much to Jeffrey's pleasure, and, from their correspondence, it appears clear that both men regarded Malthus highly.[4] That Malthus wrote several articles for the *Review* and was written of, in most favorable terms, by it, appears surprising today, since the *Edinburgh* is thought of as the fount of the Ricardian orthodoxy against which Malthus and his disciples were to fight a losing struggle. The earlier cordial relations between Malthus and the *Edinburgh Review*, which reveal a good deal concerning the development of classical economics, during a crucial period, have not received sufficient attention.

Malthus' opinions remained substantially the same both before and after 1815; it was those of the *Review* which had altered, or to be more exact, the climate of opinion in which the *Review* operated had decisively changed. Why had the *Review* permitted its pages to be turned, after 1815, from a defense of almost all of Malthus' views to McCulloch's open attacks upon them?

Before 1815, the advocates of the new science were not excessively concerned about differences of opinion within the circle of the disciples of political economy. Indeed, the foremost English economists espoused an eclectic doctrine, which can be said to have been made up of good parts of mercantilism and physiocracy, as well as elements of what might be called the "emergent classicism." Economic doctrines with a clear agricultural bias, akin in many respects to those of the earlier physiocracy, were prominent in the writings of such economists of the day as Dugald Stewart, the mentor of the *Edinburgh*'s editors, the Earl of Lauderdale, and Malthus. There had been two major strands in the thinking of Adam Smith, as is well known, one of which reveals Smith

---

[4] See especially Jeffrey's letter to Malthus, April 21, 1809, in Lord Cockburn, *Life of Lord Jeffrey* (Philadelphia, 1852), II, p. 104; also Leonard Horner, ed., *Memoirs and Correspondence of Francis Horner, M. P.* (Boston, 1853), I, pp. 446, 464-65.

as having at least one foot in the physiocratic camp. (When in 1808, the physiocrat William Spence presented his case, he referred again and again to Smith for support.) [5] Malthus and Dugald Stewart regarded themselves as disciples of Adam Smith, and yet supported one aspect or another of physiocratic doctrine without feeling disloyal to their master.[6] This is not to suggest that these economists were physiocrats. Their views, rather, represented a transitional stage in the history of economic thought. Physiocracy, believing land the only source of wealth, was, at heart, a landlord's creed. Upon its tenets, it was possible to question, for example, the value of foreign trade, upon which the commercial classes counted so much—and both Malthus and Dugald Stewart did so—and, indeed, to question the value of a commercial system, generally, which exposed a nation to dependence upon food imports and to crises caused by gluts. A more sanguine view of foreign trade as genuinely productive, a more optimistic view of the commercial system—as evidenced by their adoption of Say's Law—typified the postures of the opponents of the landed interest and supporters of commerce and the new manufacturing—men like Ricardo, Torrens, Mill, and McCulloch, who were hammering out the principles of what was to become the new orthodoxy.

It was during the course of the Napoleonic wars, that English manufacturing and commerce took an extraordinary leap forward, as a result of the virtual monopoly which war

[5] William Spence, "Britain Independent of Commerce" 1908, in *Tracts on Political Economy* (London, 1822), p. 37; also "Agriculture, The Source of the Wealth of Britain" (1808), in *Ibid.*, pp. 103-105, 175-178, and *passim*.

[6] The close ties between Malthus and physiocracy were noted in the last century by the editors of the French translations of his works: see P. and G. Prévost's notes to Malthus' *Essai sur le principe de population* (Paris, 1845), edited by Rossi and Comte, I, pp. 644, 646; also Monjean's edition of Malthus'*Principes d'économie politique* (Paris, 1846), pp. 33 f.n., 526 f.n., 416 f.n. It was understood by James Bonar, *Malthus and His Work* (New York: Macmillan, 1924), p. 248; and, more recently, it has been discussed by R. L. Meek, "Physiocracy and the Early Theories of Under-Consumption," *Economica*, August 1951, XVIII, No. 71, pp. 250-251. The first two editions of the *Essay on Population* provide especially strong evidence.

had given to them. It was the impact of this new development which spurred the prospering commercial interests to
challenge, in 1815, the supporters of agricultural protection
and to oppose the corn laws. Ricardo and Torrens were two
leaders of this cause. Malthus spoke in favor of agricultural
protection. The underlying theoretical issue was whether
high corn prices would result in abundance and high real
wages, as the physiocrats had maintained—and Malthus and
Dugald Stewart had agreed upon this point nearly fifteen
years earlier—or whether low corn prices would be preferable,
as Adam Smith, Ricardo, and other opponents of agricultural protection insisted. Here again, the issue was between
landed capital, on the one hand, and commercial and manufacturing capital on the other.

Before the debate upon the corn laws, in 1814-15, the
division of opinion between the economists who based their
views upon the different streams of thought in the *Wealth
of Nations* was sharp, but academic. No significant issue of
public policy hung in the balance.. The *Edinburgh Review*
saw no harm in publishing the special views of Malthus
whose practical political implications—a support, for example, of protection for agriculture—were yet to be sharply
drawn. At this time, Malthus' position as both a Whig and an
economist seemed sufficient *bona fides* for the *Edinburgh*.
There was no thought, as there was to be later, of excommuni-
cation of heretics who departed from one jot or tittle of the
law. We have noted that both Jeffrey and Horner regarded
themselves as disciples of Dugald Stewart—they employed the
newly acquired influence of the *Review*, in 1807, to acquire an
attractive government sinecure for him; Sydney Smith, and
Brougham had also sat at Stewart's feet.[7] Stewart, as noted, had
written rather favorably of the physiocrats and shared many
of the preconceptions of Spence, Chalmers, and Malthus[8]

[7] For Jeffrey and Stewart, see Cockburn, *Jeffrey*, I, p. 97.
[8] See Sir William Hamilton, ed., *The Collected Works of Dugald
Stewart* (Edinburgh, 1855), VIII, pp. 11, 201ff, 252, 255ff, 272f, 284, 289,
306; Stewart's approval of Malthus special notions, VIII, 205ff, and IX,
114-115 (where Stewart prefers Malthus over Smith on the issue of a
bounty on the exportation of corn), 118-20 and *passim*.

and, to a lesser degree, so did Horner.[9] The lines of economic thinking had not as yet hardened; the avenues of argument were still open. There was certainly nothing to prevent an advanced Whig journal like the *Edinburgh*—and we must remember that the Whigs were a landowning party—from looking with favor upon economists who assigned a great and even an overriding importance to the landed interest. It was only after 1815, after the controversy over the corn laws, that sharply defined rival camps were formed and unalterable dogma set. It was only then that the smallest diversion from the canons of what was becoming a Ricardian 'orthodoxy' appeared a sign of deep heresy which had to be extirpated. The acceptance of McCulloch's guardianship over the economic pages of the *Edinburgh* was a mark of the reluctant acquiescence of the review in the new Ricardian dispensation, the gospel of the commercial classes; and McCulloch proved an able scourge of those who hankered after the gods of bygone days.

The time of decision for the *Edinburgh Review* came with the publication of Malthus' defense of the corn laws in 1815. Jeffrey and Horner—the prime determiners of the policy of the *Review*—were divided on the issue. In a letter to Malthus, on May 12, 1814, Jeffrey declared that Malthus was "very much of my way of thinking on the subject," but that "Horner is much more Smithish." [10] In a letter to Murray, on January 30, 1815, Horner declared, with some annoyance, that "the most important convert"—though this is hardly the right term—"the landholders have got, is Malthus," adding that "there is not a better or more informed judgment, and it is the single authority which staggers me." [11] Horner's opinions were not always so. Only six years previously, he had commented upon "a new speculation" of Malthus' "about the importance of the people being fed dear," which "has the look of a paradox," but, he added, "I have not yet detected the fallacy, if there is one"; and even in 1815, Horner

---

[9] For Horner's attraction to physiocratic views, see *Memoirs*, I, pp. 100f, 119, 204f, and II, p. 238.

[10] Cockburn, *Jeffrey*, II, p. 120.

[11] Horner, *Memoirs*, I, p. 434, II, pp. 226-227, 222.

11

felt obliged to write Malthus to "treat me still as one of whose conversion from heresy some hopes may be entertained." However, such hopes were indeed slight as party and class controversy increasingly shaped the direction of economic argument, and Horner, clearly sympathetic to the outlook of the commercial classes, added, in this letter to Malthus, a denunciation of the "audacious and presumptuous spirit of regulating, by the wisdom of country squires." The *Edinburgh,* in 1815, published an article critical of Malthus's views on the corn laws in just this spirit—it did "not think that the great mass of the community should be taxed for the benefit or relief of the landed proprietors"—[12] as Jeffrey, relying upon Horner's superior judgment in economic matters, set aside his own preferences for Malthus and those sympathies for the landed interest which he had imbibed from Dugald Stewart.

Another Scotsman, J. R. McCulloch, must be brought into our story. It was McCulloch, who, from about 1817 to 1837 was the leading economic reviewer for the *Edinburgh,* wielding, for over a score of years, through the pages of that journal, a crushing authority in economic matters. In 1818, in a eulogistic review of Ricardo's *Principles,* McCulloch acknowledged the English stockbroker as his master, and employed the rest of his life to advancing Ricardian principles and stamping out the embers of opposition. Malthus had terribly offended McCulloch's vision of the economic verities by opposing Say's Law which held that since goods exchange for goods, all goods produced represent a demand as well as a supply, and that therefore general overproduction, glut, was impossible. Malthus, along with the French economist Sismondi, stressed that gluts were possible, and held, indeed, that the workings of a commercial system made them relatively frequent. In a letter to Ricardo on April 2, 1821, McCulloch referred to "the poisonous nostrums, for they can be called nothing else, of Messrs. Sismondi and Malthus." Nor was this the only of Malthus' opinions which disturbed McCulloch and Ricardo. There was, for example,

[12] "Malthus on Corn Laws," *Edinburgh Review,* February 1815, Vol. XXIV, No. XLVIII, Article XIII, pp. 491-505.

Malthus' refusal to acknowledge foreign trade as a prime producer of national wealth, his support for high corn prices, and other marks of sympathy for the landowning-class and of suspicion of the commercial classes; finally there were Malthus' special views on rent and taxation. Such divergences from Ricardian doctrine led McCulloch to declare that "I consider Mr. Malthus reputation as an Economist to be very much overrated," and to suggest elsewhere, in a letter to Ricardo, that Malthus "deserves to be very roughly handled." Malthus, for his part, recognized McCulloch's enmity. In a letter to Sismondi, dated March 12, 1821, Malthus wrote that because of McCulloch's recent entrenchment as the *Edinburgh*'s economic writer, "the Edinburgh Review has so entirely adopted Mr. Ricardo's system of Political Economy that it is probable neither you nor I shall be mentioned in it."

Although the *Review* was converted by McCulloch into an organ of Ricardian orthodoxy—indeed, what helped to make Ricardianism "orthodox" was the dominance of McCulloch over the pages of the highly influential *Edinburgh Review*—its editor, Jeffrey, persisted in his earlier friendliness to Malthus personally. McCulloch expostulated with annoyance that were Malthus not "a particular friend of Jeffrey's, who would most likely oppose his veto, I should attempt to reduce him [Malthus] to his just magnitude." [13] McCulloch wrote this in 1819, after having been denied by Jeffrey the opportunity to review Malthus' *Principles of Political Economy*. The fierce hostility which McCulloch felt for Malthus was climaxed, in the view of one historian of economic thought, by his entirely ceasing to write for the *Edinburgh* when that quarterly published a laudatory view of Malthus' life and work three years after his death.[14]

Malthus was driven from the pages of the *Edinburgh*—he made a brief reappearance in 1821 in defense of his unexceptionable principle of population—and was compelled

[13] These letters are to be found in Piero Sraffa, ed., *The Works and Correspondence of David Ricardo* (Cambridge University Press, 1952), Vol. VIII, pp. 366, 139, 167, 376, 139.

[14] Fetter, "Authorship of Economic Articles."

to turn to the Tory *Quarterly Review* which, recognizing his value to the landowner's cause, dropped its previous opposition to him and his views. In this way, then, in 1815, the *Edinburgh Review* prepared itself to take on the role of Defender of the Orthodox with McCulloch as its intrument.

III.

Malthus' *Edinburgh* articles have not been published in any collection of economic writings, and, although frequently referred to in the debates of the time, are relatively unknown today. Although of unequal value and importance, they all possess aspects of considerable interest in tracing the intellectual development of one of the great economists of the nineteenth century.

During the first two decades of the life of the *Edinburgh Review*, Malthus contributed five articles, rather certainly; there has been some speculation concerning two others, which, however, we hope to show, were probably written by other hands. All five of these articles are being reprinted in the present volume. During this period, there appeared three articles about Malthus and his ideas, and a fourth, biographical and eulogistic—this last is also included in this collection—three years after his death.

The articles of the *Edinburgh Review* were anonymous. There is considerable evidence for the assigning of the five articles noted above to Malthus, but we need not present it in any detail, for both Copinger, in his sometimes inaccurate listing,[16] and Fetter in his splendid article upon the authors of economic articles in the *Review,* are in agreement upon these five. In the case of two others, authorities have been in some disagreement. In January 1808, an article on Spence's tract on foreign trade appeared, and Fetter attributes this to "T. R. Malthus (probably)," basing his opinion upon a reference in a letter from Horner to Jeffrey, which, however, Fetter grants might well refer

[16] W. A. Copinger, "On the Authorship of the First Hundred Numbers of the *Edinburgh Review*" (Manchester, 1895).

14

to the Malthus article of July 1808. It seems to be more probable that Malthus did not write the January article. Many of the views of Spence were too congenial to Malthus to have received such a full-scale drubbing from him; indeed, in Spence's reply to the *Review*'s article, Spence actually turned to Malthus, quoting at length from his writings, for support against the *Review*.[17] Who, then, again "probably," wrote the article? A subsequent article on Spence was the work of Jeffrey, and, of course, he emerges as a possibility. However, this second article on Spence's views does not reveal the economic sophistication of the first, and Jeffrey, although he tried his hand at economic articles, was rather a novice in such matters. The January 1808 article is *probably* the work of Brougham, who reviewed frequently for the *Edinburgh* during this period, and had previously been employed in the writing of polemical reviews—as in the case of his article on Lauderdale in 1804.[18] It was written in Brougham's style—the style of the Lauderdale review; certain forms of thought and terminology—on such questions as colonies (it quotes from Brougham's *Inquiry* on this subject) , Say's law (an issue upon which Spence and Malthus agreed) ,[19] the "middle doctrine" of Smith,[20] and so on—resemble Brougham not Malthus.

The second article about which there is some question is the "Disquisition on Population," which appeared in 1810. Bonar, Malthus' biographer, suggested that Malthus himself had "possibly" written the article, but Fetter has turned this suggestion aside on grounds that the article speaks much too well of Malthus to have been written by him. However, aside from a reference to "the excellent work of Mr. Malthus," and to "this celebrated work," expressions which can be excused as a means of preserving anonymity, this presentation of the principle of population, occasioned by the

[17] Spence, "Agriculture the Source" in *Tracts*, pp. 129-133, and *passim*.
[18] [Brougham], "Lord Lauderdale on Public Wealth," *Edinburgh Review*, Vol. IV, No. VIII, pp. 343-377.
[19] See "Spence on Commerce," pp. 430, 434, 440ff.
[20] See, for example, H. Brougham, *An Inquiry into the Colonial Policy of the European Powers* (Edinburgh, 1803), I, p. 7.

15

writings of certain objectors, is rather matter-of-fact, with no excess praise. Nor was Malthus incapable of presenting his special views as if the presentation stemmed from another—witness his writing of the review of "Godwin on Malthus," in 1821. Still, the article does not have the ring of an author defending himself against the attack of a critic, but rather that of a journalist attempting to "digest" the principle of population for the *Edinburgh*'s readers. In no wise does it bear Malthus' special stamp, and its vagueness and little errors at several points—for instance in accounting for the eighteenth century anticipations of population theory —further indicate another author. Certainly the article on population which we know Malthus to have written for the *Review* in 1821 is entirely different in style. So Fetter is probably right in rejecting Bonar's suggestion, but he himself has offered no alternative. For many reasons, it seems quite likely that Jeffrey wrote this review. The Jeffrey-Horner correspondence was for some years full of nagging requests by Jeffrey that Horner prepare an article presenting Malthus's views to the *Edinburgh*'s audience. Despite the review's acceptance of Malthus' views upon population, the principle itself had not been fully and analytically described in its pages. Horner was reluctant to do this, and so was Jeffrey, perhaps because, being journalists, they felt it difficult to deal with a subject which had already received so much attention over so many years. Finally, Jeffrey in a letter to Horner, April 2, 1809, after over five years of vainly attempting to interest Horner in the subject, asked him for "notes or ideas," determining finally to write the article himself:

> If I am to think of reviewing Malthus myself, could you give me any notes or ideas? It is a pang to my heart to quit this hold upon you, but it is idle I fear to hope for anything better, perhaps even for this;—God mend you! [21]

[21] Horner, *Memoirs,* I, p. 488. For Bonar's contention, see James Bonar, *Malthus and His Work* (New York: Macmillan, 1924), p. 33 f.n.

16

The following year, as noted, the "disquisition" finally appeared.

Now to Malthus' articles themselves. First to appear were the two articles upon the Irish question. Malthus, somewhat surprisingly, did not, to any extent, discuss Ireland in the successive editions of his *Essay on Population,* which lends these articles heightened interest. Ireland had been for some time a grave problem, and the distress of great masses of Irishmen had produced rebellion in the 1790's and was a particular cause of concern for Englishmen engaged in a struggle with Napoleon. It was hoped that the Union of Ireland with Great Britain, consummated in 1801, would alleviate many of Ireland's problems, but this hope proved largely vain. In the first of his articles, Malthus considered the rapidly increasing Irish population—which he regarded as the key to Ireland's difficulties. His analysis of Irish conditions was an amalgam of Whiggish prejudice, the dogmatism of the new political economy, and a genuine desire to be of service to the depressed Irish multitudes. Indeed, at many points, Malthus adopted positions far in advance of his time. The Irish population multiplied so rapidly, Malthus maintained, because of the use of potatoes —so much cheaper to raise than grain crops—as the food staple. This also was the cause of the high rents which burdened the Irish tenantry, to the advantage of absentee English landlords. Because of "the small portion of land and capital necessary, upon the potato system, to support the labour employed in cultivation," the "large portion of the gross produce . . . consequently falls to the share of the landlord." The Irish cotter, as a result, had sufficient potatoes to support a large family, while he was compelled to wear rags and live in a hovel. Rents, furthermore, were very high. If there were more land available—i.e., if the population were not so great, the demand for land not so intense—the situation would be better. Rents, for one thing, would be lower.

But under the conditions which prevailed, no "man of common sense" could suggest, as some persons did, Malthus declared, that parliament act to relieve the Irish tenantry

17

from exorbitant rents. This would be "to prevent that natural rise of pecuniary rents, which takes place from the principles of free competition in the progress of wealth and population." There were only two ways out of the dilemma: a limit to the expansion of population would be reached when the Irish cotters command over potatoes appreciably declined; or the Irish peasantry could be educated to higher expectations which would result in his voluntarily limiting his numbers: "Such an elevation in the character and condition of the lower classes of society, as will make them look forward to other comforts beside the mere support of their families upon potatoes." There were actions that the parliament, Malthus asserted, could profitably take: a useful move would be to do away with the "political degradation" of Irish Catholics by granting the franchise to Catholics and by eliminating other repressive features of the Catholic Code. With Catholic 'emancipation' —and a call for this was rather extraordinary from the pen of a clergyman of the Established Church—would come the revival of self-respect which would lead Irishmen to insist upon higher living standards.

In his second article, the following year, Malthus called for the end of restrictive legislation which subordinated Irish commercial enterprise to English. Furthermore, in the manner of the new political economy, he chastized Newenham (whose books upon Ireland were the occasion for both of Malthus' articles) for being "much too fond of public grants and bounties" and for not clearly perceiving "the duty of government, which is to stand by and see fair play, and not to be actively assisting—first one party, and then another." (It is interesting to note, as Collison Black has told us, that later political economists were—contrary to the policy they advocated in England—to urge government intervention in Ireland on matters such as these, even on such questions as the regulation of rents).[22] Newenham was most particularly taken to task for recommending that bounties be given for the production of corn—Malthus seem-

[22] R. D. Collison Black, *Economic Thought and the Irish Question, 1817-1870* (Cambridge University Press, 1960).

18

ingly forgetting that he had made a similar proposal on behalf of English agriculture! (Indeed, we find Malthus opposing Newenham's desire to "propose encouragements to the exportation of corn, with high prices and profits for their ultimate object, instead of plenty," as "a gross abuse even of the system of bounties"). Malthus objected to the taxes upon the tenants of land in Ireland, and suggested, instead, one upon "the very great proportion of the whole produce possessed by the Irish landlord," assuring the landlord that "the sacrifice" was only "temporary,—as it is universally acknowledged, that all taxes upon the tenants fall upon the landlord at the renewal of a lease." Malthus insisted, however, that he was no advocate for "the territorial tax" of the physiocrats. (In the 1880's Henry George was to electrify all of Ireland by proposals similar to this.) England needed Ireland, Malthus concluded, and might obtain complete independence of foreign corn supplies through the development of Irish agriculture.

One of the most important economic questions of the day was whether the suspension of specie payment by the Bank of England in 1797 had resulted in the depreciation of bank notes. The bullionists declared it had—since a premium was given for bullion in exchange—and a Bullion Committee, which met in 1810-11 under the chairmanship of Francis Horner, issued a report embodying this conclusion. The anti-bullionist party insisted that there had been no depreciation, and this was the position of the Tory government, in defense of its policy of war-finance, and of the directors of the Bank of England. One of the leading bullionists was the stockbroker David Ricardo, then but a fledgling in the field of economic controversy, and it was to him that the *Edinburgh Review* turned for an article reviewing the pamphlet literature upon the subject. Ricardo preferred, however, to set down his conclusions in another form, and the *Edinburgh* turned to Malthus, who agreed to supply a review. In fact, he supplied two—one in February and one in August 1811—in which he carefully and closely argued the bullionist position, that is, the comparatively moderate position of the report of the Horner committee.

Indeed, we know that Horner was consulted by Malthus in the composition of his first article.

The articles mark the beginning of the personal relationship between Malthus and Ricardo, and of the controversy between the two. Two of Ricardo's pamphlets, and four other works, were discussed in Malthus' February review, and Malthus' manner of treating Ricardo's writings makes it clear that he was cognizant of the qualities of the young stockbroker. Although he agreed with Ricardo's basic position and paid tribute to his "clearness and precision," Malthus found "great fault" in "the partial view he takes of the causes which operate upon the course of Exchange." The next several pages of the review contain evidence of the two different modes of economic thinking personified by the two men, foreshadowing a divergence which would become sharper and clearer in the years that followed. Specifically, Malthus objected to Ricardo's attribution of "a favourable or unfavourable exchange *exclusively* to a redundant or deficient currency," thus overlooking the effects produced by the balance of trade between two countries. Ricardo, Malthus continued, was unable to appreciate that a country whose goods England might wish to import in an increased supply—say, corn at a time of a bad English harvest—might not be ready to receive payment in the form of a proportionally increased consumption of English "muslins, hardware, and colonial produce." (Ricardo, indeed, had gone so far as to deny that "any unwillingness should exist in the foreign country to receive our goods in exchange for their corn," adding that "if such an unwillingness were to exist," there was no reason why England should "agree to indulge it so far, as to part with our coin.") Such a situation, Malthus declared, had not, contrary to Ricardo, any necessary connection with the question of a redundant currency, although depreciation might increase foreign demand somewhat by lowering prices. Malthus agreed that "it is unquestionably true, as stated by Mr. Ricardo, that no nation will pay a debt in the precious metals, if it can do it cheaper by commodities; but the prices of commodities are liable to great depressions from a glut in the market."

20

On the question of the "efflux and influx of bullion," Malthus found that Ricardo made no provision for many causes. For example: "The wants of different nations with different climates, and different degrees of fertility, cannot, with any degree of probability, be supposed, in the first instances, *exactly* to balance each other." Although, Malthus agreed, that such a balance would probably, in time, come about, there were immediate imbalances, making necessary transfers of bullion. Malthus stressed that this error was Ricardo's alone, and not that of the Bullion Committee. In all this we can see anticipations of future discussions betwen Malthus and Ricardo on short-term and long-term effects, the issue of protection to agriculture, and, of course, Say's Law. Malthus consulted Ricardo in the writing of his August article, and this is free of cavilling at the latter; indeed Ricardo is praised on its last page.

The last article which Malthus wrote for the *Edinburgh* was a reply to Godwin's renewal of his attack upon the Malthusian principle of population. Malthus disposed of Godwin with a vigor almost unbecoming under the circumstances of an anonymous review.[23] Godwin's book was set down as "the poorest and most old-womanish performance that has fallen from the pen of any writer of name, since we first commenced our critical career." This was the last encounter between two old antagonists, for it had been largely in reply to Godwin that the *Essay on Population* had originally been written, and the tone, as we see, was frequently venomous. Malthus wrote of Godwin's "enfeebled judgment," and of his manner of treating the subject as "utterly disgraceful to any writer of character and ability." Malthus then proceeded, most ably, to demonstrate the fallacies in the statistical inferences and general reasoning of Godwin's work. "We did not think that such an instance

[23] Ricardo wrote to Trower, October 4, 1821: "I have not heard who the writer is but have no doubt that it was written by Malthus himself." Ricardo to Malthus, Sept. 18, 1821, indicated belief that Malthus was author, and Malthus replied, October 9, 1821: "I am glad you approve of Review in the Edinburgh. If you have discovered the author, don't betray the secret." See Sraffa, *Works of Ricardo*, IX.

of false reasoning could have occurred in the nineteenth century." What had especially disturbed Malthus was what he regarded as Godwin's "wilful misrepresentation" of his views. Instead of noting Malthus' insistence upon "moral restraint"—"a temporary or final abstinence from marriage on prudential considerations, with strict chastity during the single state"—Godwin had stressed that, in Malthus' view, the great preventitive check to population growth was a high rate of infant mortality as a result of vice and misery. Furthermore, Godwin had stated that, in line with the above, Malthus was an advocate of low wages. Malthus, terribly disturbed at such misrepresentation, declared: "Now, if there be one point more than another which Mr. Malthus has laboured in all his works, even to tiresome repetition, it is to show the labouring classes how they may raise their wages effectively and permanently, and become more independent or rich." Godwin's "whole work," Malthus continued, "is founded on the grand misrepresentation of asserting, that the misery and vice which Mr. Malthus has stated to be the *consequences* of an excessive population, have been proposed by him as its *remedies,* and of representing him, consequently, as a friend to misery and vice; while the letter and spirit of his work clearly show that he is their greatest enemy." Malthus concluded that his opponents—by bringing the principle of population into disrepute among the lower classes—were acting "to lower the wages of labour, and depress the condition of the poor."

IV.

In 1809, a group of Tories, under the leadership of Sir Walter Scott, joined with the London publisher John Murray to set up the *Quarterly Review* as a rival to the Whig *Edinburgh Review.* The editor of the new *Quarterly,* from its establishment to 1824, was William Gifford, a well-known man of letters. In contrast to the *Edinburgh,* the *Quarterly* at first paid little attention to economic questions; as such matters began to take on more prominence, however, the

Quarterly published an increasing number of economic articles. The Tory journal, however, was never to have that over-riding faith in the new science which the *Edinburgh* had evidenced from its earliest issues. Still, certain of the founders of the *Quarterly* were sufficiently perceptive to recognize that T. R. Malthus' economic opinions, grounded upon a favorable view of the landed interests, were most suitable for a Tory review. As early as 1808, indeed, Scott and Murray had been anxious to secure Malthus as a regular reviewer. In a letter to Gifford, dated October 28, 1808, Scott had written that "Mr. Murray seems to count upon Malthus for the department of political economy," adding that if Gifford approved of the choice, "I could when I come to town sound Malthus" out.[24] Not Malthus, however, but the poet and historian Robert Southey became the *Quarterly's* economic reviewer, and he—in good 'Tory-socialist' fashion—regarded political economists as men devoid of decent feelings, and their subject as beneath the contempt of men of good sense. The writings of Malthus were particularly abhorrent to Southey, who wrote of the law of population with a special disdain, and its supporters, critics of the poor laws, as beyond redemption.[25]

The *Quarterly* was clearly of two minds about its economic policy, generally, and, most particularly, concerning Malthus. We do not know if Malthus was, indeed, sounded out by Scott, but he did not write for the *Quarterly* until 1823. It is not difficult to understand the reasons for this delay. Malthus was a Whig, and the politics of the *Edinburgh* before 1815 were, without doubt, more congenial to him. In addition, the *Edinburgh* was decidedly the more influential journal, and was much more concerned with economic problems. Virtually all those who wrote for the *Quarterly*, and, perhaps of greater importance, virtually all who read it, regarded political economy as the highly impractical

---

[24] See H. J. C. Grierson, ed., *The Letters of Sir Walter Scott* (London: Constable, 1932), II, p. 108.

[25] See, for example, "Inquiry into the Poor Laws, & c." *Quarterly Review*, December 1812, Vol. VIII, No. XVI, Article IV; "The Poor," in *Quarterly Review*, April 1816, Vol. XV, No. XXIX, Article VIII.

ideology of the opposition party; furthermore, as indicated above, the *Quarterly*'s readers were particularly repelled by the 'hard-heartedness' of the principle of population. Southey well represented such sentiments. When Malthus, in 1815, came out upon the side of the landowners on the corn law issue, the possible usefulness of political economy dawned upon many Tories, but prejudice against 'abstract theory' was still too great. The gap between Toryism and Malthusian economics was partially bridged during the years following 1815 by two *Quarterly* articles which spoke rather favorably of the principle of population. In 1817, John Bird Sumner, who was to become Archbishop of Canterbury in 1848, wrote an article, "Malthus on Population," which was sympathetic to the principle,[26] and, in 1821, George Taylor, who was to be, for a short time in 1832, the Secretary to the Commission of Inquiry into the Poor Laws, wrote "Godwin and Malthus on Population," which attempted to compromise between full acceptance of Malthus' law of population and Southey's often-expressed hostility to it, and thus to define a proper Tory position. "The important truth of these (Malthus') principles must not be suppressed," he wrote, "because the unfeeling and the vicious may occasionally pervert them to disguise from others, and perhaps from themselves, the selfishness of their hearts." [27] In this manner, the way was cleared, and Malthus was asked to contribute. It was at this time, furthermore, as we have already noted, that Malthus was finding it difficult to obtain a hearing for his views from the *Edinburgh,* and the overtures of the Tory organ must have been rather welcome.

In 1823 and in 1824, Malthus contributed two important reviews to the *Quarterly*,[28] in both of which he set forth the leading points of difference, which had become so press-

[26] See "Malthus on Population," *Quarterly Review,* July 1817, Vol. XVII, No. XXXIV, Article IV.

[27] "Godwin and Malthus on Population," *Quarterly Review,* October 1821, Vol. XXVI, No. LI, Article VII, p. 168.

[28] For identification of articles and other relevant information, see F. W. Fetter, "The Economic Articles in the *Quarterly Review* and their Authors, 1809-52," *Journal of Political Economy,* February 1958, Vol. LXVI, No. 1, pp. 47-64; No. 2, pp. 154-170; also, Hill and H. C. Shine,

ing since 1815, between himself and the "new school" of Ricardianism. These articles are in our collection. The first, in April 1823, was an analysis of Tooke's *Thoughts and Details on the High and Low Prices of the last Thirty Years.* Malthus began by approving of Tooke's statistical method, vaunting the usefulness of such "an extensive collection of facts" to political economy at a time when, he continued, in a clear reference to Ricardian theorizing, "some of our ablest writers in this science have been deficient in that constant reference to facts and experience" on which political economy must be based. Malthus found that Tooke's statistics proved, fairly conclusively, that "exchangeable value," and therefore prices of all commodities, depended upon the relationship of supply and demand, rather than, as the Ricardians asserted, the labor which had produced them. Furthermore, Malthus continued, Tooke's statistics indicated that when the demand exceeded the supply, the economy was healthy—"the state of trade is brisk, profits are high"; when supply exceeded demand, the reverse was the case. Malthus noted that these conclusions were at variance with Say's law of markets which held that "all increase of demand depends upon increase of supply, and diminution of demand on diminution of supply." Say, and those who followed him, had paid insufficient attention to the *"effect of quantity on price and value."* Since, in Malthus' view, Tooke's statistics confirmed all this so clearly, Malthus was disappointed to find Tooke still an adherent of Say's law. In his own rejection of Say's law, Malthus, in common with other spokesmen for the landed interests, was asserting the superiority of a balanced economic development, and warning of the dangers facing an England which wished too rapidly to transform itself into a predominantly industrial and commercial state.

In the January 1824 issue of the *Quarterly Review,* Malthus outlined a fuller challenge to the views of what he

---

The Quarterly Review under Gifford; Identification of Contributors, 1809-1824 (Chapel Hill: University of North Carolina Press, 1949), pp. 84, 87.

described as the "new school" of political economy—the school of Ricardo, McCulloch, and James Mill. This article, the occasion for which was the publication of an "Essay on Political Economy" by McCulloch for the Supplement to the *Encyclopedia Britannica,* took up the cudgels on behalf of the school of "Adam Smith and Mr. Malthus." Malthus described "the specific error of the new school in England" as "the having taken so confined a view of *value* as not to include the results of demand and supply, and of the relative abundance and competition of capital." In the course of the lengthy article, Malthus, most ably, questioned those parts of Ricardian doctrine, which, it was to develop, the economic science of the future would find most faulty; yet this sharp analysis emerged from a point of view rooted in the economics and the prejudices of the past. Malthus, for example, rejecting the view of the Ricardians, agreed with Adam Smith—and with the physiocrats—that capital employed in agriculture added much greater value to the annual produce of a country, "to the real wealth and *revenue* of its inhabitants," than an equal capital employed in manufactures. "To establish the very great importance of manufactures," he declared, "it is not necessary to deny the superior importance of food and raw materials." Malthus even qualified the classical theory of rent—toward the development of which he had contributed so much—in favor of the view of Smith, and of the physiocrats, that rent was, in large part, the beneficent gift of nature.

As in his book *Measure of Value,* Malthus attacked the complete reliance of the new school upon the labor theory of value—this was "a most unwarranted deviation from Adam Smith and rests on no solid foundation"—and, as in his article on Tooke, the year previously, he stressed the importance of supply and demand as determiners of value. Malthus also insisted, in opposition to the "new" Ricardian school, that "the relative abundance and competition of capital"—as Smith had maintained and as, in his view, the events of the preceding thirty years had amply demonstrated —was of great importance as a regulator of profits. It was not the absolute amount of capital that was at issue, Malthus

26

contended, but the "relative difficulty of finding *profitable* employment for it"; "the continued increase of capital, in a limited territory, must unavoidably terminate in a fall of profits." (Malthus' role as the link between Adam Smith and the theorist of empire, Edward Gibbon Wakefield, was very clear here.) Closely related to this line of argument was Malthus' repetition of his long-standing challenge to the new school's acceptance of Say's law, with its denial of the possibility of a general glut. "The competition of capital acting on a slack demand, foreign and domestic" would "necessarily" produce "a general fall of profits accompanied by all the appearances of a general glut," Malthus insisted. Malthus concluded by attributing "all the peculiar doctrines of the new system" to the labor theory of value; he hoped, he wrote, that this "fundamental" error would be corrected and that, in time, political economy would see "the establishment of truth."

The *Quarterly Review* very nearly became the organ of heresy rather than that of simple, if intermittent, opposition to the very subject of political economy. Although Malthus wrote but two articles for it, many of the same views upon demand, and related subjects were upheld by G. Poulett Scrope, who, in the early 'thirties, appeared to be on his way toward becoming the *Quarterly's* McCulloch—he wrote about 10 articles between 1831 and 1833. However, proper Toryism reasserted itself with John Wilson Croker who, after 1832, became the leading influence upon the *Review's* politics. Croker was unhappy about Scrope's support for Free Trade, and Scrope was dropped. The *Quarterly* never did resolve its ambivalence concerning political economy.

V.

In January 1825, John Stuart Mill reviewed Malthus' *Quarterly* article of the previous year for the newly established Benthamite *Westminster Review*. Mill was merciless to the "anonymous" author of the article. Feigning ignorance of the author's identity, Mill confessed himself "considerably

27

startled at the remarkable similarity of the style to that of Mr. Malthus himself," and even the similarity of the views, but concluded, rather bitingly, that the writer "under the mask of a devoted adherent of Mr. Malthus, is, in reality, his concealed enemy, and affects to defend his doctrines, merely to have an opportunity of exhibiting them and him in a ridiculous and contemptible attitude." He added that Malthus had not disclaimed the Reviewer, "whom he probably deems altogether unworthy of his notice," nor did Mill omit to remind his readers that the *Quarterly* had not always looked so kindly at Malthus as it now appeared to.

The *Westminster* article reveals some of the cruelty of contemporary polemics; what Jeffrey had forbidden McCulloch in the pages of the *Edinburgh*, Mill had secured from the *Westminster*—the opportunity to handle Malthus "roughly." The article is marked by a blatant lack of fairness, and by a clear desire to expose an opponent to ridicule, attitudes no doubt common to spokesmen of triumphing orthodoxies when dealing with old associates whom they now regarded as heretics. We also gain a glimpse of the young Mill approaching the height of his analytical powers. His defense of the Ricardian theory of value was particularly able, and his lunges at certain ambiguities in Malthus' writings especially piercing. Mill concluded by declaring that the *Quarterly*'s author had evidently regarded it "a merit to puzzle what is plain, to render intricate that which is simple, obscure that which is clear, and difficult, that which is easy." A rather severe judgment, and unfortunately, one which later economists were, largely, to accept, without too much questioning and without a re-examination of Malthus' own writings.

It was William Empson, Malthus' colleague at Haileybury, where he served as professor of general "polity and the laws of England," a close friend and son-in-law of Jeffrey and a regular contributor to the *Edinburgh Review*, who wrote the final article in our collection, the "Life, Writings, and Character of Mr. Malthus," in response to the publication of a new edition of Malthus' *Principles*. His view of Malthus was very different from Mill's. Empson did not

28

seek to justify Malthus against Ricardo; indeed, he appears to have upheld the Ricardian position. Empson, however, wished to remind his readers that "the two great discoveries which have been made" in the science of political economy "since the days of Adam Smith—those relating to population and rent—are identified with his [Malthus'] name." He also wished to testify to his character—"for, from the sole of his foot to the crown of his head, Mr. Malthus was a perfect gentleman, at all times and under all circumstances"—to the sweetness of his disposition, and to his great capacity for friendship. (Empson dilated in particular upon the intimacy of Malthus' relationship with Ricardo.) Concluding, Empson declared of Malthus that, "taking him all in all, he was the best man and truest philosopher we ever were acquainted with." In saying this, he was stating the view of a great many of Malthus' contemporaries. Empson's judgment of Malthus comes closer by far to that of opinion to-day than does Mill's; indeed, our century has rehabilitated much of the Malthusian economics which even Empson had been so ready to set aside.

PART II

Articles by

MALTHUS

in the Edinburgh Review

From *Edinburgh Review,*
July 1808

For Semmel's commentary on this article by Malthus, see especially pp. 17-19 *supra.* (*Publisher*).

ART. IV. *A Statistical and Historical Inquiry into the Progress and Magnitude of the Population of Ireland.* By Thomas Newenham, Esq.

A Short Address to the Most Reverend and Honourable William, Lord Primate of all Ireland, recommendatory of some Commutation or Modification of the Tithes of that Country. By the Reverend H. Dudley.

A Sketch of the State of Ireland, Past and Present.

IT has long been a matter of just complaint with the public, that, among the few persons whose situations and habits have led them to an intimate knowledge of the state of Ireland, and who are daily compelled to contemplate what *is*, and to contrast it with what *might* be, that there has hitherto been so little anxiety either to collect or to circulate correct information. The attention which the affairs of Ireland have, from particular causes, excited, since the last dissolution of Parliament, and the publications relating to them, which are now daily issuing from the press, will, we earnestly hope, in no great length of time, remove this cause of complaint ; and, whatever views they may embrace, or in whatever garb they may be arrayed, we shall be disposed to hail them with satisfaction, as certainly conducing at least to one great object needful on this subject—*discussion.* The necessity, indeed, of making the British public more familiar with the state of Ireland, in all its relations, has been strikingly evinced by the allusions made to the opinions of the people, in the late debates on the Catholic petition. If it be really true, that the middling and lower ranks of society in this country are by no means prepared to consider the Irish Roman Catholics as fellow Christians worshipping the same God, and fellow subjects entitled to the same civil privileges ; if they are really so bigoted as to wish to deny the benefits of the British constitution to above a fourth part of the population of the empire, and so ignorant as to imagine they can do it with safety, the evil admits of no other remedy than that of bringing the subject repeatedly before them —of familiarizing them to a more just and rational consideration of it—and of endeavouring to work into their minds the conviction, that, in holding such opinions, they are not only violating the genuine spirit of Christianity, but blindly endangering their own security, and risking the subjugation or dismemberment of the empire. As the denunciation of offences committed against the principles of an enlightened policy, is more peculiarly within our province than the violation of religious duties, it is to the

33

former that we shall at present principally call the reader's attention.

Among the subjects peculiar to the state of Ireland, which have hitherto been comparatively but little noticed, is the extraordinary phenomenon of the very rapid increase of its population. While many of the countries of Europe have been slumbering on with a population nearly stationary, or, at most, increasing very slowly ; while even the most prosperous (except the newly civilized country of Russia) have not approached towards doubling their numbers during the course of the last century, Ireland, in the same period, has more than quadrupled them.

The proofs of this position are brought forward by Mr Newenham in a manner which does credit to his industry and information ; and we really think that the public is much indebted to him for the results of his labours. It appears that some unworthy efforts have at different times been made to *conceal* the full amount of the population of Ireland, and the rapidity of its increase. We can hardly imagine that our Government could at any time have been so weak, as directly to encourage such misrepresentations, or attempt to conceal the relative strength and importance of a particular part of the empire, for the purpose of blinding themselves and others to the dangers with which they are surrounded. It is more probable that misrepresentations of this kind should have proceeded, in the first instance, from the friends of Protestant ascendancy in Ireland, though they might afterwards be too readily adopted by the Government. But, however this may be, one of the principal motives which incited Mr Newenham to engage in these inquiries, seems to have been the fear, that even any official returns that might in future be published by authority, collected, as they probably would be, by the Protestant clergy, and revised by persons not unwilling to be deceived, might give a very incorrect statement of the real magnitude of the Catholic population in Ireland.

With the importance of knowing the whole truth on this subject, on whatever side it may lye, Mr Newenham seems fully impressed ; and, in order to ascertain it as nearly as possible, he has collected all the *data* respecting the population of Ireland, at different periods, furnished by previous inquiries ; has enlarged and extended them by his own personal researches, and those of his friends ; and has strengthened the whole by a variety of collateral information, all bearing upon the main question.

The actual population in 1804, Mr Newenham estimates at 5,400,000. This result is obtained, by applying the present apparent rate of increase, which is stated to be such as would make the period of doubling forty-six years, to the acknowledged population of 1791, deduced from the last returns for the hearth-tax. In this estimate, of course, much depends upon the correctness with which the rate of increase is determined; and though this part of the calculation is not made in a manner which bespeaks a familiar acquaintance with the technical parts of the science, yet we think it founded on sufficient evidence to justify our conviction, that it is not overrated. A still more rapid increase, indeed, seems to have taken place in all the districts of which particular surveys have been collected ; and, wherever an opportunity has occurred of procuring any accurate information respecting the number of children produced by each marriage, the earliness of marriages, and the proportion of the population under puberty, the results, which are very curious and interesting, bear unequivocal testimony to a progress in population at least as quick as that which has been stated.

The average rate of increase throughout the country, can only be correctly determined by setting out from a correct estimate at first ; and here, perhaps, the statement of Mr Newenham may be most open to objection. The estimate he adopts, as nearest the beginning of the century, and the most accurate that could be obtained, is that of Captain South in 1695, which makes the population at that time amount to 1,034,102 ; but as it was calculated from the assessments of a poll-tax, though it appears to have been done with considerable care, it is probable, or rather certain, that the usual evasions of such taxes have made it fall below the truth. And this seems to be in some degree corroborated by the result of an enumeration in 1731, from which the population appeared to amount to 2,010,221, which would imply an increase from 1695 considerably greater than the average rate of the century. This objection, however, is expressly noticed by Mr Newenham ; and in answer to it he observes, that the omissions in 1695 were probably not greater than those of 1791, relative to which, the Inspector-general of hearth-money declared to him, that there was no truth of which he was more thoroughly convinced, than that the return should have comprised a much greater number of houses exempt from the hearth-tax than it did. Were this really the case, and the proportion of omissions the same, any supposed deficiency in the computation of 1695 would not, of course, affect the average rate of increase throughout the century ; but, even allowing for some difference in these proportions, our general position, that the population of Ireland has quadrupled during the last century, cannot be on either side far from the truth.

The *causes* of this rapid increase, among a people groaning under a penal code of singular severity, and oppressed for three

fourths of the period in a manner of which history does not
furnish a second example, cannot fail of exciting our astonishment and curiosity.   We are at a loss to reconcile such an instance to those causes of increase laid down by Hume and
Smith,—' wise institutions,' and an ' increasing demand for labour.'   Under circumstances apparently the most opposite, Ireland has increased with extraordinary rapidity; and this fact
affords so striking an illustration of the doctrines which Mr
Malthus has advanced in his late Essay on Population, that we are
surprised that he did not enter into it more in detail.   Nothing,
however, that this author has said tends really to contradict these
positions of our illustrious countrymen.   It is still true that wise
institutions, and an increasing demand for labour, are most
powerful promoters of population; because, in all ordinary cases,
they most effectually tend to produce the means for its support.
But in any particular case, where such means could be produced
and distributed without the aid of these advantages, population
would still make a rapid progress under circumstances in other
respects the most adverse.

The introduction of the POTATOE into Ireland, and its becoming
the general food of the common people, seems to have formed
this particular case; and to be the single cause which has produced the effects that excite our astonishment.   At what period
potatoes became the staple support of the Irish poor, it is difficult precisely to ascertain; but, whenever this event took place,
it would necessarily occasion a most prodigious facility in the
payment and production of labour.   The way in which the means
of subsistence practically regulate the increase of population in
civilized societies, is, by limiting and determining the real wages
of the labourer, or the number of persons which the labour of
one man will support upon the staple food of the country.   In
England, at present, reckoning labour at ten shillings a week,
the quartern loaf at a shilling, and allowing a half peck loaf a
week to each individual, the earnings of a single man will support, on bread alone, five persons.   With his weekly wages he
will be able to purchase 43 pounds 7 ounces * of bread, his usual
nourishment.

In Ireland, at the time that Mr Young made his tour, the a-
verage price of labour was 6½d., and the prime cost of potatoes to
the cultivator 1½d. † the stone of 14 pounds.   At these rates, the

---

* The half peck loaf weighs 8 lib. 11 oz.

† In estimating the effect of potatoes upon the population of Ireland, it is necessary to take them at their cost to the cultivator; because, according to Mr Newenham, four fifths of the people are supported on the produce of land cultivated by themselves.   (p. 271.)

labourer would be able to procure, with his weekly earnings, 364 pounds of potatoes, and, allowing four pounds of potatoes to one of bread, 91 pounds of solid nourishment,—above double the quantity earned by the higher wages of the English labourer, and adequate to the weekly support of above double the number of persons. If either the wages of labour in England have been taken too low, or the price of bread too high for the general average ; or, if a pound of bread contain more nourishment than four pounds of potatoes, * the difference of course will not be so great as here stated ; but, at all events, it will be prodigious, and sufficient to account at once for the much more rapid increase of population in the one country than in the other.

According to Mr Young, four times the quantity of land is required in Ireland to yield the same nourishment in wheat as in potatoes. † in the cottar system, which is almost necessarily adopted in every agricultural country deficient in capital, this circumstance must afford incalculable advantages. The farmer would be able, by letting a very small proportion of his land, to provide that most important branch of capital, the wages of labour ; and the facility with which labour could thus be paid, would naturally prompt him to procure it in abundance ; more solicitous to have an ample supply in seasons of pressure, than fearful of not being able to keep all his cottars constantly employed. The latter consideration, indeed, would chiefly rest with the labourer himself. The farmer would at all events receive a fair price for his land, and would only deduct so much from the rent of it, as the number of days labour which he had required might amount to. It would depend upon the judge-

---

* Mr Newenham is of opinion, that three pounds of good mealy potatoes are more than an equivalent for one pound of bread ; but, in allowing thirty-six pounds of potatoes for the daily consumption of a family of six persons (p. 340.), he does not seem to adhere to this estimate, unless indeed we suppose with Mr Young, that the Irishman has always a bellyful, and the Englishman not. We understand that, in England, a half peck loaf a week, or 8 lib. 11 oz. in seven days, is considered as a fair average allowance for each individual of those families that live almost wholly on bread ; but we know, at the same time, that a young and healthy labourer will eat double the quantity. We believe that the Irish labourer in general lives more exclusively upon potatoes than the English labourer upon bread ; and this is probably the chief reason why the allowance to an Irish family is greater in weight than the proportion of 4 to 1, though, as to the comparative nourishment of the two kinds of food, Mr Newenham's estimate is probably nearer the truth than ours.

† Tour in Ireland, vol. II. p. 120.

ment of the labourer to decide, whether the work of the farm on which he was settled, and the occasional employment which he might elsewhere obtain, would enable him to pay his rent, and procure the proper assistance for the cultivation of his potatoes In this state of things, aided by the singular advantage, that in the cultivation of potatoes in Ireland, the attention of the cottar is directed to a small portion of good land, instead of a comparatively large portion of poor land, as in most other countries, great scope would naturally be given to the principle of increase ; and the abundance of labour thus produced, would react upon the agriculture of the country, and force on a production of capital, and of funds for the maintenance of labour, in spite of every disadvantage of government.

The indolence of the Irish peasantry, which has been so frequently the subject of remark, has naturally been occasioned by this redundancy of labour, combined with the habit of working for the farmers, on whose lands they are settled at a fixed and under price. But, paradoxical as it may at first appear, it is probable, that this indolence, and the number of holidays that it prompts them to keep, has rather tended to improve, than to lower their condition, and has been one, among other causes, which has prevented the price of labour from falling, in proportion to the cheapness of the food on which it is supported.

But though it is certainly true that the Irish peasant has hitherto been able to command a greater quantity of the food to which he is accustomed, than the English labourer can of bread, yet it by no means follows that his general condition should be proportionably better. Something else besides food is required to make life comfortable ; and the surplus potatoes of the Irishman, when converted into money, will have but a small power in purchasing other articles. Owing to the deficiency of manufacturing capital in Ireland, and the indolent habits of workmen in general, the conveniences of clothing, furniture, &c. are as dear as in England ; while the pecuniary wages of the Irish labourer are not equal to half the earnings of the Englishman. * Hence arises the unsparing meal of potatoes noticed by Mr Young, at which the beggar, the pig, the dog, the cat, and the poultry, seem all equally welcome ; while the cabin that affords shelter to all these vari-

---

* Mr Newenham says in a note, page 273, that labour is more than twice as high as in the year 1777 ; but, as far as we have been able to learn, the average is rather under than over 10d. There is a great difference in the prices both of potatoes and labour in the towns of Ireland, compared with the country, on account of the bulk and weight of potatoes, and the consequent expense of carriage.

ous inhabitants, is hardly fuperior to an Englifh pigftye ;—its furniture confined almoft exclufively to the pot in which the potatoes
are boiled ; and the clothing of its human inmates as deficient in
quantity as it is wretched in quality.   Mr Young obferves, that an
Irifhman and his wife are much more folicitous to feed than to
clothe their children ; but the fact is, that they have the power of
doing the one, and not that of doing the other.

This kind of fupport, though it might be fufficient to give play
to the ftrong principle of increafe among a people long opprefled
and degraded, could never prefent very flattering profpects of happinefs ; and when joined to the occafional difficulty of getting fufficient employment to enable them to pay the rent of their potatoe
grounds, would naturally prompt them to emigration.   Ireland
has, in confequence, long been confidered as the great *officina mi-
litum,* not only for England, but for other countries.

It has been calculated, though it is probably an exaggeration,
that, from 1691 to 1745, 450,000 Irifhmen perifhed in the fervice
of France ; and, for fifty years of the laft century, the annual e-
migration to America is eftimated, by Mr Newenham, at 4000.
During three years from 1771, of which there are accurate accounts, the average annual emigrations to America alone, were
9533.   Additional encouragement would, of courfe, be given by
thefe emigrations, to the habit of early marriages, the prevalence
of which in Ireland Mr Newenham particularly notices : and
though fuch drains muft neceffarily prevent the poffibility of a full
development of the power of increafe in the country where they
take place ; yet it is probable, that, in the actual ftate of things,
the population of Ireland was not diminifhed by them ; and that
the remaining inhabitants were always as numerous as the progrefs
of its refources would enable it to employ and fupport.

Thefe emigrations of different kinds were checked by the American war ; but about the fame time, the difgraceful code under
which the Catholics had been fo long opprefled, began to be relax-
ed ; and fhortly after, under a lefs fhackled trade, and a fome-
what improved government, a new life was given to induftry ; and
the rapid increafe of agriculture, manufactures, and commerce,
found employment for a great increafe of people at home.   Thefe
advantages, the effects of which are detailed at large by Mr Newenham, appear to have more than counterbalanced any difadvan-
tages which may be fuppofed to have arifen from the increafing
dearnefs and fcarcity of land : and, on the whole, there feems to
be good reafon to believe, that, in fpite of the late rebellion, and
the two years of fcarcity, the progrefs of population fince 1777
has been decidedly above the average rate of the century.

The confequences of fuch a rapid rate of increafe deferve our moſt ſerious attention.   Either the increaſe will continue at its preſent rate, or it will not.   If the rate continue, Ireland will contain *twenty millions* of people in the courſe of the preſent century; and we need not inſiſt upon the reſult.   With ſuch a phyſical force, it is quite impoſſible that it ſhould remain united to Great Britain, without ſharing, in every reſpeȼt, the full benefits of its conſtitution.

If the rate do not continue to the end of the century, which is certainly the more probable ſuppoſition, it will be intereſting to aſk ourſelves, what will be the principal cauſes of its retardation, and in what manner they will practically operate?   The cauſe firſt generally felt, will be the dearneſs of land ; and the advance of rent will continue, till the uſual quantity of land conſidered as neceſſary to ſupport a large family, cannot be obtained for the a-mount of the average earnings of a year's labour.   Smaller portions will then be taken; but even theſe, in time, becoming ſcarce, and difficult to be procured, the cottar ſyſtem will be gradually deſtroyed, and give place to a ſet of labourers earning their pecuniary wages like the peaſantry of England, but ſtill living upon potatoes as their principal food.   Theſe potatoes will then be raiſed by the farmers, and will become a principal object of cultivation for the market, as the great ſtaple food of the country.

The other, and ultimate cauſe of retardation, will be ſuch a riſe in the price of potatoes, compared with the price of labour, as will give the labourer no greater command over ſubſiſtence in the ſhape of potatoes, than he has at preſent over corn, in ſome of the ſtationary, or ſlowly-increaſing countries of Europe.   When the Iriſh peaſant can only earn the maintenance of five, inſtead of ten perſons, the habit of early marriages will neceſſarily be checked ; the rearing of families will be impeded ; and the cabins will ceaſe to ſwarm, as they do at preſent, with overflowing broods of healthy children.

But before this laſt cauſe has produced an approach to a ſtationary population, Ireland will contain, in proportion to its ſize, a prodigious maſs of people.   It is the firſt and only country that has yet fully taken to a ſpecies of food, which, at the moſt, requires only one third of the land neceſſary to yield the ſame nouriſhment in wheat. *   Its effects, hitherto, have been truly aſto-

---

* According to Mr Young, the average produce of the whole kingdom is 82 barrels per Irish acre, (Irish Tour, vol. ii p. 120.) each barrel weighing 20 stone.   This, in pounds, amounts to 22,960, and divided by 4 to reduce it to the solid nourishment of wheat, will be 5740 pounds.   The average produce of an Irish acre in wheat,

nifhing ; and, in its future progrefs, it may be expected to produce proportionate refults.   We fhould not wonder if Ireland
were deftined to become an inftance of the greateft denfity of population yet known in the world : and it has fometimes ftruck us
as poffible, that the prodigious phyfical force thus created in a particular country, might, like the ftanding armies introduced into
modern Europe by France, occafion the adoption of the fame fyftem in the neighbouring ftates.   We own that we do not contemplate fuch a change as favourable to the happinefs of mankind.
That fo great an increafe of human beings, if they could be well
fupported, would be highly defirable, cannot admit of a doubt ;
but it feems fcarcely poffible that they fhould be fo fupported; and
we feel convinced, that if the lower claffes of fociety lived exclufively upon potatoes, they would not only have lefs power to purchafe the conveniences and comforts of life, but would be much
more expofed to the preffure of fcarcity than they are at prefent.
As long as potatoes can be kept to act only as fubfidiaries to the
main food of the country, they appear to be calculated to produce
the higheft benefits to the poor, as affording a moft admirable and
timely fupply to thofe who have larger families than ufual ; and
the beft and cheapeft refource in feafons of fcarcity.   Thefe advantages would be ftill further extended in England, if cattle, pigs
and poultry were more generally fed upon them ; as the ftore
would then be greater in a deficiency of corn.   In the actual ftate of things, however, both in England and Scotland, the
poor derive great benefit from them.   But when once they
fhall have become the main food of the country, fo as to be
the principal regulator of the price of labour, the fcene will
be moft decidedly changed.   The never-failing bellyful to all the
children of a family, noticed by Mr Young, as the circumftance
which must ever recommend potatoes, was procured, not by
any quality necessarily and unalterably inherent in this kind
of food, but by the rapid increase of the funds for the maintenance of labour in Ireland, at the time that he made his

---

is 4 quarters, which, at 460 pounds the quarter, amounts to 1840,
less than one third of the solid nourishment yielded by an acre of
potatoes ; independently of the important circumstance, that the cultivation of wheat requires the intervention of more fallows or green
crops, than that of potatoes.   If we take Mr Newenham's estimate
of three pounds of potatoes to one of bread, the produce of an acre
of potatoes will be at once more than quadruple that of an acre of
wheat.   A certain weight of wheat will yield nearly the same weight
of bread, on account of the water absorbed in its composition, which
about balances the loss of the bran and coarse parts.

tour,—by causes, in short, similar to those which secure to the American labourer, and all his children, a never-failing bellyful of bread. But, when these funds cease to advance with the same rapidity, which they necessarily must do in time, there is no reason why potatoes should not ultimately be as scarce, and as economically consumed, as the bread and cheese of the English labourer. And, under such circumstances, there can be no doubt, that the lot of the labouring poor would be worse, than if they had still continued to live upon bread corn.

But to return from this digression, which has led us further than we intended. Although it is quite certain that the population of Ireland cannot continue permanently to increase at its present rate, yet it is as certain that it will not *suddenly* come to a stop. Mr Newenham, assuming that it will go on for some time, at least, as it has done of late years, supposes that the country will contain 8,413,224 inhabitants in 1837; and enters into an elaborate calculation to show that it is fully capable of maintaining such a number. Knowing the uncertainty of all particular estimates of future population, we shall not give our sanction to the present, though it is certainly not impossible, nor even very improbable; and we feel confident, that a much greater population might in time be supported in that country if potatoes continue to be its staple food. But what we wish to notice at present is, that Mr Newenham stops short with 1837, the period of doubling from 1791, and, satisfied with having proved that Ireland will be able to maintain the numbers which he supposes it will then have, dismisses the subject without consideration of further consequences. It is quite clear, however, that if Ireland can only maintain the number which the present rate of increase will produce in 1837, such a number will *not* be found in it in so short a period. Both theory and experience uniformly instruct us, that a less abundant supply of food operates with a gradually increasing pressure for a very long time before its progress is stopt. It is difficult indeed to conceive a more tremendous shock to society, than the event of its coming at once to the limits of the means of subsistence, with all the habits of abundance and early marriages which accompany a rapidly increasing population. But, happily for mankind, this never is, nor ever can be the case. The event is provided for by the concurrent interests and feelings of individuals long before it arrives; and the gradual diminution of the real wages of the labouring classes of society, slowly, and almost insensibly, generates the habits necessary for an order of things in which the funds for the maintenance of labour are stationary.

We may be quite certain, therefore, that, without external

42

violence, the period when the population of Ireland will become stationary is yet at a very considerable distance; that in the mean time it will continue increasing, with a movement sometimes quicker and sometimes slower, from varying circumstances, but, on the whole, gradually retarded; and that the causes of its retardation will be generally felt, and generate a change of habits long before the period in question arrives.

The two most obvious causes of this retardation have already been suggested, and they must be allowed to be of a nature to aggravate the discontents of a people not firmly attached to the government under which they live.

Mr Dudley, in his address to the Primate of Ireland on the subject of a commutation for tithes, has gone so far as to write the following strange sentence. ' Whatever the enemies of their country may advance for the purposes of delusion, relief from the harassing system of *tithes,* and the increasing pressure of *exorbitant rent,* is the real emancipation on which the hearts of the Irish people are principally fixed. ' That every effort should be used to relieve the people from the pressure of tithes, we are most ready to allow. It is not the sum collected, but the mode of its collection, that is the grievance; and this grievance, on many accounts, produces infinitely worse consequences in Ireland than in England. Such an evil is the proper subject of legislative interference; and we earnestly hope, that no difficulties, however great they may at first appear, will be allowed to stand in the way of its removal. But that any man of common sense should talk as Mr Dudley does about *rents,* is quite inconceivable. A Legislature might, perhaps, fairly enough interfere to relieve a people from the pressure of rents paid in kind; but to prevent that natural rise of pecuniary rents, which takes place from the principles of free competition in the progress of wealth and population, would be tantamount to saying, either that land shall be for ever in the same plenty, however the population may increase, or that one part of the society shall always be extremely favoured, to the utter exclusion of other competitors, whatever may be their talents, industry, and farming skill.

The very general clamour that has lately been raised about high rents and middlemen, however natural it may be to the poor of Ireland, cannot be supported and propagated by persons in the higher classes of society, but from the most evil designs, or the most consummate ignorance. The middlemen who took long leases, when land was much cheaper than it is now, are undoubtedly making great profits; but if the leases were expired, the same, or nearly the same, profits would be made by the landlords. This system of letting lands, which formerly prevailed in

Ireland, arose, almost necessarily, from the extreme poverty of the tenantry; and as soon as this cause is removed by the progress of improvement and the increase of capital, we may be certain, that the landlord will feel no disposition to divide his rents with another person. The effect of the middleman in raising rents has always, we conceive, been greatly exaggerated. Some difference will, of course, always prevail in the indulgence granted to tenantry from the personal character of the landlord, from his easy or distressed circumstances, or from the customs of particular countries. In all these respects, we are ready to allow that Ireland is not favourably circumstanced. But these are comparatively inefficient; and the main cause of high rent in Ireland, is, certainly, neither the extortion of the middleman nor of the landlord, but the small portion of land and capital necessary, upon the potatoe system, to support the labour employed in cultivation, and the large portion of the gross produce which consequently falls to the share of the landlord. In former times, when the population of Ireland was scanty, the great plenty of land naturally counterbalanced this cause; but the increasing demand arising from an increasing population could not fail of making its effects apparent. What is now taking place in Ireland with regard to rents, is merely an exemplification of an obvious principle in political economy, long ago laid down by Dr Smith, who expressly notices the very case before us; and, speaking of the great produce of potatoes, says, ' Should this root ever become, in any part of Europe, like rice in some rice countries, the common and favourite vegetable food of the people, so as to occupy the same proportion of the lands in tillage, which wheat and other sorts of grain for human food do at present, the same quantity of cultivated land would maintain a much greater number of people; and the labourers being generally fed with potatoes, a greater surplus would remain after replacing all the stock and maintaining all the labour employed in cultivation. A greater share of this surplus too would belong to the landlord. Population would increase, and *rents would rise* much beyond what they are at present.' *
The situation of things here contemplated, is not as yet fully accomplished in Ireland, but a regular progress is making towards it; and as, in this progress, a continued rise of rents is in the natural and necessary order of things, to clamour against it is folly, —to interfere in it would be madness.

It is still less possible to interfere in the ultimate cause which practically regulates and limits the population of all civilized states, the real price of labour. As long as the Irish peasant can

---

* Wealth of Nations, Vol. I. p. 250.

earn the support of eight or ten persons, and his condition in other respects remains the same, it is not probable that the habit of early marriages, now so generally prevalent, will experience any material change ; and if we could succeed in preventing the wages of labour from falling, we are reduced to the conclusion, that Ireland will be able to support a population increasing for ever at the rate which it does at present.   But this is manifestly an absurdity ; and any attempt to alter the natural results arising from an increased supply of labour compared with the funds which are to support it, would just be an attempt to reverse the laws of nature.

The distress, therefore, which may prevail among the labouring classes of Ireland, from these two causes, is evidently beyond the power of the Legislature *directly* to relieve.   But still, it will be widely and sensibly felt.   And the point to which we wish particularly to direct the reader's attention, is, that so long as any civil distinctions remain between the Protestants and the Catholics, so long, we may depend upon it, will the cruel and foolish refusal of complete emancipation be charged, not only with all the evils which really belong to it, but all the others which are confessedly irremediable.   The really disaffected among the Irish, the real advocates for the separation of the two countries, must hail with delight the short-sighted policy of the British government, as it gives them a power of exciting the lower classes of the people far beyond what they could possibly obtain otherwise. The causes of distress to which we have particularly adverted, cannot be made intelligible to every poor peasant who suffers from their effects ; but the Catholic poor readily see, that a marked line of distinction is drawn between them and the Protestants ; they see that they are regarded with fear and suspicion, and do not partake the full benefits of the British constitution ; and, with these obvious causes of depression before their eyes, it can require little art to direct all their discontents, from whatever source they may be derived, exclusively to the Government.   In the peculiar circumstances of Ireland, with its poor labouring under the pressure of increasing rents and decreasing wages, what an incalculable advantage it would be to the British government to have no line of separation in civil rights capable of giving the colour of truth and justice to the most unfounded accusations !   The mere pressure of poverty alone, though it has been felt with varied weight in every part of the world, has never, we believe, in a single instance, produced a general spirit of insurrection and rebellion against Government , but when other specific and removeable causes of complaint have existed at the same time, it has invariably added to them tenfold

45

strength, and often been productive of the most tremendous effects. The distresses of the common people of Ireland will ever continue a weapon of mighty and increasing force in the hands of the political agitator, till it is wrested from him, or its point turned aside, by the complete abolition of all civil distinctions between the Protestant and Catholic subjects of the British empire. If to this consideration be added, that of the rapidly increasing physical force of the Irish Catholics, it seems scarcely possible to imagine a case in which the views of policy and security so imperiously dictate the same line of conduct as those of justice and humanity.

When all the arguments which at different times have been brought to bear upon this question are duly weighed, no thinking man can seriously be of opinion that the present system with regard to Ireland can be permanently adhered to. If a French army do not step in, and decide the matter at once, the increasing physical force of the Catholics cannot fail, ultimately, of effecting either a change in this system, or a separation of the two countries. We doubt, even, whether those who, with Lord Hawkesbury, profess to take their stand at the Union, feel really confident of being able to maintain the station they have chosen; and, notwithstanding a few bold declarations to the contrary, we think we see symptoms of fear and distrust among the most strenuous enemies of emancipation, as to the final success of their measures. But if it be conceded, that a time may come when it will be absolutely necessary to alter these measures, the arguments for doing it immediately, and while it is yet in our power, receive such an accession of weight as absolutely to exclude all rational opposition.

Every year that elapses under the present system, tends to aggravate all the causes of discontent in Ireland, and to accumulate materials of insurrection and rebellion, which, however quiescent at present, are at all times liable to burst into a flame before our concessions are granted. Every year the proportion of the Catholics to the Protestants is rapidly augmenting,—a circumstance which might be contemplated without fear if they were once conciliated; but, till that time arrives, must be regarded with increasing apprehension, as daily diminishing the prospect of a cordial and permanent union between the two countries. *

---

* In 1731, it appeared, from actual returns, that the proportion of Catholics to Protestants was two to one. It is now generally acknowledged to be four to one. This change of proportions was to be expected from the manner in which the population of Ireland increases ; and from the same cause it may be expected to continue.

Every year fifty thousand youths rise to the military age in Ireland; and as comparatively few in the same time go off the stage, or become unfit for service, the military part of the population is receiving every year a great accession of strength. What additional number of British soldiers may be necessary every year to guard the increasing numbers of the Irish, we will not pretend accurately to calculate. But it cannot be denied, that, in the present state of the two countries, the increasing strength of Ireland is the increasing weakness of England; and that each passing year, while it adds both to the disposition and the power of Ireland to resist the wrongs she suffers, diminishes, in a still greater proportion, the power of England to enforce them. In this unequal race, if it continue much longer, England must necessarily be left behind : the danger is of a nature to admit of no delay; and unless this contest of vigour be exchanged, and that very shortly, for a contest of kindness and conciliation, she will inevitably have to rue her folly in the conquest or dismemberment of a fourth part of the empire, and the probable subjugation of the whole.

It is impossible ever to speak of the chance of foreign subjugation, and think, at the same time, of the peculiar situation of Ireland, without feeling the most bitter regret at that short-sighted policy which has made enemies of a gallant people, from whom, as friends, we might have received services of the most inestimable value. If England had been to choose a territory calculated to afford her the most effectual assistance, in this awful crisis of her fate, we doubt if she could have fixed upon any portion of land, of the same extent, so peculiarly suited to her wants as Ireland; with the single change, that the hearts of the people were with her, instead of against her. The manufacturing habits of England have, in some degree, been unfavourable to her warlike habits. Her agricultural population is comparatively small; and her artificers, accustomed to high wages, from the late unexampled prosperity of commerce, are unwilling to exchange their good food and warm workshops, for the coarse fare and damp lodging of a camp : and when they do exchange them, under the temptations of high bounties, or a temporary slackness of trade, they are not likely to make the best and most hardy soldiers. In all these particulars Ireland presents a contrast, which, for the object in view, is in the highest degree favourable. Her agricultural population is redundant, and rapidly increasing; the pecuniary wages of her labourers are lower than the pay of the British army, and offer almost irresistible temptations to enlist; and the habitations and food of her peasantry are such, as to make a British camp appear an abode of much superior comfort, and the fare of the common soldier a luxurious repast. Even the present peculiar causes of distress in Ireland, would be so many sources of strength to the armies of the empire ; and the destruction of the cottar system, and the diminution of the wages of labour; would only circle the British standard with additional crowds of willing followers. The facility, indeed, which the peculiar state of Ireland gives to military levies, is so preeminent, that it breaks through all discouragements ; and in the actual state of things, a very large proportion of Irish is to be found both in our army and navy. But if, even under the present system, in spite of the irritation they are taught to feel at the power which degrades them ; in spite of their exclusion from military distinctions; the discouragement of their priests and friends, and the inconveniences to which they are subject in the performance of their religious duties, they still offer their services in considerable numbers ; what would they do, if these causes of alienation were removed, and their hearts were really and cordially with us ?

That the affections of the Irish might have been conciliated by wise and benignant councils ;—that the golden opportunity, though every day receding, is not yet beyond our grasp, can scarcely admit of a doubt. Whatever might have been the hopes indulged by the visionary, at the commencement of the French revolution, the complete failure of that tremendous experiment must have blasted them ; and the scenes which have been since passing in Europe, are such as to give every advantage in the comparison to the British constitution. It is impossible to imagine that the Irish Catholics could really prefer the arbitrary sway of Bonaparte, or any of his subject kings, to the government of the laws of England,—if they had once been allowed to feel the full benefit of their salutary influence. Irritation and resentment will, we know, often precipitate a people into measures the most contrary to their interests ; but a deliberate choice of this kind is inconceivable. Every principle that is known to influence human conduct, seems to assure us, that if the Irish Catholics were raised from their present political degradation, and admitted to all the rights and privileges of British subjects ; if the career of honours and distinctions of every kind were fully and fairly opened to them, and they were allowed to feel the same motives of love and veneration for the Government under which they live, as their Protestant brethren,—they would soon be found among the most loyal, willing, and powerful supporters of the Crown and the empire. Then would Ireland indeed be united to Great Britain ; and they might then, like ' the Douglas and the Percy both together,' be ' confident against the world in arms. '

We have said, that some of the principal causes of the distresses of the Irish poor, and of their present discontents, are beyond the power of the Legislature *directly* to remove. In expressing ourselves in this manner, it will be observed, that we have advanced a qualified position ; and we wish the reader to attend to the import of the term *directly*, as contradistinguished from *indirectly ;* because it is really our opinion, that, *indirectly*, Government has great influence on the causes of distress here particularly alluded to. Universally it will be found, that political degradation is accompanied by excessive poverty ; and that the opposite state of society is the most efficient cause of the general spread of comforts among the lower classes. We have little doubt, that the political degradation of the Irish poor powerfully contributed to make them adopt potatoes as their principal food ; and in the curious question, whether, at a future distant period, the greater part of the population of Europe will be supported upon potatoes ? much will depend upon the character of the governments in which the present convulsions may terminate. The establishment of an universal despotism, and the exclusion of the lower and middle classes of society from all share in the government, by annihilating in a great degree individual importance and dignity, would have a strong tendency to make the poor submit to the lowest and cheapest kind of sustenance ; and it is quite certain, that if they once consent to produce an adequate supply of labour on the cheapest sort of food, they never will be able to obtain any thing better. On the other hand, if the present convulsions of the civilized world should leave behind them improved forms of government, it is probable, that the decent pride occasioned by a superior political condition, will make the lower classes of society look forward to something besides mere support, and not only prevent them from falling to potatoes, but raise the quality of their food above what it is at present. The causes which, independently of soil and climate, have actually determined the chief food of the common people in the different kingdoms of Europe, seem to have been their political state, and the periods of prosperity or adversity, with regard to the funds for the maintenance of labour, which they may have gone through. And when the character of the food has been determined in any particular country by these causes, though it continues always susceptible of change, yet it changes slowly and with difficulty, and a union of favourable circumstances is necessary to produce the effect. A country which, from a previous state of general depression, had been long in the habit of living upon the lowest kind of food, might pass through a period of considerable agricultural prosperity, and feel it chiefly in the rapid increase of population, and not in an improvement of the diet and comforts of the lower classes. On the other hand, a people which, from a course of favourable circumstances, had been in the habit of living upon the best wheaten bread, might, from checks to their agriculture or commerce, suffer long and severe want, before they would consent to change their diet; and the effect of such checks would be felt rather in the retardation of the population, than in the adoption of an inferior kind of food, or a different standard of comfort.

With regard to the population of Ireland, it is quite evident that it cannot continue permanently to increase as it does at prefent; but it can only be retarded, either by the operation of the two caufes before mentioned, which will give the labourer a fmaller command over the means of fubfiftence, or by fuch an elevation in the character and condition of the lower claffes of fociety, as will make them look forwards to other comforts befide the mere fupport of their families upon potatoes. When we confider the actual fituation of the poor in Ireland, notwithftanding fuch an increafe in the funds for the maintenance of labour, as would, if they did not confift of the loweft kind of food, produce general profperity, we cannot but contemplate with difmay the flackening of the increafe of thefe funds, if aggravated poverty *alone* be left to effect the neceffary retardation of the population. We muft furely hope, that the caufe laft noticed will co-operate in producing this retardation, and, by the introduction of more prudential habits, alleviate the fevere diftrefs which will otherwife be unavoidable. But if we allow ourfelves to indulge a hope of this kind, it is quite clear, that *the firft ftep* towards its accomplifhment muft be the full and complete emancipation of the Catholics, as the radical caufe of the prefent moral and political degradation of the mafs of the Irifh poor.

We are difpofed to agree very nearly with the author of the *Sketch of the State of Ireland, Paft and Prefent,* in what he calls the fprings of his country's misfortune, which he thus enumerates. 1. The ignorance. 2. The poverty. 3. The political debafement of the inferior orders. 4. The Catholic code. 5. The provinciality of the government. But we by no means agree with him in the relative importance which he appears to attach to each, nor in the order in which he propofes to remove them. We fhould without hefitation fay, of thefe five caufes of Irifh mifery, that the Catholic code, and the provinciality of the government, had produced the political debafement of the inferior orders; and that this political debafement had been the chief inftrument in producing the *peculiar* ignorance and poverty of the lower claffes of the Irifh. If this be true, and we conceive that it can fcarcely admit of a doubt, nothing can be more abfurd than what the author of the *Sketch* afferts as his mature opinion, that without the removal of the other caufes which he has named, Catholic emancipation would *not* tranquillize the country ; but that they without it *would.* To begin with the ignorance and poverty, is manifeftly to begin at the wrong end, and to labour in vain. However ardently we may wifh to fpread the advantages of education among the Irifh poor, we cannot rationally expect the fuccefs of any general fyftem of inftruction, while the prefent civil and religious animofities remain unallayed, by the continuance of the Catholic code. The poverty of the Irifh, as we have before obferved, is an evil, the direct removal of which is not in the power of the Legiflature ; and if it be true, as our author ftates, that the competitors for land offer the whole value of the produce *minus* their daily potatoe, there is clearly no other remedy than the removal of that ftate of moral and political degradation which makes them fatisfied with fo fcanty a refervation. The only poffible relief, then, that can be applied to the poverty of Ireland, is the abolition of the Catholic code, and the improvement of the government. In looking to the third caufe here ftated of the misfortunes of Ireland, the political debafement of the inferior orders, we are immediately directed to the fame quarter for its removal ; fo that wherever we begin, or to whatever grievance we turn our eyes, the Catholic code, and the provinciality of the government, invariably prefent themfelves as the primary and radical caufes of the mifchiefs we deplore ; and without the removal of thefe caufes, it is quite certain that no efforts of the Legiflature can effentially relieve the misfortunes of Ireland, nor make it contribute to the ftrength of the empire, in proportion to its magnitude, its fertility, and its population.

We have left ourfelves no room to notice further the ' *Sketch of the State of Ireland.* ' It contains a few juft, and many ftriking obfervations, and a defcription and character certainly highly picturefque and impreffive, of the Irifh peafantry ; but it is written in fo antithetical and fantaftic a ftyle, and truth and confiftency are fo frequently facrificed to brilliancy of language, or an affectation of candour and impartiality, that it poffeffes very little merit as a whole.

Though we difapprove of fome parts of Mr Dudley's pamphlet, we moft certainly wifh him fuccefs in his main object. We are inclined, however, to think with the author of the *Sketch*, that a poundage upon rents would, on the whole, be a lefs difficult and objectionable commutation for tithes than the purchafe of land.

Mr Newenham's work, we are difpofed to recommend for a quality which we always confider as very valuable,—that of containing the beft information to be found on an interefting fubject

little known.   His reafonings and conclufions, it muft be confeffed,
do not always fhow a thorough acquaintance with the general
principles of his fubject; and with regard to facts, much is ftill
wanting to give us a full view of the ftate of population in Ireland; but, confidering the difficulty of getting information of this
kind in the peculiar circumftances of the country, we really think
that the induftry and exertions of Mr Newenham have been
crowned with a fair portion of fuccefs; and we owe him fome
apology for not having noticed his work before.

From *Edinburgh Review,*
April 1809

For Semmel's commentary on this article by Malthus, see especially
pp. 17-19 *supra. (Publisher).*

Art. XII.   *A View of the Natural, Political and Commercial
circumstances of Ireland.* By Thomas Newenham, Esq.   4to.
pp. 355.   London.   1808.

HAD we not been prepared, by Mr Newenham's former work,
to expect some valuable matter in the present, we confess
that we should have been a little alarmed by the style in which
the preface is written, and particularly by the manner in which
the qualifications of a statesman are discussed in the opening pa-
ragraph.

He begins by observing, that, ' Under a well-established go-
' vernment, exempt from popular controul, an accurate and com-
' prehensive knowledge of the various circumstances of a coun-
' try, on the part of those who exercise the principal functions of
' the state, does not appear to be indispensably necessary, when
' the obedience of the people is the sole or paramount object of
' concern.   To ensure that obedience, a due proficiency in the art
' of government is the chief, or perhaps the only requisite.   To
' promote the prosperity of a nation, a much more diversified
' knowledge than that of the mere statesman must unquestion-
' ably be attained. '

Now, we apprehend, that, in the best established governments,
and those the most exempt from popular controul, a comprehen-

52

sive knowledge of the circumstances of the country to be governed, is indispensably necessary to enable the sovereign, or the minister who acts for him, to do his duty: nor can we attach any
other idea to a due proficiency in the art of government, either
in despotic or in free countries, than such a degree of knowledge
as will not only insure the obedience of the subject, but tend to
promote the wealth, power and happiness of the state. The great
advantage of a free country does not consist in its requiring higher qualities in its governors, but in its being better secured against
their bad qualities ;—in being better fenced against the folly or
wickedness of a sovereign,—and having better means of removing a foolish or wicked minister.

We do not perfectly understand what Mr Newenham means by
the expression *mere* statesman. We know of no situation which
presents a grander and more varied field for the exercise of talents, than that of a leading statesman ; and none in which a
more diversified knowledge is required to enable him to do his
duty. The materials which he has to work upon are so various ;
—he is so continually assailed by partial and individual interests
in all their different combinations, that nothing but an enlarged
and comprehensive view of the true state of his own and other
countries—and, above all, a thorough acquaintance with the general principles by which the relative value of contrasted good and
evil may be determined—can qualify him so to influence the legislative provisions of his time, and so to direct their equal execution, as to give full play to the industry of all the parts of a
great empire, and allow it to develop all its energies. All this,
indeed, seems so obvious, that we cannot help suspecting that
Mr Newenham has here said what he did not intend,—or that the
Irish idea of a statesman is different from the common one. Upon this supposition, we venture to suggest a correction, which, as
it appears to us, will make the observation accord much more
nearly with the author's general sentiments, and at the same time
give us an opportunity of agreeing with him most cordially. We
have, indeed, sometimes felt, and we think he has felt too, that
‘ to promote the prosperity of a nation, a much more diversified
‘ knowledge than is *possessed by those who at present have the
‘ chief influence in state affairs*, must unquestionably be attained. ’

We beg the reader's pardon for detaining him so long at the
threshold ; and proceed without further delay to the body of the
work. It is not by its style, or even its reasonings and opinions,
that a publication of this kind should be judged. What we want
with regard to Ireland, is a collection of well authenticated *facts*;
and the author who professes to give us this, will always have a
strong claim on our attention. We confess, however, that even

in this respect, the expectations which we have formed from Mr Newenham's former publication, have been a little disappointed in going over the present.   Not that it is without valuable information, which it is at all times desirable to bring before the public ; but the information, on this occasion, is neither so full nor so new as we had been inclined to expect ; and is, besides, clogged with a good deal of very indifferent reasoning.   In justice, however, to Mr Newenham, we should state, that a part of our disappointment has almost necessarily arisen from the nature of his former subject, compared with the present.   He was, we believe, the first who brought together all the facts relating to the population of Ireland, during the course of the last century.   But, in treating of its natural, political and commercial circumstances, he has had, in some parts of his subject, most able precursors, particularly Arthur Young, and the two Mr Parnells.

Mr Newenham has divided his work into four parts ; the firſt, treating " of the natural advantages which qualify Ireland for the acquifition of commercial wealth : " the fecond, " of the caufes which frustrate the natural advantages of Ireland : " the third, " of the remote caufe which eventually fruſtrated the natural advantages of Ireland : " and the fourth, " of the circumſtances which have tended to prevent a complete fruition of the natural advantages of Ireland, fince the removal of the principal caufes which operated in rendering them comparatively abortive,—and of the effects refulting from thefe circumſtances. "

Thefe divifions, the reader will fee, are not very luminous and diſtinct ; and imply at once too much of hiſtory, and too little detail of the actual circumſtances of Ireland, and of the condition of the lower claffes of the people, to fatisfy the particular wants of the Britiſh public.   In fact, the greateſt ſhare of the information of this latter kind, to be found in the work, is fcattered about in the form of notes, or thrown together in the tables of the appendix, which renders thefe parts of the book the moſt valuable of the whole.

The very great advantages for commercial intercourfe, particularly with the Weſtern world, which Ireland poffeffes from her geographical pofition, are evident, from the infpection of the map ; and her numerous and commodious harbours, which are reprefented by Mr Newenham, and we believe juſtly, as much fuperior to thofe of England, would enable her, under favourable aufpices, to reap the full benefit of her fortunate fituation.   Her deeply indented coaſt, her extenfive lakes, and the number, fize, and direction of her rivers will inevitably fecure to her a moſt excellent fyſtem of inland navigation, as foon as the capitals of individuals are fufficiently large, the profits of employing them in other ways fufficiently reduced, and, above all, the quantity of goods to be carried fufficiently confiderable, to encourage private fubfcriptions, and fecure their effective application. But that this great object cannot be completed until this period arrives, is nearly certain ; and how far, under all the circumftances of the cafe, a very beneficial ftimulus can be given to it by the Government advances recommended by Mr Newenham, may reafonably be queftioned, when we hear fo much of the inveterate propenfity to jobbing, which prevails in Ireland, in the expenditure of the public money. It was no longer ago than the end of laft March, that Sir John Newport ftated in Parliament, that of the 500,000l. granted at the Union for the inland navigation of Ireland, only about 27,000l. had been drawn for, in the courfe of the eight years that had fince elapfed, of which 6000l. had gone in falaries ; fo that the fuperintendance of the expenditure of 21,000l. for public purpofes, had already coft 6000l.

The land carriage of Ireland, which is the subject to which Mr Newenham next proceeds, has been in a very good state for some time ; partly owing to the excellent materials for making roads, which are almost every where at hand,—partly to their being made and repaired from funds raised by the grand juries, instead of the old plan of compulsory labour,—and partly to the use of onehorse cars, instead of heavy waggons. When any system seems to have answered the end proposed, we are naturally prejudiced in its favour. But even good roads may be purchased too dear ; and we have reason to believe, that very just and well-founded complaints prevail respecting the powers of taxation possessed by these grand juries,—the partiality with which the money raised by them is expended,—and the weight and inequality of its pressure on the farmers. In answer to the first part of this complaint, which is slighty adverted to, Mr Newenham, to our utter astonishment, gravely enters into a discussion of the comparative merits of grand jurors and members of Parliament, and seems to determine that the former are as well qualified for imposing taxes as the latter. It is not necessary to refute so very strange an opinion ; but being in search of facts and information, we have to complain of what we consider as a more serious offence. He has no where explained to us the manner in which the sums to be raised by the grand juries are levied. We are hardly qualified to supply this omission ; but we have understood, that in some counties the assessment is made by the plough lands, and in others by the acre. These plough lands, though extremely various in their extent and quality, are all rated alike. It is scarcely credible, but we have been told from good authority, that there is one plough land in the county of Cork, containing 1360 acres, and another in the same county containing only 100 acres; and that these two properties pay the same sum in rates. The extreme injustice and partiality of such a system of taxation need not be insisted on. But even the assessment by the acre, which prevails, we believe, in the greater number of the counties, is in the highest degree objectionable. When a man takes land, as he always must do, according to its *quality*, it must be productive of a most unequal kind of pressure, to tax him afterwards according to its *quantity*. We are surprised that Mr Newenham should speak in so favourable a manner of these assessments. To have good roads, it cannot surely be necessary to commit acts of injustice; and the subject evidently requires legislative interference.

To the great natural richness of the soil of Ireland all writers bear strong testimony. Mr Young, who paid great attention to the subject, and will be allowed to be a competent judge of such matters, says, that, taking acre for acre over the two kingdoms, the comparison will be decidedly in favour of Ireland; and Mr Newenham produces such statements of its fertility, that it must be allowed to vie with the richest in Europe, and surpass any of which England can boast. Nor is it only that the cultivated land of Ireland is superior in its natural quality to that of England; but the parts which have hitherto been neglected are more capable of being brought into a good state, at a much less expense. Of the whole area of Ireland, consisting, according to Dr Beaufort, of 19,439,960 English acres, 13,454,375 acres are considered as cultivated and fertile land; only 1,185,585 acres as inapplicable to the sustenance of man, being the sites of lakes, rivers, roads, towns, &c.; and 4,800,000 acres, as unreclaimed, and at present comparatively unproductive land. Of this latter division, a very large portion, from its nature, situation, and the abundance of natural manures with which it is almost every where surrounded, might be easily reclaimed. It is to these tracts of desert mountains and bogs that Mr Young refers, when he says, ' Upon these lands is to be practised the most profitable husbandry in the King's dominions;' and, according to Mr Newenham, the authors of the Seventeen Statistical Surveys, lately published, speak of the condition and circumstances of these waste lands in similar terms.

Of the cultivated soil of Ireland, by far the greater portion has hitherto had to contend against the united disadvantages of want of capital, and want of skill. It is at once a proof of uncommon fertility of soil, and of excessively bad management, that ten or twelve crops of oats are not unfrequently taken, in uninterrupted succession, from the same fields; and it appears, that only two or three years are necessary to recover the large portion of arable land, of average quality, which is successively reduced

56

to sterility by a long and ruinous continuance of grain crops without dressing, owing to the mismanagement and poverty of the small tenantry. There is reason to believe, that such treatment would render a vast proportion of the land of England altogether useless for at least double the time.

On the whole, if we compare the present produce of the land of Ireland with what it seems easily capable of producing, it will appear to present prodigious resources for agricultural improvements; and to be destined to contribute, much more than in proportion to its size, to the funds of subsistence, and the raw materials of manufactures, raised for the use of the empire.

On the subject, however, of the causes which tend to produce a surplus quantity of food, and regulate the increase of population, Mr Newenham's ideas in this section, are not very distinct. He begins by observing justly, that men, like other animals, will multiply in proportion to their means of subsistence; yet a little further on he says, ' It is generally admitted, that the increase of ' food, though in some rich countries it actually falls short of, ' may yet be made to surpass, the greatest probable increase of ' people ;' and afterwards he intimates, that if only one eighth part of the waste lands of Ireland had been cultivated, the whole supply required by England, in 1799 and 1800, might have been furnished without foreign assistance. Now, the second of these remarks seems evidently in contradiction to the first ; and if the first be true, the last will be more than doubtful; as it will by no means follow, that an additional cultivation to a certain extent will occasion a proportionate excess of produce above consumption. But though we cannot admit the justice of these two last remarks, as here stated, it is still true, that a country, under certain circumstances, may continue to possess an exportable surplus of corn. In an early period of civilization and improvement, the growth of corn is carried on by farmers rather as a profitable manufacture, than as the means of subsistence. It is the nature of this manufacture to produce more food than is consumed by the persons employed in it ; and the surplus will of course be sold at the best market, wherever that may be. If the country be surrounded by rich nations in want of corn, and if its other manufactures be not in a flourishing state, it will generally answer better to the farmer to sell his corn abroad than at home. In this case, the effective demand for a common manufacturing population will be comparatively inconsiderable ; and the wages of labour will be such as to regulate the increase of labourers, not according to the increase of agriculture, but to the increase of agricultural employment. The means of subsistence to the population within the country will consist, not of what the country may grow, but of what this population can purchase; and, of course, the continuance of a redundant growth will in no respect invalidate the general principle, that men, like all other animals, will multiply in proportion to their means of subsistence.

Mr Newenham finishes this first part of his work with the following recapitulation, which may be produced as a useful sketch of the various subjects to which he has adverted, and a favourable specimen of his style.

' With a situation, then, so eminently favourable to foreign commerce ; with a coast so free from danger, and every where presenting safer and more capacious harbours and bays than are to be found in any other country of equal extent in the world ; with so many noble rivers flowing through the land in all directions,—through the richest parts of it,—through as fertile districts as any in Europe, and terminating in harbours, calculated not only by locality, but by every other requisite, for the prosecution of the most extensive traffick with every other nation under the canopy of heaven ; with such vast advantages in respect of artificial navigations ; with such unequalled means of bringing all the parts of the country, as it were, into contact one with another, and affording to each the varied markets of all the rest ; with a climate so far removed from the extremes of heat and cold, as to permit the unhoused labourer to pursue his occupation, without danger or obstruction, throughout the year, and to insure an almost perpetual verdure to the pastures ; with such an abundant supply of those minerals and fossils which are most necessary to the wellbeing of man, and on which human labour and ingenuity may be exerted with the fullest effect ; with such productive fisheries, both off the coasts, and in the rivers and lakes ; with a soil so luxurious and inexhaustible in many places, so fertile in most, and so capable, in all others, of being rendered, at a trifling expense, highly and permanently profitable ; with a singular assemblage of all the various requisites for becoming the great emporium of the commercial world, the theatre of industry and arts, the granary of the West of Europe, and the successful rival of all other countries, antient or modern, in commercial opulence and national strength :—How has it happened, that Ireland was not long since, what the sagacious Sir William Temple affirmed she might become, " one of the richest countries in Europe ? " How has it happened, that she did not long since make, what he affirmed she was capable of making, " a mighty increase of strength and revenue to the Crown of England ? How did it happen, that this fair island, so profusely gifted with all the more valuable boons of nature, continued, until near the close of the last century, in a state of comparative obscurity and national poverty ? How did it happen, that a spirit of industry, and a spirit of commercial enterprize, became completely extinguished among the active, quicksighted, and adventurous people of Ireland ? " The solution of these questions is far from being either difficult or uninteresting. It will constitute the following part. '

Mr Newenham then proceeds to the caufes which have hitherto fruftrated the natural advantages of Ireland. It is of courfe impoffible, in this place, to go through the difgufting detail of the various commercial regulations, which, aided by the penal laws, have produced this melancholy effect. They were dictated by Englifh traders, and were among the worft that ever came from fuch fufpicious advifers. The natural advantages of Ireland feem very early to have excited an alarm in this jealous body; and even the liberality of Sir William Temple, and the knowledge of Dr Davenant yielded, after a fhort ftruggle, to the prevailing fentiment.

Among the many acts dictated by this narrow fpirit, and fubmitted to by the fervile parliament of Ireland, we cannot help alluding to the introduction of one, on account of its being accompanied with a circumftance which puts the commercial intolerance of the times in a very ftriking point of view. We wifh we could fay that fuch times were now entirely over.

The progrefs of the Irifh woollen manufactures, notwithftanding many reftrictions, having ftill continued to give increafing inquietude to the monopolizers of England, the Parliament, under the influence of the Englifh manufacturers, refolved to take decifive meafures to preclude all competition with them on the part of Ireland in foreign markets. The Englifh Lords accordingly prefented an addrefs to William III., ftating, ' that the growing ma-
' nufacture of cloth in Ireland, both by the cheapnefs of all forts
' of the neceffaries of life, and the *goodnefs of materials* for making
' *all manner of cloth*, doth invite his fubjects of England, with their
' families and fervants, to leave their habitation to fettle there, to
' the increafe of the woollen manufacture in Ireland, which makes
' his loyal fubjects in this kingdom very apprehenfive that the
' further growth of it may greatly prejudice the faid manufacture
' here; and praying that his Majefty would be pleafed, in the
' moft public and effectual way that may be, to declare to all his
' fubjects of Ireland, that the growth and increafe of the woollen
' manufacture there hath long, and will ever, be looked upon with
' great jealoufy by all his fubjects of this kingdom.' A fimilar addrefs was prefented by the Commons; and his Majefty was pleafed to fay in anfwer, ' *Gentlemen, I will do all that in me lies*
' *to discourage the woollen manufacture of Ireland.*'

This, it will be obferved, was the anfwer of the moft liberal and enlightened prince of his age; and was fpoken, not of an enemy's country, as from the language one might naturally fuppofe, nor even of a diftant colony likely to be feparated from the parent ftate,—but of a part of the dominions of the crown of England, fo fituated, that its lofs would at all times endanger the fafety of the whole, and every acceffion to the wealth, ftrength and happinefs of which, fhould therefore always be confidered as an acceffion to the wealth, ftrength and fecurity of Great Britain. It was in this manner that, even without the plea of religious animofity, the intereft of the Britifh and Irifh confumers, involving the whole population of the two countries, was facrificed to a few Englifh traders; and the woollen manufacture, for which Ireland poffeffed great facilities, was thus, *by particular desire*, completely crufhed. The fame fyftem was uniformly purfued; and the monopolizers of England alone liftened to, not only with regard to many other manufactures peculiarly fuited to Ireland, but even with regard to the raw produce of its land, and its trade in provifions. The poor refource of a poor country in the neighbourhood of a rich one, was denied to it; and by the 18th of Charles II., which was not repealed till the reign of George III., the importation into England of great cattle, fheep and fwine, beef, pork, and bacon, and, fhortly after, of mutton, lamb, butter and cheefe, was declared a common nuifance, and forbidden on pain of forfeiture.

Hateful as religious animofities are, their connexion with the greater paffions renders them perhaps lefs uniformly difgufting, than that mean and pitiful jealoufy of trade which is thus allowed to crufh the induftry, and reprefs the wealth, of thofe who ought to be confidered as friends and brothers; and there is nothing that the great interefts of fociety more imperioufly call for, than the appointment of governors, who have knowledge to detect, and vigour to refift, thofe mercantile clamours, the uniform object of which is to facrifice the whole to a part.

In the third divifion of his work, Mr Newenham traces thofe acts which have benumbed the induftry, and almoft rendered abortive the natural advantages of Ireland, to religious animofities;—of the rife and progrefs of which he gives an account. We have indeed feen that fome of thefe acts appear to have had another origin. But it may fafely be afferted, that fuch a fyftem of oppreffion as that defcribed by Mr Newenham, could never have been fubmitted to by a Proteftant parliament, and the Proteftant part of the population of Ireland,—if their numerical feeblenefs, compared with the Catholics, and the dread of offending the Britifh government, which was to affift them in oppreffing and keeping down fo large a proportion of their countrymen, had not paralyzed all refiftance. But,

——' even handed justice
Returned the ingredients of their poisoned chalice
To their own lips. '

The fetters which they had been forging for others, neceffarily fhackled their own advances. The eftates of the rich Proteftants felt the want of a free vent for their produce, as well as the farms of the poor Catholics. Time brought to their conviction, that, by a daftardly, fervile and ufelefs compromife, they had facrificed their own wealth and honour by facrificing their country : and this conviction, joined to the very critical fituation of Great Britain, which at once made her unable to affift the dominant party in Ireland, or to punifh their difobedience, gave rife to a fpirit of conciliation between the Proteftants and Catholics, which opened (in 1780), a new era in the hiftory of Ireland. A few acts had indeed been previoufly paffed by the Irifh legiflature, purporting to encourage the induftry of the country, but abfolutely inefficient in their operation ; and a few others had been reluctantly conceded by Great Britain on account of her preffing wants and neceffities, under a change in the courfe of the corn and provifion trade ; but it was not till this period that a regular fyftem of conceffion was begun, which, however the event may be delayed by accidental circumftances, *must* terminate either in *complete emancipation,* or *complete separation.*

It is unnecessary to refer more particularly to the well known acts passed in favour of Ireland about this time ; but it is juftly observed by Mr Newenham, that ' for the liberation of their trade, and the establishment of legislative independence, Irishmen, who advert to the spirit and unanimity of the volunteers in 1779 and 1782, can scarcely fail to experience a considerable diminution of their gratitude for these boons to Britain. '—' The truth is, ' (he goes on to say), ' that had it not been for want in the former case, and fear in the latter, on the part of Britain, we should, in 1800, have been in no respect better than fifty years before ; and to want and fear, it is certain that many Irishmen look for such further improvements of their condition as may be necessary, rather than to liberality or sound policy, the effects whereof they have certainly not been in the habit of experiencing. '

Of all the beneficial acts which were passed by the newly independent Legislature of Ireland, there are none which seem to make so great an impression on Mr Newenham, as the corn laws. He devotes, in consequence, two sections to a digression concerning the bounties on the exportation of corn granted in the session of 1783-4, and their effects. We really believe, that, in the circumstances in which Ireland was placed, a beneficial stimulus was given to its agriculture by these regulations. Though we do not assent to the doctrine, that corn measures the value of silver ; yet, in those countries in which corn is the principal food of the lower classes of society, it must be allowed to influence the value of silver. But in Ireland, where the principal food is potatoes, this influence cannot be felt in the same degree ; and a more effective stimulus on the production of corn would of course be given by a bounty upon its exportation. We cannot however by any means agree with Mr Newenham, in attributing, as he seems to do, the greatest part of the prosperity of Ireland, since 1784, to this cause. The history which he has himself given of the commercial injustice of Great Britain, amply accounts for the low state of Irish agriculture during the greatest part of the century ; and the happy period, which produced a change of measures, and abrogated the penal laws against the Catholics relating to land, accompanied, as it happened to be, by the increasing wants of Great Britain for corn, could not fail of turning a considerable quantity of fresh capital to the cultivation of the soil.

Without determining, however, how much is to be attributed to bounties, and how much to other causes, the fact seems to be certain, that the tillage of Ireland has been increasing at a very rapid rate, while the exports of its pasture products have remained undiminished, and the internal consumption of them has been daily augmented. The natural effect of a great increase of produce, is a great increase of rents. And this effect, in the case of Ireland, has been rendered more remarkable by the cooperation of other causes,—the natural fertility of the soil,—the small capitals required to work it,—the use of potatoes as the principal food of the common people,—and the absence of poor laws. Mr Young, in 1778, computed the rental of Ireland at six millions ; Mr Newenham, partly from some surveys, the results of which he has given in tables in his appendix, partly from information which he says he received from various quarters, and partly, as we conceive, from conjecture, states the present rental at fifteen millions, exclusive of the ground rents of the houses in the different towns. This is, to be sure, a prodigious increase, though we think it highly probable that it is not overrated. It is nearly certain, that if the lands of Ireland were relet at the present moment, a larger share of the whole produce would, from the causes above mentioned, fairly belong to the landlord, than would fall to his lot in any other country of Europe. This share of the whole produce is indeed probably as large now, as it ever will be.

In the progress of improvement, the increasing capitals of the tenantry will require a larger remuneration ; and though, from these increasing capitals, produce will continue to increase, and rents to rise, yet the future proportion of rent to produce may not be so great as at present.

Among the most beneficial consequences of the extension of agriculture, which Mr Newenham strangely perseveres in referring almost exclusively to Mr Foster's acts, he dwells particularly on its effects upon the Catholic population.   It has contributed so much, he thinks, to increase their numbers, wealth and influence, and has connected their prosperity so closely with the general prosperity of agriculture, and the interests of the Protestant landlords, the Protestant clergy, and the Protestant manufacturers, that as they can never again be kept down as they were formerly, their daily increasing strength must ultimately obtain for them that justice which has been so long refused.

In a note to a previous section (p. 185), Mr Newenham produces some facts relating to the proportion of the Roman Catholic to the Protestant population.   From some of these it appears, that not only the *proportion*, but the actual *number* of the Protestants, has diminished since the middle of the last century. This we should not have expected; and the facts stated are hardly sufficient to convince us of its truth.   But there are the most obvious reasons, as we stated in a former article, why the Catholic part of the population should have been increasing much more rapidly than the Protestant part.

The endeavours which were used in former times to banish the Roman Catholics from the towns, had the effect of rendering the rural population chiefly Catholic ; and it is upon this part of the people, consisting of the poorest in Ireland, that the peculiar facility of increase, occasioned by the use of potatoes, has naturally operated with the greatest force.   Wherever the Protestants are situated, whether in the towns, where they are principally to be found, or in the country, they uniformly seem to consider themselves as persons belonging to a class in the community superior to that of the lower orders of the Catholics.   Even the linen weavers of the North, who are probably among the poorest of the Protestants, earn, according to Mr Young, about double the wages of the labourers in husbandry, and feel so much of the pride belonging to a superior condition, that they have generally preferred emigration, * to being reduced much below their usual rank in society, although there might be little chance of their wanting the means of subsistence for their families.   But the humiliated Catholic, with no rank in society to support, has sought only these means of subsistence ; and finding, without much difficulty, potatoes, milk, and a hovel, he has vegetated in the country of his ancestors, and overspread the land with his descendants.   If to this consideration we add a circumstance, in which all writers seem to agree, that of the great encouragement

---

* According to Arthur Young, the emigrations to America, which were at one time so considerable, consisted almost exclusively of the Protestants of the North of Ireland.

given to the marriages of the Catholic poor by the parish priest, on account of his deriving a very considerable part of his revenue from them, we shall see no reason to be surprised at the increasing proportion of the Catholics to the Protestants. And there can be no doubt, that while the same causes continue to operate, this proportion will continue yearly to increase.

With respect to the general amount of the population of Ireland, Mr Newenham seems inclined to adhere to his former computations, which, he says, subsequent researches have strongly conduced to substantiate. No new statements are given on the subject in the body of the work; but, in the Appendix, some interesting statistical tables are added, which, as far as they go, and as far as they can be depended on, certainly tend to confirm his computations, and mark, in particular, a very rapid increase of population.

In the town and diocese of Cork, the proportion of Catholic births to the Catholic population, is nearly as high as 1 to 23 ; and of marriages to births as 1 to above 5 ;—both indications of early marriages, large families, and full houses. In the diocese of Ross, the survey of which, Mr Newenham says, may entirely be depended on, the number of persons to a house appeared, by enumeration, to be 6 and a small fraction ; and the proportion of births to the population was as 1 to 24 and a fraction; the proportion of Catholics to Protestants as 31 to 1. Of the accuracy of the other surveys, Mr Newenham cannot speak, from his own knowledge, with so much certainty ; but sees no reason to doubt them. In one of them, which relates to the diocese of Limerick, the proportion of births to deaths is stated as above $2\frac{3}{4}$ to 1 ; though the proportion of baptisms to the population is not so great as in the diocese of Cork, which makes the account rather doubtful. These surveys, which are unfortunately too confined as to their extent, to warrant very general inferences, were made by the Catholic clergy of the different parishes, at the request of Mr Newenham ; and, besides the particulars above alluded to, contain other interesting information,—such as, the wages of labour,—the rent of land,—the number of acres cultivated, uncultivated, and barren, &c. &c. Before the enumerations relating to parochial registers were proceeded on, Mr Newenham observed to one of the superiors of the Roman Catholic clergy, by whose influence the business was pursued, that the detection of an exaggeration in any one instance, would obviously have the effect of bringing discredit on all the returns, and, consequently, that of weakening whatever reasoning might be employed in behalf of the Roman Catholics, founded upon their numerical importance. To this it was replied, that, generally speaking, the parochial Roman Catholic clergy concerned themselves but very little in political speculations ; and that there existed rather more reason to apprehend, that they would underrate, than overrate, the numbers of their parishioners ; as, in the latter event, they would impress their Bishop with the expediency of appointing coadjutors, who would participate in their scanty incomes, as well as in their labours.

On the whole, there seems to be no doubt of the very rapid increase of population in the Southern and Western parts of Ireland ; and if Mr Newenham's former computations are in any respect exaggerated, which we have sometimes heard suggested, particularly with regard to the number of persons which he allows to a house, we think it must have arisen from his applying the proportions which he has found in the Southern and Western counties too generally to the other parts of the kingdom.

On the subject of the general condition of the Catholic labourers, we have to complain that Mr Newenham has nowhere given us sufficient information. We wished much to have the means of judging, whether the increase of tillage, and the increase of rents occasioned by it, has essentially contracted the abundance of the Irish cotter ; or whether the increase of his wages, which is generally acknowledged, has as yet fully counteracted the increased price which he pays for his land. But though Mr Newenham states very distinctly, that the wages of labour in husbandry have risen, since the time of Mr Young's tour, from 6½d. to 10½d. a day, yet he has not given us, as Mr Young did, a list of prices with which to compare these earnings. We have understood, that the growing price and the market price of potatoes have hardly risen in proportion to the rise of wages ; but that milk, which is almost a necessary addition to a potatoe diet, has become so scarce in the tillage districts, as to occasion a great diminution of comfort and health ; and it seems to be generally agreed, that all other articles, except potatoes, have advanced in price faster than the advance of wages. It is indeed one of the radical evils of the use of potatoes, as the principal food of the lower classes, that the abundance in which they are supplied, and their consequent cheapness, by no means occasions a proportional cheapness of other commodities. On the contrary, this very abundance contributes to the high rent of land, which, of course, must tend to raise the price of the cattle, wood, or materials of manufactures which are raised upon it ;—a proof, by the by, among many others, that the price of the common food of the labouring classes cannot be considered as regulating the prices of other commodities.

It is not improbable, that the scarcity of milk above alluded to,

65

combined with the increasing quantity of corn grown, from the extension of tillage, may gradually induce the Irish labourer to mix a greater quantity of oats or other corn with his potatoe diet, than has hitherto been usual; and we are convinced that such a change would, on the whole, be favourable to his general condition; but, whether any approaches to it are taking place at present, we are not informed.

We have heard from some quarters, that a decided improvement, of late years, may be observed in the dress of the peasantry, and the furniture of their cabins. From other sources we have been informed, that their general condition has been unquestionably deteriorated, by an advance of rents and prices greater than the advance in their wages. On these points, authentic information extending to the whole kingdom is much wanted; and it is a great fault in Mr Newenham's work, that he has not endeavoured more fully to supply it. We should rejoice to hear, that the check to the present rapid increafe of population, which must necessarily soon take place, had begun to operate from an increasing taste for comforts and conveniences, before it was forced from the absolute want of food; but we own we have not much hope of any marked and striking change of this kind, till the Protestant and Catholic are in every respect put on a level.

On the important subject of the education of the Catholic poor, Mr Newenham has produced some information which has at once surprised and gratified us. He has asserted that, in point of literary attainments, they are far above the level of the same classes in England; and this assertion seems to be confirmed by some of the tables in his Appendix. In one of these tables, it appears that, in the dioceses of Cloyne and Ross alone, there are no less than 316 parochial schools kept by Catholics; and that they are attended, during the summer, by 21,892 scholars. It is pleasing to have this information accompanied by such other statements respecting the county of Cork, as to lead us to believe that its criminal calendar is, in proportion to its population, unusually free from great crimes. The Protestant schools in Ireland, with all the aid which they have received from government, seem to be by no means in a flourishing state; and the scholars which attend them do not equal, by 6000, the number that attend the Catholic schools in the diocese of Cloyne and Ross alone.

This increased attention to education among the lower classes of the Irish, Mr Newenham attributes to the care and industry of the Catholic clergy, of whose general conduct, politeness, erudition, and pastoral exertions as a body, he speaks in the highest terms. How far he may be unduly biassed by the civilities which he appears to have received from them, we will not pretend to say;

but if we might in any respect judge of them, by a letter which he has produced in the Appendix, we should think that his picture was by no means overcharged. This letter, which gives an account of the present state of the Catholic church, and Catholic clergy, in Ireland, which is very little known in England, we particularly recommend to the reader's attention ; and we should insert the whole of it, if it were not too long for our limits. We earnestly wish that Mr Perceval would attend to those parts of this letter which relate to the causes which have affected, and may be expected to affect, the influence of the Catholic clergy in Ireland over their flocks.

The last division of Mr Newenham's work, consisting of eight sections, contains the Rebellion, the Union, and a great deal of miscellaneous matter which we have not room to comment upon. In his proposals for the improvement of Ireland, which occupy the three last sections, he is much too fond of public grants and bounties ; and seems entirely to mistake the duty of government, which is to stand by and see fair play, and not to be actively assisting—first one party, and then another, as its caprice may direct. In the true mercantile spirit, and with a view, we imagine, to conciliate a nation of merchants, he proposes to the Legislature to give additional encouragements to the tillage of Ireland, as the occupation least likely to interfere with the manufacturers of Great Britain ; and most preposterously recommends that the present high prices of corn should be maintained by fresh bounties, even after the surplus of Ireland should exceed the supply required by Great Britain, in order that the Irish farmers should gain fifteen millions for further improvements ! It is unnecessary, we hope, to comment upon such proposals. To act under the dread of interfering with Great Britain, is directly contrary to the spirit of the Union ; and to propose encouragements to the exportation of corn, with high prices and profits for their ultimate object, instead of plenty, is a gross abuse even of the system of bounties.

We are friends to the agriculture of Ireland ; but should propose to encourage it with other views, and in other ways. Among the grievances which are felt by the small tenantry, none press so hard, nor give occasion to such constant irritation, as the unexpected demands so frequently occasioned by new county rates, and new valuations of tithe. The insurrections of the *Oak Boys* and *Steel Boys*, according to Arthur Young, were owing, in a considerable degree, to oppressive county cesses ; and it is well known, that the long-protracted commotions of the White Boys, originated in the grievance of tithes. It may be asserted as a general truth, that the taxes which fall on the tenantry of a

country, are, of all others, the most prejudicial to the individual, and the most disadvantageous to the public; because the
tenant of land has rarely the power, like other traders, of raising
the price of the produce in which he deals, in proportion to the
tax,—or of resorting to the alternative of withdrawing his capital;
and if he had this power, the public would most materially suffer from it. But this truth, which is not sufficiently attended to
in general, applies with peculiar force to the state of Ireland, on
account of the extreme poverty of a large portion of the tenants.
The competition for land, and the improvidence of the competitors, seem to be such, that they are willing to take farms, if they
have but a tolerable prospect of getting on, under the existing
outgoings at the time of taking the lease; and in such circumstances, a new demand must often find them absolutely unable
to answer it. The very great proportion of the whole produce
possessed by the Irish landlord, contrasted with the very scanty
proportion possessed by his tenants, presents, we conceive, the
natural remedy to this evil. And if he were obliged to take the
burden of all permanent taxes on the land, upon their first impo-
sition, we are convinced that he would be amply remunerated,
not only by the happiness of his tenants, but by the superior
state of his farms when they came to be relet, and the consequent greater advance of his rents.

The sacrifice, it is evident, would only be temporary,—as it is
universally acknowledged, that all taxes upon tenants fall upon
the landlord at the renewal of a lease; but the misfortune is,
that a pressure during a few years, which would scarcely be felt
by a man of property, is sometimes sufficient, in Ireland, to ruin
both the farmer and the farm, and to spread dissatisfaction and
irritation far and wide over the country.

We are no advocates for the territorial tax of the Economists;
but we certainly think, that the peculiar state of Ireland calls
upon the Legislature, by every principle of justice and policy,
to remove the burden of the partial and oppressive county rates,
and the still heavier and more oppressive burden of tithes, from
the poor tenantry, to the rich landlords. Such a measure would
be an effective and permanent encouragement to agriculture; and
would go further in allaying the discontents of Ireland, than any
thing short of complete emancipation,—which, at all events, it
ought to accompany.

The tables in the Appendix, relating to the corn trade of Ireland, exhibit a very promifing picture of its increafing exports, and
explain in great meafure the caufe of the decreafing wants of the
empire for foreign corn. According to *Chalmers's estimate,* the
annual importation of all forts of corn, for the five years previous

to the fcarcity of 1800, was 1,191,131 quarters. In the committee on diftilleries, the foreign corn imported during five years ending with the 5th of January 1808, was calculated at only 700,000 quarters annually. This beneficial change has undoubtedly arifen, in part, from the ftimulus given to Britifh agriculture by the late high prices ; but by far the greater part will be found to be attributable to the increafing fupplies of corn from Ireland, and the circumftance of Irifh corn being included in the foreign imports before the Union. During the laft year, Ireland exported 875,096 barrels of corn, (about 540,000 quarters), nearly the whole of which came to Britain. If this quantity be added to the 700,000 quarters of foreign corn at prefent imported, the amount will exceed the average importations of the five years before the fcarcity, and fhow clearly in what manner the change in queftion has arifen. There can be little doubt, from the progreffive ftate of the Irifh exports of corn, that if things remain quiet fome years, the empire will be entirely independent of foreign fupplies, except in times of fcarcity ; and for this independence it will be indebted to Ireland.

In our review of Mr Newenham's former work, we obferved, that if England were to choofe a territory calculated to afford her the moft effectual affiftance, fhe could not have fixed upon a portion of land of the fame extent, fo peculiarly fuited to her wants as Ireland. We were then alluding principally to the defence of the empire ; but the fame thought forces itfelf upon us when we advert to its refources ; and it is impoffible to contemplate the immenfe fupplies of the very firft importance, which we receive from this fruitful ifland, and their prodigious capability of increafe, without feeling the conviction that it fhould ever be prized and cherifhed by us as our richeft mine of wealth, as well as our ftrongeft pillar of defence.

And yet this is the country the lofs of which is daily rifked by the inhuman cry of no popery,—by the bigotry and littlenefs of one part of an adminiftration, and by the tergiverfation and inconfiftency of the other. It is really fickening to think, that at a period when every heart and hand is wanted to rally round the laft remains of liberty in Europe, a fet of men fhould be found at the head of affairs, who are either abfolutely incapable, from narrownefs of intellect, of profiting by the great leffons of experience that are daily unfolding themfelves ; or, whatever their opinions may be, are willing to facrifice them and their country at the fhrine of prefent place and emolument !

We have all juftly reprobated the impolicy of the Supreme Junta of Spain, in not anticipating the offers of Bonaparte ; and in leaving it a matter of rational doubt to the people, whether it might

not be for their happinefs to accept them.   But in fpite of the
glaring bad effects of fuch conduct on the fateful ftruggle in Spain,
are we not acting with infinitely greater folly and feeblenefs towards a part of our own empire ?   Are we not even, by repeated
infults and difappointments, taking the moft effectual means to
alienate, difguft, and irritate a people who will foon have the fame
offers made to them from the fame quarter ?   The blaze of hope
and of joy which lately illumined the horizon of Spain, is now
funk into a few feeble gleams ; the impending effort of Auftria
feems to be but the prelude to her final extinction ; and what fhall
then prevent the ruthlefs victor from turning his conquering arms
towards the weft ?   We own that we fhould fee with dread even
a very fmall French army in Ireland, after the councils of the empire had been for fome time guided by the prefent Chancellor of
the Exchequer,—by a man, who thinks he can fave Ireland by ir-
ritating its clergy, and being fparing in his grants to the College of
Maynooth.

There is one, and one only way, of rendering all the offers and
efforts of Bonaparte powerlefs.   The time is fhort ; but it may yet
be fufficient.   Before the conquering legions of France return
from the Danube, let us, by a great and generous act, prepare the
hearts of the Irifh for their reception.   Let the reign of George III.
be diftinguifhed by the glorious completion of thofe conceffions
which it commenced.   Let the Irifh Catholics have all that they
have demanded ; for they have afked nothing but what ftrict juftice and good policy fhould concede to them.   Let them not only
enjoy all the civil advantages of the Britifh conftitution, but give
them a church eftablifhment, like Scotland ; and we venture to
predict, that the increafing proportion of the Catholics will foon be
lefs perceptible.   Let the fpirit of the Union, or what ought to
have been its fpirit, be carried into execution without fear or jealoufy, till Ireland is in no refpect to be diftinguifhed from any
other part of the empire, but by its fituation, and fuperior fertility.

Such a train of meafures, begun by the Government with earneft-
nefs and good faith, and while yet the power of the fword is in
its hand, would foon work a change in the feelings of men who
are known to be highly fufceptible of gratitude and affection, and
who could receive no fuch offers from other quarters; and though
we will not affirm that all the difcontented would be immediately
conciliated, yet we are confident that they would be reduced to fo
few as to be perfectly infignificant, and that the country would
then be completely fecure againft foreign invafion or domeftic trea-
fon.   Notwithftanding the known capricioufnefs and perverfenefs
of man, we believe that not a fingle inftance can be produced in
hiftory, of an eftablifhed government being unable to fupprefs dif-
contents, when juftice was clearly and entirely on its fide.

In the prefent wreck of empires, and under the extinction of all international law, no *small* ftate can hope to maintain its independence. Great Britain and Ireland, from their fituation, their language, and their mutual necessities, feem naturally deftined to fupport each other's ftrength, and fupply each other's wants ; and we are quite convinced, that nothing but extreme mifgovernment can feparate them. Heavy indeed, then, will be the refponfibility of thofe men, under whofe adminiftration, or by whofe previous unconciliatory meafures fuch a feparation is effected—whether the immediate caufe of it be foreign conqueft, or internal commotion.

From *Edinburgh Review,* February 1811

For Semmel's commentary on this article by Malthus, see especially pp. 19-21 *supra*. (*Publisher*).

ART. V.   *An Inquiry into the Effects produced on the National Currency and Rates of Exchange by the Bank Restriction Bill.* By Robert Mushet.

The High Price of Bullion a Proof of the Depreciation of Bank Notes. By David Ricardo.

Observations on the Principles which regulate the Course of the Exchange. By William Blake.

The Question concerning the Depreciation of our Currency stated and examined. By William Huskisson, Esq. M. P.

Practical Observations on the Report of the Bullion Committee.
By Charles Bosanquet.

Reply to Mr Bosanquet's Obervations on the Report of the Bullion Committee. By David Ricardo.

THE two first of these pamphlets deserve particular commendation, for having given a beginning to the interesting discussion which is still going on, with regard to the present extraordinary depreciation of our paper currency. The attention which
was drawn to the same important question a few years ago, by
the very clear and masterly view of the subject given by Lord
King, and the uncommon combination of extensive knowledge
of detail with just principles, exhibited in the work of Mr H.
Thornton, seems to have had the effect of checking the progress
of the evil, though not of entirely removing it. The great subsequent prosperity of our commerce, owing to our peculiarly fortunate situation compared with the rest of Europe, having improved our foreign exchanges, the depreciation of our currency,
which still existed in a certain degree, was no longer thought of;
and the subject, as might be expected, was allowed to drop.

Within the last two years, however, the progress of depreciation has been so rapid, as to force itself on the attention of all
who were in any degree acquainted with its symptoms; and
as it is not the practice of the public to resort to advice called
forth on temporary occasions when similar occasions recur, Mr
Mushet and Mr Ricardo seem to have been fully justified in their
endeavours to excite fresh attention to so important a subject by
new publications.

Nor are their *endeavours* alone entitled to our commendation :
the manner in which they have executed their tasks, deserves
a very considerable degree of praise. Mr Mushet has the great
merit of stating some very important truths in so clear and simple
a manner, as admirably to fit them for admission into the minds
of those who are not very familiar with such investigations; while
his errors are so inconsiderable, that the reader is in no danger of
being led far from the right course. His suggestions respecting
a recoinage of silver, and the mode of preserving it from degradation, well deserve the attention of the government. It should
also be observed, that the judicious selection of tables subjoined
to this publication, give it a very great additional interest, which
has not been superseded even by the valuable Appendix to the
Report of the Bullion Committee.

Mr Ricardo's pamphlet contains an excellent view of the general principles of circulation, and of the various results which

are occasioned in different countries by the variations in their respective currencies. He is, in our opinion, particularly entitled to praise for the manner in which he has laid down two most important docrines,—long known, indeed, and acknowledged by those who have maturely considered these subjects, but not unfrequently overlooked by others.

The first is the grand doctrine, which may be said to be the main hinge on which the principles of circulation, whether consisting of a paper currency, or of the precious metals, must necessarily turn ;—the doctrine, that every kind of circulating medium, as well as every other kind of commodity, is necessarily depreciated by excess, and raised in value by deficiency, compared with the demand, without reference either to confidence or intrinsic use. This doctrine follows immediately from the general principles of supply and demand, which are unquestionably the foundation on which the whole superstructure of political economy is built. And if we deny the application of these principles to the currencies of different countries, it will be quite impossible to explain the reason why the wants of some countries do not absolutely exhaust them of the precious metals, and the desireable products of others overload them with bullion ;—and why, instead of such a state of things, the precious metals are, on the whole, maintained in such proportions in the different countries of the commercial world, as, in reference to the commodities which form the subjects of their mutual intercourse, to be nearly of the same value in each.

The other doctrine, to which we have alluded, nearly connected with the former, and, from its being less generally known, even more important on the present occasion, is the doctrine, that excess and deficiency of currency are only *relative* terms ; that the circulation of a country can never be superabundant, except in relation to other countries ; that, as, after the discovery of the American mines, the different countries of Europe absorbed into their circulation three or four times the quantity of gold and silver which they before possessed, so, if the paper currency of one country would pass in another, or if proportional issues were made in all the different countries of the commercial world at the same time, there is no limit to the quantity which might be absorbed, without any such redundancy as would overfill the circulation, and occasion the efflux of the precious metals, though it might be continually occasioning the melting of coin into bullion.

A clear understanding of this doctrine is absolutely necessary, in order to explain what is meant by *excessive* issues of paper ;

and to enable us fully to comprehend the grand distinction, between the wants of the circulation, in order to maintain it on a level with bullion or the currencies of surrounding countries,—and the wants of private merchants, and of the government for the purposes of business, and national expenditure.

These two important doctrines are, in the course of Mr Ricardo's discussion, explained with great clearness and precision; and both he and Mr Mushet appear to us to have completely succeeded in proving the actual depretiation of our currency, and in tracing it to its true cause. They have both also the satisfaction of having seen their main views of the subject, and the remedy which they recommend, sanctioned by a Report, drawn up with great care and ability by a committee of the House of Commons, consisting of some of the best informed men of their time; and founded upon a body of curious evidence, and a set of instructive documents, which would have been utterly beyond the reach of private individuals.

The great fault of Mr Ricardo's performance, is the partial view which he takes of the causes which operate upon the course of Exchange.

Independently of the wearing or the adulteration of the coin, the effects of which are readily intelligible, there are, we conceive, two causes, perfectly distinct in their origin, though nearly similar in their effects, by which the exchange is affected. The first, and the most ordinary, is the varying demand for different sorts of produce arising from the varying desires and necessities of the nations connected with each other by commerce : The second is a comparative redundancy or deficiency of currency, in whatever way it may be occasioned.

If, for instance, in consequence of the sudden adoption of some foreign commodity into general use, or the sudden deficiency of some commodity of home growth, which must be supplied from abroad, the imports of a particular country should exceed its exports, the exchange might be turned greatly against it ; and it might be obliged to make some of its payments in bullion, although, previous to the extraordinary imports occasioned by these new desires or new wants, both its bullion and its currency might have been precisely of the same value as those of the country into which they were now flowing.

In this case, it is quite clear, that the exportation of bullion was the *effect of a balance of trade*, originating in causes which may exist without any relation whatever to redundancy or deficiency of currency.

In other cases, a redundancy or deficiency of currency is the exciting *cause of the balance of trade* and payments, and of the exportation or the importation of bullion.

An efflux or influx of the precious metals, for instance, originating in the first cause, could exist but a very short time, before it would produce a comparative deficiency in one country, and redundancy in the other ; and, by the convertibility of bullion into coin, and coin into bullion, a proportional change in the bullion value of their respective currencies.

But the country, with a diminishing quantity of bullion, would evidently soon be limited in its powers of paying with the precious metals, while, at the same time, it would be encouraged to sell by the low bullion prices of its goods, and the foreign demand for them, occasioned by the fall in its bills. On the other hand, the country, with an increasing quantity of bullion, would have its power of purchasing with the precious metals increased, and its encouragement to sell diminished, by the advanced bullion prices of its goods, and the diminished foreign demand for them occasioned by the premium upon its bills. This state of things could not fail to have a speedy effect in changing the direction of the balance of payments, and in restoring that equilibrium of the precious metals, which had been for a time disturbed by the naturally unequal wants and necessities of the countries which trade with each other.

A similar effect would be produced upon the imports and exports, by the discovery of a new mine, or the increased issues of paper, as long as such issues continued to throw coin out of circulation. In these cases, the redundancy or deficiency of currency is the *cause* of an unfavourable or favourable balance of trade, an unfavourable or favourable course of the real exchanges, and the consequent exportation or importation of bullion.

It is of the utmost importance to keep these two distinct causes, which affect the course of exchange, constantly in view ; because they sometimes act in conjunction, and sometimes in opposition to each other; and the results produced by their sum, or their difference, cannot of course be accounted for by either the one or the other taken separately. Mr Ricardo, however, instead of directing his attention to both these causes, confines it to only one of them. He attributes a favourable or unfavourable exchange *exclusively* to a redundant or deficient currency, and overlooks the varying desires and wants of different societies, as an original cause of a temporary excess of imports above exports, or exports above imports.

To point out more explicitly the effects of these partial views on the reasoning of Mr Ricardo, we will quote his criticism on a passage in Mr Thornton's work on *Paper credit*, in which the error of his principles appears in a very striking light.

Mr Thornton had stated in substance, that a very unfavourable balance of trade might be occasioned in this country by a bad harvest ; that there might be at the same time an unwillingness in the country to which we were indebted, to receive our goods in payment ; and that, under these circumstances, the balance due must be paid in part by bullion. On this statement Mr Ricardo observes, that ' Mr Thornton has not explained to us, ' why any unwillingness should exist in the foreign country to ' receive our goods in exchange for their corn ; and it would be ' necessary for him to show, that if such an unwillingness were ' to exist, we should agree to indulge it so far, as to part with ' our coin. If we consent to give coin in exchange for goods, ' it must be from choice, not necessity. We should not import ' more goods than we export, unless we had a redundancy of ' currency which it therefore suits us to make a part of our ex- ' ports. The exportation of coin is caused by its cheapness ; ' and is not the effect, but the cause, of an unfavourable balance. ' We should not export it, if we did not send it to a better mar- ' ket ; or if we had any commodity which we could export more ' profitably. It is a salutary remedy for a redundant currency ; ' and as I have endeavoured to prove that redundancy or excess ' is only a relative term, it follows, that the demand for it abroad ' arises only from the comparative deficiency of the currency of ' the importing country which there causes its superior value. ' This reasoning, Mr Ricardo applies equally to the stronger case of the payment of a subsidy to a foreign power.

Now, we would ask, what necessary connexion there is between the wants of a nation for unusual importations of corn, occasioned by a bad harvest, or its desire to transmit a large subsidy to a foreign power occasioned by a treaty to that effect,—and the question of redundant or deficient currencies ? Surely, such wants or desires might occur in one of two countries, where, immediately previous to their existence, the precious metals circulated as nearly as possible on a level. And the unwillingness of the country to which the debt is owing, to receive in payment a great quantity of goods, beyond what it is in the habit of giving orders for, and consuming, stands much less in need of explanation, than that a bad harvest, or the necessity of paying a subsidy in one country, should be immediately and invariably accompanied by an unusual demand for muslins, hardware, and colonial produce in some other. We know indeed, that such a demand will to a certain degree exist, owing to the fall in the bills upon the debtor country, and the consequent opportunity of purchasing its commodities at a cheaper rate than usual. But if the debt for the corn or the subsidy be considerable, and require prompt payment, the bills on the debtor country will fall below the price of the transport of the precious metals. A part of the debt will be paid in these metals; and a part by the increased exports of commodities. But, as far as it is paid by the transmission of bullion, this transmission does not merely originate in redundancy of currency. It is not occasioned by its cheapness. It is not, as Mr Ricardo endeavours to persuade us, the cause of the unfavourable balance, instead of the effect. It is not merely a salutary remedy for a redundant currency : But it is owing precisely to the cause mentioned by Mr Thornton—the unwillingness of the creditor nation to receive a great additional quantity of goods not wanted for immediate consumption, without being bribed to it by excessive cheapness; and its willingness to receive bullion—the currency of the commercial world —without any such bribe. It is unquestionably true, as stated by Mr Ricardo, that no nation will pay a debt in the precious metals, if it can do it cheaper by commodities ; but the prices of commodities are liable to great depressions from a glut in the market ;—whereas the precious metals, on account of their having been constituted, by the universal consent of society, the general medium of exchange, and instrument of commerce, will pay a debt of the largest amount at its nominal estimation, according to the quantity of bullion contained in the respective currencies of the countries in question. And, whatever variations between the quantity of currency and commodities, may be stated to take place subsequent to the commencement of these transactions, it cannot be for a moment doubted, that the cause of them is to be found in the wants and desires of one of the two nations, and not in any original redundancy or deficiency of currency in either of them.

The same kind of error which we have here noticed, pervades other parts of Mr Ricardo's pamphlet, particularly the opening of his subject. He seems to think, that when once the precious metals have been divided among the different countries of the earth, according to their relative wealth and commerce, that each having an equal necessity for the quantity actually in use, no temptation would be offered for their importation or exportation, till either a new mine, or a new bank was opened; or till some marked change had taken place in their relative prosperity.

That the discovery of a new mine, or the opening of a new bank, on which Mr Ricardo lays his principal stress, are most powerful causes of the efflux and influx of bullion, we are most ready to acknowledge ; but they certainly are not the sole causes. The wants of different nations with different climates, and dif-

ferent degrees of fertility, cannot, with any degree of probability, be supposed, in the first instance, *exactly* to balance each
other. They are only forced to this kind of level by the absolute impossibility, if they have no mines, of continuing to purchase more than they sell; and the rapid effect which the exportation of even a very moderate quantity of the precious metals has in raising the currency of the exporting, and lowering
that of the importing country. But, while this level is, on the
whole, maintained, we cannot doubt that the varying wants of
these nations frequently subject them to unfavourable or favourable balances of payment, beyond what can be easily settled by
bills : and that to settle these, and to carry on the various roundabout foreign trades of consumption, there ever has been, and
always will be, a quantity of the precious metals in use destined
to perform the same part with regard to the different nations
connected with each other by commerce, which the currency of
a particular country performs with regard to its distant provinces.

To the pamphlet of Mr Ricardo succeeded, we believe, the
able and original observations of Mr Blake, on the principles
which regulate the course of exchange ; and the public is certainly indebted to him for a very valuable addition to their stock
of information on the important subject which now occupies so
much of their attention. We wish that we had room to point
out to the reader many of the clear and masterly statements contained in this publication ; but when we consider the quantity
of matter still before us, we are compelled to confine ourselves
chiefly to the more invidious task of pointing out what we conceive to be its errors. Mr Blake observes, in his introduction, that
‘ the computed exchange varies from two causes totally distinct
from each other. The first, arising from the abundance or scarcity of bills in the market, is the foundation of what may be
called the *real* exchange ; which depends upon the payments
which a country has to make, compared with those it has to receive, and has no reference to the state of the currency. The
second, arising from alterations in the value of the currency,
is the foundation of what may be called the *nominal* exchange ;
which has no reference whatever to the state of debt and credit
of the country. ’ He then proceeds, in three distinct sections,
to comment, first, upon the real exchange ; secondly, upon the
nominal exchange ; and, thirdly, upon the computed exchange,
or the combined results of both, as they appear in the printed
accounts.

In discussing the first branch of his subject, he has entirely
avoided the error of Mr Ricardo, and has traced the causes of

78

the real exchange to the varying desires and necessities of different nations, which naturally make them sometimes debtors, and sometimes creditors, to the countries with which they deal, although their respective currencies may be in a state of the most perfect equality of value. The great fault which appears in this part of Mr Blake's work, is, that though he has explained certain causes of the real exchange, and their various effects on mercantile transactions, in the clearest and most satisfactory manner, yet, he has omitted to notice one of the principal causes; and, so far, has left his section on the real exchange incomplete.

In proceeding to the discussion of the nominal exchange, he assumes as a postulatum, for the sake of clearness, that the real exchange remains unaltered : he, at the same time, considers an alteration in the total amount of the currency of a country, without a corresponding alteration of the commodities to be circulated by it, as the main cause which, in the present times, affects the nominal exchange ; and the cause, therefore, to which he intends to direct his chief attention. He is thus at once led into the grave error of implying, what indeed he distinctly maintains afterwards, that an alteration in the amount of the currency of a country, without a corresponding alteration in its commodities, has no tendency to affect the real exchange, and to cause an exportation or importation of bullion.

We are quite ready to agree with Mr Blake, that the *nominal* exchange, as far as it is *merely nominal*, has no tendency of this kind ; but, we are firmly persuaded, with Mr Ricardo, that, as long as there is any quantity of coin to be displaced, and converted into bullion by increased issues of paper, so long will such increased issues continue to raise the bullion, as well as the nominal prices of commodities ; that if the bullion prices of commodities be raised, what Mr Blake calls the real prices current will be raised; and the raising of the real prices current cannot fail to discourage the sale of home produce, and encourage the purchase of foreign produce, occasion a discount upon home bills, and a premium on foreign bills, affect unfavourably the real exchange, and terminate in the exportation of bullion.

Connected with this important error, of supposing that the real exchange is not affected by a redundancy or deficiency of currency, is another, which supposes that the bullion trade may be carried on between two countries while their real exchanges are at par. Now, we would ask, in the first place, whether it is readily conceivable that such a difference should exist between the real prices of bullion in two countries connected with each other, as to cover the expenses of transport, and offer a fair profit to the bullion merchant, without affecting the real prices of commodities in such countries. By the real prices of commodities, in the present discussion, Mr Blake explains himself to mean (p. 48) ' the prices at which those commodities would be bought and sold, if no depreciation of currency existed, which, from the convertibility of coin into bullion, and bullion into coin, can be no other than what we should call the bullion prices. But if the bullion prices, or real prices current, were lowered in one of two countries, so as more than to cover the expense of transport, the exports would undoubtedly exceed the imports, and the exchange could no longer remain at par.

Secondly, We would ask, in what manner the bullion merchant pays for the bullion which he imports ? It can only be by the purchase and remittance of a foreign bill, or by ordering a bill to be drawn upon him. In either case, funds in goods must have gone out, or must go out, to provide for the payment of these bills ; and if a balance of goods had not gone out before, that is, if the exchange had not before been favourable, the additional quantity which must go out to pay for the bullion would at once make the exports exceed the imports, and prevent the exchange from being at par. It appears, therefore, from the very terms of the proposition, that bullion cannot be purchased for importation without an excess of exports, and a consequent favourable exchange. We are aware, indeed, that on the supposition of the exports and imports of the produce of two countries being exactly balanced, and the exchange at par, the fresh competition of a bullion merchant for a bill to pay for the bullion which he wished to import, would rather tend to raise the price of foreign bills, and render the exchange unfavourable ; but this only shows that such a competition at such a time could never occur. It is indeed impossible to suppose, with Mr Blake, that the bullion dealer would be the most engaged at the time that the real exchange was at its least deviation from par, (p. 35.), when, in the purchase of a commodity for which there is rarely any very urgent and sudden demand, by waiting till the exchange was decidedly favourable, he could import any quantity that he might want, with so much greater profit. Mr Blake seems to be quite unconscious of the grand difference between bullion and other commodities. The bullion prices of particular commodities may easily vary in such a manner, from plenty or scarcity, as to make it answer to import them when the exchange is at par, or even decidedly unfavourable. But how can the bullion prices of *bullion* experience such variations ? The prices of that commodity, which is the general medium of exchange, can properly be said to vary only in reference to the sum of all other commodities ; but a variation in the sum of all other commodities compared with bullion, cannot take place in any country which has a ready communication with others, without affecting the exchange.   To us, therefore, it appears quite clear, that there are really no other variations in the prices at which bullion can be bought and sold for import or export, than those which appear in the exchange.

In our commerce with all those countries which are nearly connected with the mines, and where, in consequence, bullion is comparatively cheap, the real exchange has been almost invariably in our favour ; and we believe it may be laid down as a rule that admits of no exception, that, whenever the real exchange with any country is either at par, or unfavourable, it is cheaper to purchase bullion in the home markets than to import it from such country.

To the same error of Mr Blake is to be ascribed his criticism upon Lord King (p. 35.), who has stated, if we recollect, in substance, that the bullion sent to India has a tendency to render our exchanges with Europe favourable.   Now, if, from what we have just said, it appears that bullion cannot flow into a country except in consequence of a favourable real exchange ; and if any unusual demand for bullion in a particular country must tend to render bullion scarcer and dearer, and, by lowering the real prices of commodities, to encourage an excess of exports above imports, and to render the real exchange favourable, we conceive that Lord King must be right, and Mr Blake's correction unfounded.

We are fearful that the subject of exchanges will not admit of that distinctness and simplicity of division with which Mr Blake has treated it ; because it is unquestionable, that one of the most powerful causes of the nominal exchange—a redundancy or deficiency of currency—invariably influences the real exchange, as long as there is any coin that can be converted with advantage into bullion, or any bullion to be converted into coin.   All that can be done, as it appears to us, is, to rank among the causes of the real exchange, not only the varying desires and necessities of different nations, but every such alteration in their currencies as tends to affect the bullion prices of commodities.   The causes of the nominal exchange will then be all that part of every alteration in the currencies of different countries, which does not affect the bullion prices of commodities ; and the computed exchange will of course be the result of both.   Notwithstanding the errors in Mr Blake's pamphlet which we have here ventured to point out, and which, if our criticisms be just, are not unimportant, we still think it a very valuable publication, and earnestly recommend it to the attention of our readers, particularly the first and last sections.

Mr Huskisson's pamphlet has been published since the Report of the Committee, and was written, as he intimates, to satisfy the minds of some of his friends, and to support the conclusions which he had formed upon so interesting a question, against the clamours of those who were inimical to the Report. There was not, indeed, much that remained to be done after the publication of the Report itself, and the body of evidence with which it was accompanied. But what Mr Huskisson has done, he has done, on the whole, exceedingly well; and we have little doubt that his authority, as a practical statesman bred in the school of Mr Pitt, will be of essential service to the cause of truth on the present occasion; both by giving a wider circulation to the discussion, and by calming, in some degree, the fears of those who strangely imagine, that the present deranged system of our currency is necessary to the collection of our revenue. We are disposed, therefore, to give Mr Huskisson very great credit, both for the liberal and manly spirit which prompted him to undertake the task, and which pervades the whole performance; and for the general ability with which it is executed; though we think it necessary to begin with some corrections, which appear to us to be material, of his elementary doctrine.

As a very proper and sufficient reason for some explanations relating to the fundamental principles of money, with which Mr Huskisson opens his pamphlet, he intimates, that it is of great importance that the ground should be properly cleared for a discussion of this kind; and that those who engage in it, should be agreed in their first principles. The same reason makes it necessary for us to offer a few remarks on these explanations.

Mr Huskisson, in stating that it is of the very essence of *money* to possess intrinsic value, on account of its being the *common and universal equivalent*, observes, that ' the quality, of being a *common measure*, does not necessarily imply such value, any more than the possession of a foot-rule implies the power of acquiring whatever it enables us to measure.' In this observation, we neither see how the illustration applies, nor are we disposed to acknowledge the truth of the position which it is intended to establish. To us it appears absolutely necessary, that the commodity which measures exchangeable *value*, must itself possess *value* in exchange; in the same manner as a foot-rule, which measures length, must itself possess length. A pound of gold might be said to measure the nominal value, or value in gold, of all the commodities in the country, by stating how many pounds they would exchange for at their market prices :—but it does not follow, that the possessor of a pound of gold, although it has intrinsic value, should be able to acquire *all* the articles of value with which it might be successively compared.

One of the moft important functions of the precious metals, is that of acting as a meafure of value in exchanges; and if paper, or any other article poffeffing little or no intrinfic value, appears fometimes to ufurp this important function, it is folely and ex-clufively on account of its conftant reference to the intrinfic value of the precious metals. Nor do we conceive it *possible*, that a paper currency could be eftablifhed, and perform the part of mea-furing the exchangeable value of commodities, without imminent rifk of the moft tremendous convulfions of property, if there were not fome article of intrinfic value in exchange, with which it was conftantly compared; and which, therefore, and not the paper, would be the real meafure of value.

We have no great objection to the term, *universal equivalent,* which Mr Hufkiffon confiders as the quality which moft pre-eminently diftinguifhes the precious metals from all other com-modities; but we doubt whether it advantageoufly fupplies the place of the term *medium of exchange,* or *instrument of commerce ;* becaufe it is precifely on account of their being adopted by the common confent of fociety as the general medium of exchange, that they are received as a univerfal equivalent. Were it not for this confent, it is quite clear, that they would only be accepted as an equivalent for other commodities, of equal exchangeable value, by thofe who wifhed to make ufe of them as plate.

Mr Hufkiffon further ftates, that paper currency ' is fo much circulating credit,' that ' whoever buys, gives—whoever fells, receives—fuch a quantity of pure gold, as is equivalent to the ar-ticle bought or fold :—or, if he gives or receives paper inftead of money, he gives or receives that which is valuable only as it fti-pulates the payment of a given quantity of gold or filver......that money alone is the univerfal equivalent; paper currency the re-prefentative of that money.' This account appears to us exactly to fuit the ftate of circulation which is reprefented to have pre-vailed in Holland before the revolution, arifing from a Bank of Depofit; but it does not apply to the fyftem of banking, and of paper currency, which has been adopted in this and moft other countries. In Holland, it was really true, that every Bank credit reprefented a certain weight of coins, or of bullion of a known finenefs; that no part of thefe coins or bullion was exported in confequence of the fubftitution of Bank money for bullion; and that, if all the creditors of the Bank required at once what thofe credits reprefented, the whole of the bullion and coins that had been depofited would be forthcoming at a moment's notice. But every perfon who is acquainted with the fyftem of banking in this country, knows perfectly well, that fuch a realization could never have taken place here; he knows perfectly well, that the peculiar advantages which we derive from this fyftem, depend chiefly upon the fubftitution of a very cheap inftrument for a very dear one ; and that, confequently, when this fubftitution has once taken place, there feldom has been, nor ever will be, a fufficient quantity of coin in the country to realize in the precious metals the whole of its paper currency. It is true, that, in the healthy ftate of our circulation, Bank notes are, and always fhould be, exchangeable for coin at the option of the holder ; but it is found by experience, that, in all ordinary times, the option of the holder is fatisfied with a very moderate portion of coin, compared with the whole currency. It is found by experience, that a bank-note is not confidered as valuable, only becaufe it enables him to obtain a given quantity of the precious metals. The holder is in general fatisfied, if he feels quite fure of always obtaining for his note a quantity of commodities *equal in value* to the quantity of the precious metals fpecified in it. This is, in fact, what, ninety-nine times out of a hundred, he really wants ; and what alone, in reference to the whole body of notes in circulation, the country poffeffes the means of effecting.

The reason why his wants are, for the most part, directed to the value, rather than the substance, of the precious metals, depends upon a quality which peculiarly distinguishes that commodity, whatever it is, which has once been constituted by the common consent of society the general medium of exchange. This is, that every person is a dealer in it ; and that men want it most frequently, not for its intrinsic uses, but in order to obtain other commodities for it ; in the same manner as a dealer in corn, as far as he is only a dealer, wants it, not on account of its intrinsic use in supporting human creatures, but in order to obtain the necessaries, conveniences, and comforts of life in exchange for it. And if such a person dealt in pieces of paper marked with bushels and quarters of corn, provided that, by any process, they could be kept always on a level with the varying market prices of real corn, he would carry on his trade with exactly the same advantage to himself as he does at present. But it is quite clear, that, with regard to corn, no possible process could preserve the level of value here supposed ; and precisely, because very few, comparatively, are dealers in corn, and the great majority of mankind want it to eat, not to sell ; whereas the very simple process of making every bank which issues notes, perform its promise of paying them in specie, at the option of the holder, under the penalty of complete loss of credit in case of failure, is known to be sufficient to effect a level of value between bank-notes and the precious metals ; and precisely because, with regard to the precious metals, in their character of a circulating medium, every man is a dealer, and wants them to sell—not to use.

This is a view of the subject which has not been sufficiently attended to, although it appears to us to afford the only satisfactory explanation of the great quantity of paper which may be substituted for the precious metals, in the common systems of banking. In fact, we believe, that the circumstance of our being chiefly dealers in the medium of exchange, not consumers of it, is the very foundation of all those systems of paper currency, the great advantage of which consists in the substitution of a cheap for a dear instrument of commerce.

It will be observed, that this circumstance does not, in any degree, tend to impeach the necessity of the obligation upon all bankers to pay their notes in specie, whenever they are called upon ; as in no other way would it be *possible* so to regulate the quantity of bank notes, as *uniformly* and *certainly* to maintain them of the same value as coin. It is merely a somewhat different, and, in our opinion, a more correct view of what actually takes place in those countries where banking establishments prevail, than that which considers the usual kinds of paper-currency in the light of the bank money of Amsterdam, as representing so much coin or bullion at all times forthcoming, and which affirms, that whoever buys, gives, whoever sells, receives, such a quantity of pure gold or silver as is equivalent to the article bought or sold ; when it is perfectly well known that the fact is not, and cannot be so, according to the principle of substitution. The precious metals, therefore, in our opinion, perform a more important part in society, and are more frequently called into action, as a measure of exchangeable value, than as a universal equivalent.

But, notwithstanding the little elementary inaccuracy which has given rise to these observations, we must again repeat, that Mr Huskisson's doctrines appear to us to be on the whole quite sound and satisfactory. Nothing can be clearer, or more convincing, than the statements in proof of the actual depreciation of our currency, from p. 12. to p. 17, to which we particularly refer our readers. If a pound of gold, which being coined, according to the law of the country, into forty-four guineas and a half, must, in an undegraded state of the currency, be equal in value to 46*l*. 14s. 6d., cannot now be purchased for less than 56*l*. of our actual currency : —if a *light* guinea, which, by being legally convertible into bullion, represents the value of the currencies of surrounding countries, be worth above 24s. in our currency, while the few heavy guineas which are current, being forced to partake of the degradation of the general currency, are worth only 21s. :—if the only reason why a solitary guinea here and there remains in our circulation, and purchases only the same quantity of goods as a one pound note and a shilling, is, that the law will punish, by fine and imprisonment, every man who dares to sell his commodity for what it is really worth :—if, by the act of 1774, gold, which for many years had been the practical measure of value in this country, was made the only legal tender for payments above a certain sum; and if no repeal or alteration in this act took place in consequence of the restriction bill in 1797 :—if our foreign exchanges have been, for a considerable period, permanently against us, to the amount of between 15 and 20 per cent., which, when the highest expense of transmitting gold was about 7 per cent., could not possibly have happened if gold could have been had in exchange for notes at the Bank, and our currency had been of the same value as the currencies of surrounding countries :—if what alone can be meant by the term ‘ depreciated currency,’ is a depreciation below the value of that metal which has long formed the effective legal tender of the realm, or below the currencies of the different nations of the commercial world, which, being always estimated in one or other of the precious metals, can admit only of the slight variations that affect the relative values of gold and silver :——If, we say, these things are so, whatever may be urged in favour of the benefits to be derived from a redundant currency, or the inconvenience of returning to payments in specie, *the fact* of such redundancy, and the propriety of applying the term ‘ depreciated ’ to the present state of our currency, appears to us to be placed beyond the possibility of doubt.

In answer to the decisive argument suggested by the high price of gold when compared with our currency, it has been confidently asserted, that this high price is not occasioned by the depreciation of that currency, but by the unusual demand for gold abroad. These assertions, Mr Huskisson considers in a subsequent part of his pamphlet, and denies their having any foundation either in fact or probability. But he does not seem to be sufficiently aware, that, even if they were admitted, they have nothing to do with the *existence* of the depreciation, though they have with its *cause*. And this is a point of view which ought to be by no means omitted in our consideration of the subject.

The precious metals are the currency of the commercial world ; and whatever variations may take place in their value, either from a greater or less supply of them from the mines, or a greater or less use of them in commerce, it is clear, that all the nations which have a mutual intercourse with each other, must partake of them. If any have currencies, consisting partly of coin and partly of paper, convertible, at the will of the holder, into coin, it is equally clear, that this paper must partake in all the changes that affect the coin. Let us suppose, now, the case of a more abundant supply from the mines.—An influx of the precious metals would evidently take place, which, for a short time, would sink the market price of bullion below the mint price ; but more bullion would be immediately converted into coin, and each bank would find that it might issue more of its notes without risk. The consequence would be, that the whole of the currency, retaining probably the same proportions of paper and coin, would be enlarged ; the market price of bullion would quickly be raised to the mint price ; the exchanges which had been very favourable, would return to their usual state ; and no other effect would be experienced, than a general rise of prices throughout the commercial world.

On the other hand, in the case of a diminished supply from the mines, or a greater consumption of the precious metals in some of the principal states of Europe, an immediate demand would be felt in the rest for bullion to be exported ; the market price of bullion would be raised for a time above the mint price ; the notes of the different banks would return upon them, to be exchanged for coin, which would be sent abroad. The consequence would be, that the whole currency, consisting still of the same proportion of paper to coin, would be diminished in quantity, and raised in value ; the market price of bullion would soon sink to the mint price ; the exchanges, which had been unusually unfavourable, would be restored to their accustomed state ; and no other effect would be felt, than a general fall of prices throughout the commercial world.

Now, if, in the case last supposed, the paper of one of these countries were not convertible into coin, and very little specie remained in circulation, it is quite clear, that the currency would not have the means of assimilating itself to the currencies of the nations with which it was connected. The market price of bullion would rise very greatly above its mint price ; all the gold which could be readily collected would be exported. But as this would be inconsiderable, and as the great mass of paper would remain undiminished, or perhaps be slightly increased, to supply the vacancies occasioned by the gold exported, the great excess of the market price of bullion above the mint price, and the very unfavourable exchanges, would become permanent, (subject however, still, to variations occasioned by the balance of trade, and payments) ; and the currency of such a country would be to all intents and purposes depreciated, when compared with gold and silver and the currencies of other countries, just as it would be from an original excess of paper issues ; although, on the whole, taking paper and guineas together, the amount of the currency might not be increased by a single pound.

It is material to observe, that, under all possible variations in the value of the precious metals, whether they are increased in quantity tenfold, or diminished to one tenth, the defect or ex-cess of the market price of the precious metals, compared with the mint price, always ceases as soon as the level is effected ; and *nothing* but a depretiated currency *can* render gold in bullion per-manently of greater value than gold in coin.

Whether any rise has really taken place in the value of the precious metals on the Continent during the last few years, and has contributed, in a slight degree, to the present state of our currency, we will not take upon ourselves to determine. We cer-tainly do not think it quite so improbable as Mr Huskisson does ; as we conceive, that the great shock which mercantile credit has suffered, by the difficulties thrown in the way of commercial in-tercourse, may have operated something like a return to a less advanced period of civilization, and occasioned the necessity of employing a greater quantity of the precious metals, in propor-tion to the number of exchanges to be transacted. We think, also, that in the evidence before the Bullion Committee, there are some symptons of a rise of this kind, which are not sufficiently noticed in the Report. As, however, the effect derived from this cause, appears, at any rate, to be very inconsiderable, com-pared with the degree of actual depreciation, an attempt to as-certain its proportion to the whole would certainly be very diffi-cult, and could not be very important. But it appears to us to be extremely important to know, that the Bank directors cannot, with any degree of propriety, urge the argument of a great de-mand for gold on the Continent, to justify the comparative de-preciation of their notes. Whatever may be the variations in the value of the precious metals, their business is to regulate the issue of their notes, so as always to maintain them of the same value. To this course they would be forced, by considerations of personal interest, if the restriction bill had not passed ; and, after its enactment, to this course they ought to be impelled, by a sense of their duty to the public, and a proper estimate of the high responsibility that must attach to a set of men, to whose discretion, during the continuance of this act, the entire regu-lation of the national currency is entrusted.

We had intended to point out to our readers, many parts of Mr Huskisson's pamphlet in which we think he has been very fuccefsful; and a few, in which we do not agree with him, befides his doctrine of equivalents in trade. * But our limits oblige us to haften to Mr

---

* We trust that we shall not be suspected, because we disapprove of the doctrine of equivalents, of adopting the old mercantile no-tion, that the profits of foreign trade are derived from a balance

Bofanquet, whofe various alleged facts and defultory obfervations, we confefs, excited in us, at firft, a confiderable degree of alarm ; —not, however, on account of their formidable nature—for, though he very correctly defcribes himfelf as ' a partizan,' we cannot help thinking that he is a little incorrect in adding that he is ' a fuccefsful' one ; but on account of their mere number, and the confequent time and fpace which the fhorteft remarks upon them would take up.   Fortunately, however, the fecond edition of his pamphlet fell into our hands ; and, in reading his fupplementary obfervations, we found ourfelves relieved from the tafk we had undertaken, by the *concessions* of Mr Bofanquet himfelf.

We had conceived, that the great object of the various facts and obfervations which he had brought forward, was to fhow, that the prefent phenomena relating to the market price of gold bullion, and the courfe of our foreign exchanges, were of the fame temporary nature as thofe of a fimilar kind which had often occurred before,—though, from an unufual concurrence of circumftances, they had been aggravated, both in degree and duration ; and that the Report of the Bullion Committee was not juftified in reprefenting them as indications of a permanent depreciation of our currency below the legal tender of the realm, and the currencies of furrounding countries.   What then was our furprife to find him, on fecond thoughts, *giving up completely the question of depreciation,* in reference to our legal tender,—*acknowledging fairly* that the gold contained in a guinea is now of more value than $\frac{2\frac{1}{4}}{5}$th parts of a two pound note, and, without any allufion to it as a temporary occurrence, propofing an entirely new ftandard of value, from a comparifon with which it appears that our currency is not depreciated !

What this ftandard is, we are quite fure that our readers would never guefs ; and we cannot but confider it as one of the moft curious inftances of felf-deception that we have ever met with, and a moft unlucky fpecimen of the reafoning of practical men, that *the interest of* 33*l.* 6*s.* 8*d. in the* 3 *per cent. stocks,* fhould be gravely propofed as the ftandard meafure of the value of our currency ; that is, that *a one pound note*

---

paid in the precious metals ; which Mr Huskisson very oddly seems to think is the alternative.   Our opinion is, that, in all commercial transactions, both parties gain what, in the estimation of each, is decidedly more than an equivalent for what it has given ; and that it is out of this excess, that the gains of the merchants concerned are taken, who, it appears to us, would be very badly off, and would be little disposed to continue their business, if what they imported were not worth more to the purchasers of it, and would confequently sell for more, than what had been exported.

of the Bank of England, which is the intereft of this fum, and the kind of currency in which it is paid, fhould be the criterion by which we are to judge of the depreciation of—*a one pound note of the Bank of England!*

It may be true, as fuggefted in the Report of the Committee, that, ever fince 1797, Bank of England notes have been the practical medium of exchange, and the meafure of relative value in all our fales and purchafes at home. But the public has always flattered itfelf, that during the temporary fufpenfion of payments in fpecie, the quantity and value of thefe notes would be regulated by a conftant comparifon with the legal tender of the realm. Let the reader for a moment confider, in what a dreadfully critical ftate muft the property and contracts of a country be placed, which has a paper currency not referrible to *any commodity of intrinsic worth* for the correction of its quantity, and the maintenance of its value, and which might confequently fink, in the courfe of a few months, 50 or 100 per cent. below the value of the precious metals, and deprive individuals of half their fortunes, and yet appear to be unchangeable. The moment we quit the precious metals as the conftant ftandard of reference, there is no fancy fo wild, refpecting a paper circulation, which may not be indulged, and no limit to the degree of depreciation which may not in time be expected. Yet, *of this ftandard*, to our utter furprife and grief, the Bank Directors, and their friends, have openly avowed their neglect before a Committee of the Houfe of Commons. What they mean to fubftitute, we are not informed ; nor do we know whether or not Mr Bofanquet is fanctioned by their authority in the new ftandard which *he* has brought forward. But it is unqueftionable, that, except in regard to the integrity of a few individuals, on which the great mafs of the property of a country ought never to be made to depend, even the affignats of France refted upon a better foundation than that on which it is now propofed to place the paper circulation of Great Britain. In fact, what fecurity have we, except in this integrity, that the Bank Directors may not agree to create and divide 24 millions in notes among them for their private fortunes ? Or, to put a lefs ftrong, and not fo improbable a cafe ; What fecurity have we that the Bank, when releafed from all obligation to keep their notes of the value of the precious metals, may not alter their mode of conducting bufinefs, and lend money for longer terms than they do at prefent, and on any fair perfonal fecurity ? Mr Bofanquet, in the courfe of his work, has given us an elaborate explanation of the manner in which the demand for difcounts at the Bank naturally limits itfelf ; for which we are really much obliged to him, though we do not think that it proves fufficiently what he intends ; and, in one refpect, it is rather unfortunate for his general argument, as he appears to have been led by it, unintentionally, to let 'out fome of the fecrets of his ' prifon houfe, ' by talking of a recurrence of demand for notes by the *first class* of difcounters ; which he explains to be ' thofe which the Directors diftinguifh as folid paper for real tranfactions ; ' from which we may fairly conclude, that there are other claffes well known, and not always rejected at the Bank, which are probably diftinguifhed as accommodation paper. But whatever faith Mr Bofanquet may attach to his natural limit, we are quite fure, that neither he, nor any man of bufinefs, will venture to deny, that there are thoufands and thoufands of traders in the kingdom, who would eagerly feize the opportunity of borrowing capital on their perfonal fecurity at 5 per cent. ; and that the immenfe profits of the Bank, in lending fuch fums, would beyond all comparifon counterbalance the rifk : Yet, while the country was thus abfolutely inundated with paper, a one pound note would be ftill worth the intereft of 33l. 6s. 8d. 3 per cents.

We cannot believe that Mr Bofanquet would have reforted to fo very ftrange a folution of his difficulties, if he had felt any real confidence in his practical obfervations againft the doctrines of the Report. We do not therefore think it neceffary to combat arguments which the author himfelf gives up. But, to thofe who have only read the firft edition of his pamphlet, or have a greater faith in the correctnefs and efficacy of his facts than he has himfelf, we would recommend the careful perufal of the able reply of Mr Ricardo, accompanied by the remarks of Mr Blake, on the real, nominal, and computed exchange, and corrected by the few obfervations which we have ventured to fuggeft in a former part of this article. With thefe helps, we are perfuaded, that an impartial and attentive inquirer after truth will fee, that the facts of Mr Bofanquet, as far as they are ftated correctly, may be eafily explained, in perfect accordance with the main doctrines of the Report.

We do not, however, think, that thefe facts are at all fatisfactorily explicable upon the principles of Mr Ricardo alone, who, in his Reply, ftill perfeveres in the confined view which he had before taken of the caufes that operate upon exchange, and in confidering redundancy or deficiency of currency as the mainfpring of all commercial movements. According to this view of the fubject, it is certainly not eafy to explain an improving exchange under an obvioufly increafing iffue of notes ; an event that not unfrequently happens, and was much infifted upon by the Deputy-governor of the Bank, as a proof that our foreign exchanges had no connexion with the ftate of our currency. Nothing, however, is more eafy of explanation, if we take into our confideration the effects produced upon the real exchange by the payments neceffary to be made, for the fupply of paft or prefent wants ; which effects, in fuch inftances, will always be found operating in a direction exactly oppofite to the effects of redundancy of currency. If the Bank were paying in fpecie, the precife period when it could keep the greateft quantity of its notes in circulation, would be that in which the ftate of mercantile tranfactions was occafioning a current of payments in bullion into the country. The increafed iffue of notes, under fuch circumftances, would for a time be imperceptible ; though its tendency would undoubtedly be to raife prices at home, and thus to fhorten the duration of the favourable exchange ; and, when it turned, to increafe the ftrength of the current in the oppofite direction. The real ftate of the cafe feems to be, that though the effects of a redundancy of currency upon the exchange are fure, they are flow, compared with the effects of thofe mercantile tranfactions not connected with the queftion of currency ; and, while the former of thefe caufes is proceeding in its operations with a fteady and generally uniform pace, the more rapid movements of the latter are oppofing, aggravating or modifying thefe operations in various ways, and producing all thofe complex, and foemingly inconfiftent appearances, which are to be found in the computed exchange.

We agree, therefore, entirely in opinion with the Report of the Bullion Committee, that the great and sudden depression of the exchange in the summer and autumn of 1809, is to be traced principally to mercantile causes. A depreciation of the currency to a certain degree, had existed for many years before ; because, of all the symptoms of such depreciation, there is none so completely unequivocal as an excess of the market price above the mint price of that metal which is the standard measure of the country, accompanied by a favourable state of foreign exchanges, which, we believe, took place for six years, from 1802 to 1808. But this depreciation, a considerable part of which was probably concealed from view by the favourable exchange, was not sufficient to excite alarm, till it operated in conjuncion with an unfavourable one, occasioned by mercantile difficulties and great purchases ; and till the restoration of the exchange in the usual way was prevented, by the impossibility of getting specie at the Bank, and the fresh issues of notes for mercantile speculations. Since this time, however, the exchanges have occasionally improved, from the debts for our great exports being in the course of payment, and our bills consequently in request. And now, again, we understand they have rapidly fallen, owing perhaps to the diminished competition for our bills, from the loss of funds occasioned by the late severe decrees of Bonaparte, and his occupation of Hamburgh and Holstein; while, during the whole of the time the depreciation of our currency may have been proceeding with a steady and uniform pace, or, if it has occasionally been stationary or retrograde, has certainly not been subject to those great fluctuations which have been observed in our exchanges.

One of the principal faults which we have remarked in almost all the writers that are unfavourable to the Bank restriction, is, that they have not made sufficient concessions to the mercantile classes in some points where they appear to have truth on their side. We have already adverted to the error (confined, however, principally to Mr Ricardo, and from which the Report is entirely free) of denying the existence of a balance of trade or of payments, not connected with some original redundancy or deficiency of currency. A practical merchant must, to be sure, be extremely surprised at such a denial, and feel more than ever confirmed in his preference of practice to theory. But there is another point in which also almost all the writers on this side of the question concur, where, notwithstanding, we cannot agree with them, and feel more inclined to the mercantile view of the subject. Though they acknowledge that bullion occasionally passes from one country to another, from causes connected with the exchange, yet they represent these transactions as quite inconsiderable in degree. Mr Huskisson observes, that ' the operations ' in the trade of bullion originate almost entirely in the fresh ' supplies which are yearly poured in from the mines of the New ' World, and are chiefly confined to the distribution of those sup- ' plies through the different parts of Europe. If this supply ' were to cease altogether, the dealings in gold and silver, as ob- ' jects of foreign trade, would be very few, and those of short ' duration. '

Mr Ricardo, in his reply to Mr Bosanquet, refers to this passage with particular approbation. Mr Blake seems inclined to separate the dealer in bills of exchange, from the dealers in bullion; and the latter he considers as exclusively employed in supplying the manufacturers, though he says that the purchases made for this purpose are sometimes seized upon by the bill-merchants to pay an unfavourable balance.

Now, though we are perfectly ready to acknowledge, that an unfavourable exchange has a tendency to right itself, without the transmission of the precious metals, and that the transmission of a moderate quantity has a considerable effect ; yet we cannot believe that these transactions are altogether, either few in number, or small in amount. If the precious metals did not pass from one country to another, in consequence of the state of the exchange, the varying necessities of these countries would frequently raise the rate of the exchange very far above the expense of transport; and it would be impossible for the debtor country to make its payments at the time promised. But if the precious metals *do* pass readily from one country to another, from this cause, we cannot help thinking, that the same varying desires and necessities must render these transactions not very unfrequent. Every peculiar failure, or peculiar abundance of produce, in any of the states of the great mercantile republic; every subsidy to be paid or received; and every movement of a considerable army from one country to another, must almost inevitably give some employment to the bullion trade: and when the level of the precious metals has been in some degree destroyed by these necessary operations, the bullion dealer is again called into action to restore the balance. But, not only on such occasions as these, does bullion pass from one country to another, but it is well known that most states, in their usual relations of commercial intercourse, have an almost constantly favourable exchange with some countries, and an almost constantly unfavourable one with others. And Dr A. Smith has justly observed, that bullion forms, in general, the most convenient medium for carrying on the various roundabout foreign trades of consumption which a country finds it necessary to engage in; and is, in consequence, greatly used for this purpose. It appears, then, that in the most permanent and ordinary relations of countries with each other, the bullion trader will always have something to do.

The quantity of the precious metals employed in supplying and maintaining the coins of different nations, and making payments in the currency of the commercial world, far exceeds, we conceive, the quantity used in manufactures. Though the intrinsic value of these metals was first founded, and is still supported, by their use for plate and ornaments; yet, their much more general use, as a medium of exchange, has rendered the supply of the manufacturer a subordinate branch of the bullion trade. But, for whatever purpose the precious metals may be wanted, as the only variations in the prices at which they can be purchased are those which show themselves in the exchange, it is to this quarter that the bullion dealer always directs his attention. He imports or exports, according as the exchange is sufficiently favourable, or sufficiently unfavourable, to afford him an adequate profit in the transaction. And, in so doing, his main operations, we believe, will be found to consist in facilitating the purchases of those nations which have not, at the moment, any other commodities that they can give, or that will be readily accepted in return; and in restoring that level of the precious metals which has been temporarily destroyed by the unequal desires and necessities, and the unequal advantages and disadvantages of the different nations between which the trade of the world is carried on. In this view of the effect of the exchange upon the bullion trade, we think we shall be supported by the practical merchants; and it seems to us to have been confirmed by the evidence before the Bullion Committee, where it appears that the quantity of the precious metals sold for home consumption in manufactures, is quite inconsiderable, compared with the quantity imported and exported by the bullion merchants.

There is yet another point, still more important, where the experience of the merchant will be apt to lead him to a conclusion quite different from that which is generally maintained by the writers in question. A merchant, or manufacturer, obtains a loan in paper from a bank; and, with this loan, he is able to command materials to work upon, tools to work with, and wherewithal to pay the wages of labour; and yet, he is told that this transaction does not tend, in the slightest degree, to increase the capital of the country.

The question, of how far, and in what manner, an increase of currency tends to increase capital, appears to us so very important, as fully to warrant our attempt to explain it. No writer that we are acquainted with, has ever seemed sufficiently aware of the influence which a different distribution of the circulating medium of a country must have on those accumulations which are destined to facilitate future productions; although it follows, as a direct consequence, from the most correct and legitimate view of capital that can be taken.

Dr A. Smith justly observes, that ' though the whole annual produce of the land and labour of every country is, no doubt, ultimately destined for supplying the consumption of its inhabitants, and for procuring a revenue to them; yet, when it first comes, either from the ground, or from the hands of the productive labourers, it naturally divides itself into two parts. One of them is, in the first place, destined for replacing a capital, and for renewing the materials, provisions and finished work, which had been withdrawn from a capital; the other for constituting a revenue;' which, of course, is destined to be spent without any view to reproduction.

Now, it is quite certain, that any thing like an equal distribution of the circulating medium among all the members of the society, would almost destroy the power of collecting any considerable quantity of materials;—of constructing proper machinery, warehouses, shipping, &c.;—and of maintaining a sufficient quantity of hands, to introduce an effective division of labour. The proportion between capital and revenue would evidently, by this diftribution, be altered greatly to the difadvantage of capital; and in a few years, the produce of the country would experience a rapid diminution. On the other hand, if fuch a diftribution of the circulating medium were to take place, as to throw the command of the produce of the country chiefly into the hands of the productive claffes,—that is, if confiderable portions of the currency were taken from the idle, and thofe who live upon fixed incomes, and transferred to farmers, manufacturers and merchants,—the proportion between capital and revenue would be greatly altered to the advantage of capital; and in a fhort time, the produce of the country would be greatly augmented.

Whenever, in the actual ftate of things, a frefh iffue of notes comes into the hands of thofe who mean to employ them in the profecution and extenfion of a profitable bufinefs, a difference in the diftribution of the circulating medium takes place, fimilar in kind to that which has been laft fuppofed; and produces fimilar, though of courfe comparatively inconfiderable effects, in altering the proportion between capital and revenue in favour of the former. The new notes go into the market, as fo much additional capital, to purchafe what is neceffary for the conduct of the concern. But before the produce of the country has been increafed, it is impoffible for one perfon to have more of it, without diminifhing the fhares of fome others. This diminution is effected by the rife of prices, occafioned by the competition of the new notes, which puts it out of the power of thofe who are only buyers, and not fellers, to purchafe as much of the annual produce as before: While all the induftrious claffes,—all thofe that fell as well as buy, are, during the progreffive rife of prices, making unufual profits; and, even when this progreffion ftops, are left with the command of a greater portion of the annual produce than they poffeffed previous to the new iffues.

It muft always be recollected, that it is not the *quantity* of the circulating medium which produces the effect here defcribed, but the *different distribution* of it. If a thoufand millions of notes were added to the circulation, and diftributed to the various claffes of fociety exactly in the fame proportions as before, neither the capital of the country, nor the facility of borrowing, would be in the flighteft degree increafed. But, on every frefh iffue of notes, not only is the quantity of the circulating medium increafed, but the diftribution of the whole mafs is altered. A larger proportion falls into the hands of thofe who confume and produce, and a fmaller proportion into the hands of thofe who only confume. And as we have always confidered capital as that portion of the national accumulations and annual produce, which is at the command of those who mean to employ it with a view to reproduction, we are bound to acknowledge, that an increased issue of notes tends to increase the national capital, and by an almost, though not strictly necessary consequence, to lower the rate of interest.

It may perhaps fairly be questioned, whether the late unusual facility of obtaining discounts, though it has undoubtedly tended to increase the capital of the country, may not have given it so unsafe a direction, as to subject it to losses which may more than counterbalance its first gains;—whether, in short, it has not obliged some of the most respectable mercantile capitalists, who, in the way in which they were in the habit of carrying on their trade, scarcely ever failed of increasing the national accumulation, to yield the competition to a new and very different set of merchants, who may be said to gamble in trade,—who, in the hope of great profits, will risk any quantity of capital that they can command,—and in whose hands, therefore, the national accumulation is quite uncertain. Much, we think, might be said on this view of the subject.

But the grand and paramount objection to the stimulus which is applied to the productive powers of a country, by an excessive increase of currency, is, that it is accomplished at the expense of a manifest injustice. The observations we have made may afford a rational explanation of the facts, that countries are often increasing in riches amidst an increasing quantity of individual misery; that a rise of prices is generally found conjoined with public prosperity; and a fall of prices with national decline. But whatever phenomena they may assist to explain, they cannot alter the foundations of right and wrong, or give the slightest sanction to unjust transfers of property.

When the paper currency of a country is regulated in such a manner as to maintain it of the same value as the precious metals, the evil which the possessor of a fixed income may still suffer from depreciation occasioned by banking, is so inconsiderable, and so strictly limited, as probably to be more than counterbalanced, even to him, by the advantage which the country derives from it. It is true, however, that, upon the issue of every fresh quantity of notes, prices rise sufficiently to send a quantity of coin out of the circulation, though not, certainly, a quantity equal in amount to the notes; and the currency is at first left greater in quantity, and consequently lower in value, compared with the commodities which it has to circulate, than before. But it frequently happens, we conceive, that the beneficial employment of the coin set free, and the increased command of the produce transferred to the industrious classes by the increase of prices, gives such a stimulus to the productive powers of the country, that, in a short time, the balance between commodities and currency is restored, by the great multiplication of the former,—and prices return to their former level.

We cannot help thinking, that an effect of this kind took place in Scotland in the interval of two periods alluded to by Hume and Smith. In 1751 and 1752, when Hume published his Political Discourses, and soon after the great multiplication of paper money in Scotland, there was a very sensible rise in the price of provisions; and this was naturally, and probably justly, attributed by him, in part, to the abundance of paper. In 1759, when the paper currency had probably not been diminished, Dr Smith notices a different state of prices; and observes that, for a long period, provisions had never been cheaper. The dearness at the time that Hume wrote, he attributes carelessly, and without any inquiry about the fact, to the badness of the seasons; and intimates, that it could not be occasioned by the multiplication of paper money. The probability, however, seems to be, that the high prices of 1751 and 1752 were influenced by the paper,—as we do not see how it is possible for the substitution of paper for coin to take place, without an increase of prices; but that the new stimulus given to industry by this increase of capital, had so increased the quantity of commodities in the interval between 1752 and 1759, as to restore them to a level with the increased currency.

Independently, however, of the chance of the prices of commodities being restored by the influence of increased capital, the possessor of a fixed income cannot consider himself as unjustly treated, while the currency in which his revenue is paid is maintained on a level with the precious metals. These metals are indeed liable to change in their power of commanding the necessaries and conveniences of life; but the principal changes to which they are subject, depend upon causes so entirely beyond control, that the evils which he may suffer from these changes must be considered as necessarily belonging to the kind of property which he possesses. And if his revenue continues to be paid in the same quantity of coin, or in paper of equal value, however he may occasionally complain of increased prices, he will not feel himself warranted in complaining of injustice. As long, therefore, as the currency of a country is maintained on a level with the precious metals, the increase of national capital, and of national industry, derived from banking establishments, is unaccompanied by any essential drawbacks; but as soon as a positive depreciation takes place, the injustice committed towards one portion of the society is so unquestionable, that, though it may be concealed for a time, it cannot, when known, admit of excuse.

If, for all the commodities in this country, two prices were established, one in bullion and one in paper, and if the paper price were fifteen or twenty per cent. higher than the bullion price, we can hardly conceive that our Legislature, so famed as it is for its justice, would think it consistent with its good faith, to pay the numerous servants of the government, and the public creditors, with the same nominal amount of a currency, so obviously below the value of that in which it had contracted to pay them. And yet this is really and truly what it is now doing; and the only reason why the fact is in some degree concealed, is, that a bullion price of commodities not being as yet regularly established, the difference between the value of our legal tender and of our actual currency, is not daily forced on the attention: And, in order to be fully aware of its existence and extent, the evidence of the merchants examined before the Bullion Committee must be consulted ; where, it must be allowed, that the difference is as clearly established, as if it appeared in sales and purchases from morning to night. The circumstance of there being no current bullion price of commodities, does not, in the slightest degree, tend to affect the prices in our actual currency. These prices would not be rendered higher by the establishment of another price which was lower ; and, consequently, the real injury at present sustained by the classes of society before alluded to, is precisely the same as if it were rendered more obvious by the establishment of a bullion price and a paper price for every article sold.

The fact, however, of there being only one price, has been much insisted upon as a decisive proof that there is no depreciation. But the reasons why no distinction has as yet been openly made, are sufficiently obvious. They are, first and chiefly, the law of the land, which, applied to the present unlooked-for state of things, has the most singular and unjust operation ; which forces a heavy guinea to pass for less than a light one, and would oblige any person who could obtain coin for his commodities, to forego all advantage from it, and part with it again for fifteen per cent. less than it was fairly worth : And, secondly, the natural unwillingness of all people in trade, if the depreciation of the currency arises merely from excess, and not from want of confidence, to alter, in any degree, a state of things, and a progression of prices, from which, as being sellers as well as buyers, they are known to receive considerable advantages. And this feeling will of course be powerfully increased and confirmed by the consciousness, that the first person who was to ask two prices for his goods, would, as the law now stands, be considered as intending to make an illegal use of the coin which he might obtain, and would, in consequence, incur such odium, and deter so many customers, that the attempt would probably end in his ruin.

Yet, notwithstanding these reasons, if the Bank Directors continue to conduct their establishment upon the principles which they have openly avowed before the Committee, we do not entertain the slightest doubt, that, in a short time, two prices *must* be established, or the country will be entirely deprived of the power of making its smaller payments. In every state in Europe where a depreciated currency has circulated, it has been found absolutely necessary to allow of an open difference of price between bullion and paper, as the only mean of retaining any coin in the country. The expulsion of the legitimate coin of the realm, has, we really believe, proceeded further in this country than it ever did in any other, before this only remedy for the evil was applied. Gold may be said to be already quite banished from our circulation ; and nothing but the very extraordinary degraded state of our silver coin, and the high premium which is daily given even for this, in spite of the law, by bankers and merchants who want small change, could retain an ounce of it in circulation. We touch upon the period, when it will be no longer possible to avoid an open discount upon paper, without such a degree of embarrassment to commerce, as will much more than counterbalance the late advantages which it has derived from a redundant currency. If our silver coin had approximated, in any tolerable degree, to its mint value, there is no doubt that it would long since have disappeared ; and all ranks of society would have joined in petitioning the Legislature, if it still thought the Bank unable to pay in specie, either to repeal the law which prohibits an open discount upon paper, or to enjoin the issuing of shilling notes. And the question now is, Whether the Bank Directors, by continuing to act upon their present principles, will submit to one of these two disgraceful alternatives, under the merited reproach of having created the necessity for them by their own mismanagement ; or consent to tread back their steps, and return to payments in specie ; which may unquestionably be done, without any other evil, either to themselves or their mercantile connexions, than that of foregoing an unfair advantage ; which, as it ought never to have been possessed, ought, in honour and justice, as soon as possible to be relinquished.

The principles of banking avowed before the Bullion Committee, belong to so bold a class of projectors, and to times of such questionable authority with regard to the proper foundation of paper credit, that we were never more surprised than to find them brought forward by the Directors of the Bank of England. It is well known, that the celebrated Mr Law proposed to supply Scotland with money, by means of notes to be coined by certain commiffioners appointed by Parliament ; which notes were to be given out to all who demanded them upon the fecurity of land. In anfwer to the fuppofition, that they might be depreciated by excefs of quantity, Mr Law obferves, that ' the commiffioners giving out what fums are demanded, and taking back what fums are offered to be returned, this paper money will keep its value, and there will always be as much money as there is occafion or employment for, and no more.' * This, we conceive, is precifely the language of the prefent Bank Directors ; and they in no refpect fall fhort of Mr Law in the grand miftake, of confounding the quantity of good fecurity in the country, and the quantity of money which people may want to borrow at the legal intereft, particularly during a time of mercantile fpeculation or diftrefs, with the quantity neceffary for the circulation, fo as to keep it on a level with the precious metals, and the currencies of furrounding countries.

The fchool of Mr Law is certainly not that in which we fhould either have wifhed or expected the Directors to learn their principles of banking. But the real truth, we believe, is, that principles have very little to do with the regulation of the Bank concerns ; that every thing is done by a kind of practical routine ; and that, moft fortunately for the country, and for the credit of the Directors themfelves, this practice is ftill very much influenced by the habits of thofe wholefome times, when the Bank paid in specie, and was obliged to attend to the fafety of its eftablifhment. In no other way can we account for our not having a ftill greater excefs of paper, under the fanction of principles which lead to almoft unlimited iffues. But, greatly as we have reafon to rejoice, that the practice of the Bank does not accord with its principles, it is of the utmoft importance to recollect, that the falutary influence of a practice formed and eftablifhed while the Bank was at all times liable to pay its notes in fpecie, will, in the very nature of things, gradually ceafe to act, under other, and very different circumftances. In fact, the weakening of this influence is already but too manifeft, and muft be expected to be daily and hourly progreffive ; and if the Legiflature, by declining to enforce the recommendation of the Committee, fhould relieve the Bank from all immediate profpect of a return to cafh payments, the diforder in our currency which we have at prefent experienced, will be abfolutely nothing, compared with that which we muft then look forward to. Of courfe, the longer the term is protracted, and the greater is the previous depreciation of the currency, the greater will be the difficulty to the Bank, and the greater the hardfhip to

---

* *Money and Trade confidered :* With a Proposal for supplying the Nation with Money. By John Law esq. p. 167. Glasgow, 1750.

the perfons who benefit by the prefent fyftem, of a return to the old one.

We were, at first, inclined to approve of the recommendation of the Committee, to leave to the knowledge and discretion of the Bank Directors the mode of preparing themselves to re-sume their payments in cash at the time proposed. But it has been suggested, and the language and conduct of their friends have not sufficiently repelled the suspicion, that, under cover of this liberty, they might purposely keep the same, or a greater quantity of notes in circulation, with a view of compelling the legislature to continue the Restriction Act, as there, would, of course, be a great unwillingness in all quarters to enforce a law which at the time could not be obeyed, and the attempt to obey which, in such a state of things, would produce very serious inconveniences to the public, as well as to the Bank. We real-ly think, that if any disposition of this kind should be discover-able in the Bank direction, it would be the bounden duty of the legislature to take immediate steps for *the establishment of one or more other banks;* and it cannot be doubted, that both the business of the government and of the public might be carried on, as in America, with equal convenience, and less chance of restriction acts, without the assistance, and very improper in-fluence, of so overgrown an establishment as the Bank of Eng-land. It is, indeed, a monstrous deformity in the state, that an incorporated body of individuals should have the power of hold-ing out a threat to the legislature, that if it does not persevere in sanctioning the nonfulfilment of their engagements, they would find the means of embarrassing and punishing the govern-ment and the public. We cannot, however, conceive it possible that such an idea should be seriously entertained. At the same time, it is certain, that the Bank Directors have openly shown an unconquerable reluctance to acknowledge that there is any connexion between the market price of bullion, and an excessive paper circulation; and it may be necessary, in consequence, to direct their attention specifically to this main point. There is certainly some objection to a positive limitation of the number of notes; because the only proper criterion of excess, is depre-ciation below the value of the precious metals, and not any par-ticular amount of notes. But as, from the fact of depreciation, we are quite sure that there is at present excess, though it is impossible to say to what precise amount; perhaps, it might be the best mode of proceeding, in the present state of the know-ledge and temper of the Bank Directors, to oblige them, every successive half year, to diminish the average quantity of their notes in circulation by half a million, and to continue this diminution till the market price of bullion was restored to its mint price; and then the resumption of cash payments might take place with perfect safety and convenience, both to the Bank and the public; and the evil of any great and sudden diminution of the currency be completely avoided. We should be inclined to prefer this mode to another, which we have heard suggested, that of beginning by obliging the Bank to pay a small per centage in cash upon its notes, at the option of the holder, and increasing this per centage gradually; as we believe that great difficulties and losses would attend the execution of this plan, from the great scarcity of change in the present state of our silver coinage, and the certainty of the rapid disappearance from the circulation, of all the gold issued, till the number of notes were sufficiently reduced to bring the market and mint prices of gold nearly to a level.

We cannot conclude, without adverting, for a moment, to what has been often urged, both in print and conversation, that the Bullion Committee ought to have attended more to the opinions of those able and experienced merchants and men of business whom they examined. We decidedly think, that, in this respect, they did precisely what it was their duty to do. It was their duty to get at as large and correct a body of facts as possible, from the evidence of the best authorities which could be consulted. It was also their duty to hear the *opinions* of all those who were examined, in order that they might see the subject in the different lights in which it would naturally present itself to different understandings, and under different circumstances. But, having so done, it was most unquestionably their duty to form their own conclusions, without further deference to mercantile authorities. And we have no hesitation in saying, that the gentlemen who composed the Committee, both from their general characters, and the advantageous situation in which they stood, after having heard the evidence and opinions before mentioned, were very much better qualified to come to a just conclusion, than any body of practical merchants that could be chosen. The habits of practical detail have a natural and almost necessary tendency to direct the view to particular, rather than to general consequences, and to identify the interests of the few, with the interests of the many. If, in addition to this almost unavoidable effect of constant habits of business, we take into our consideration, that the mercantile classes are greatly interested, both in the facility of obtaining paper loans, and in the progressive rise of prices which this facility occasions, it is quite impossible to affirm, with truth, that they are either the most capable, or the most impartial judges in the present question. And if, when it comes to be determined by the legislature, the authority of merchants shall have more weight in the decision, than that of those who, from a more elevated seat of judgment, and free from the possible influence of interested motives, have taken a more commanding and impartial view of the subject, the consequences will not fail to show that the trust reposed in the great Assembly of the nation, to dispense impartial justice, and attend equally to the happiness of all the classes of the community, has been, in one instance at least, unfulfilled.

From *Edinburgh Review,*
August 1811

For Semmel's commentary on this article by Malthus, see especially pp. 19-21 *supra.* (*Publisher*).

ART. X. *Review of the Controversy respecting the High Price of Bullion.*

————

A short Investigation of the alleged superfluous Issue of Bank Notes, and the unfavourable State of Foreign Exchanges. 8vo. London, 1811.

————

The Theory of Money; or a Practical Inquiry into the present State of the Circulating Medium. 8vo. 1811.

————

Defence of Abstract Currencies; in Reply to the Bullion Report, and Mr Huskisson.

————

A Plain Statement of the Bullion Question. By Davis Giddy, Esq. M. P.

————

The Expediency and Practicability of the Resumption of Cash Payments by the Bank of England. By J. L. Tavers.

THOUGH we did not quite agree with the Chancellor of the Exchequer, in thinking that the question respecting the depreciation of our currency was set at rest by the decision of the House of Commons on the report of the Bullion Committee; yet, as so much had been written and said on the subject at that time, and so little apparently digested, we thought it right to give our readers some respite; and this respite we should perhaps have been inclined to continue till towards the opening of the next session of Parliament, if the subject had not been brought again under discussion sooner than was expected, and under circumstances calculated to make a considerable impression on the public mind.

The House of Commons had, on the 13th of May 1811, declared in a resolution, that the promissory notes of the Bank of England had hitherto been, and were at that time, held, in public estimation, to be equivalent to the legal coin of the realm, and generally accepted as such in all pecuniary transactions to which such coin was legally applicable;—yet, in so short a time as six or seven weeks, the Ministers found it necessary to interfere in support of this equivalency, not only by the most indecent clamour, but by the most formidable legal obstacles; while, at the same time, the measures which they proposed, and carried, avowedly in consequence of the decision of the Judges in the case of De Yonge, clearly and unequivocally evinced, that the fact stated in the resolution above

alluded to, had been occasioned entirely by the laudable unwillingness of British subjects to violate what they conceived to be
the law; and that those who had voted for it were conscious,
that, as soon as this fear was removed, the public estimation
would be as different as possible from that which had been asserted.

When the last poor plea of those who had maintained that
a one pound Bank note and a shilling were equivalent to a guinea, was thus obviously and practically contradicted;—when,
according to their own public acknowledgments, nothing but a
law of a similar nature to one which might declare a shilling
equivalent to a guinea, could any longer maintain the equivalency, in public estimation, of Bank notes, and the legal coin
of the realm; it might have been expected, that whatever difference of opinion might prevail as to the measures necessary to
be adopted in consequence of a depreciated currency, there
could be none respecting the fact of the depreciation itself.
Yet, strange to say, this fact has been still gravely denied, both
in and out of Parliament; and before we proceed further, it
seems to be necessary, even in this late stage of the discussion,
to define what we mean, and what we conceive ought always to
be meant, by a depreciated paper currency.

All the paper currencies that we have ever seen or heard of,
are either promissory notes to pay on demand certain coins of
a known weight and fineness, which are mentioned upon the
face of them; or they are intended to represent, and, on their
first issue, generally do represent, the value of such coins in all
the exchanges of commodities for which they may serve as a
medium. A Russian note of 100 roubles, or a Swedish note of
100 rixdollars, is intended to pass in exchange at the same value
as 100 silver roubles, or 100 silver rixdollars, to purchase the
same quantity of commodities, and, of course, the same quantity of silver bullion; and the moment it ceases to do so, it is
clearly and unquestionably depreciated. A comparison with the
coin, or the bullion value of the coin, which the note professes
to represent, is the only comparison to be made in such a case;
and when the paper currencies of Russia, Sweden and Austria,
would no longer exchange at par with the coins which they professed to represent, or purchase the quantity of bullion contained in those coins, we believe it never entered into the conception of a continental merchant to institute an elaborate inquiry
into the bullion prices of commodities, before he ventured to
pronounce such paper depreciated. In this view of what we
conceive ought to be understood, and has hitherto, we believe,
been almost universally understood by a depreciated paper cur-

rency, the question respecting the actual depreciation of our own currency is just as clearly determined as the fact, that the market price of gold purchased in Bank of England notes is 4*l.* 14s., instead of 3*l.* 17s. 10½d. per ounce.

What is it, then, that can be meant by those who still continue to maintain the undepreciated state of our paper circulation ? They can only mean, and this indeed they profess to mean, that in the separation which they acknowledge to have taken place between gold and paper, it is the gold alone that has varied ; it is the standard with which we compare the paper that has changed,—not the paper itself. According to what we have just stated, and we believe correctly, to be the proper criterion of a depreciated paper currency, the variations which may take place in the real price of bullion form quite a separate question ; and when we consider the immense mass of the precious metals existing in the commercial world, and the small proportion which the annual supplies bear to this mass, a variation of 17 * per cent. during the last three years seems certainly incredible.

But, improbable as such a change is, and utterly inconsistent with the actual phenomena, as we shall presently show ; let us for a moment suppose it to have happened. Would such a change, we would ask, justify us in separating ourselves at once from the rest of the commercial world in relation to our measure of value, and resorting to an imaginary standard, which no foreign nations could acknowledge, and which might be subject, not only to all the variations which can be supposed to take place in gold, but to others beyond comparison more sudden and more extensive ? It has always been considered as a most desirable thing, that nations should possess as many of the same scales of measurement as possible. Unfortunately, the measures of length, of capacity, of superficial extent, are but seldom the same in different countries ; but, what is of more importance in the commercial intercourse of society, all civilized nations have happily agreed in the selection of the precious metals as their measure of *value.* And yet, on account of a supposed, though very improbable change, in the value of these metals at present, we propose, at once, to preclude ourselves from the advantage which we have hitherto enjoyed, of possessing a measure of value common to other nations, and to de-

---

* According to the testimony of Mr Aaron Asher Goldsmid, (Bullion Report, p. 55.), the price of foreign gold in bars, and of Portugal gold in coin, was, during the years 1806, 1807 and 1808, 4*l.* At present, it is 4*l.* 14s., which is a rise of between 17 and 18 per cent. during the last three years.

prive ourselves entirely of the use of gold, and almost entirely of the use of silver, in our circulating medium. That we must be so deprived, if we do not conform our bank notes to the value of gold bullion, cannot admit of a doubt. From whatever cause the separation between bank notes and gold has taken place, it is equally certain, that while a guinea will only pass for twenty-one shillings as currency, and will sell for twenty-six or twenty-seven when melted, no guineas will appear in the circulation ; and consequently, for whatever purposes we may want the precious metals, whether to discharge what is called an unfavourable balance of trade, or to pay our armies on the Continent, while our paper currency is not of the value which it purports to be, our supply of them must always be most scanty and precarious.

To us, therefore, it appears perfectly clear, that if such a change as we have just supposed had really taken place in the value of gold in Europe, it would be the obvious dictate of common sense and good policy to conform our notes to it, and to insist rigidly that the Bank should so regulate its issues, as to produce the same equality between bank notes and guineas, as it would be compelled to do, if the Restriction bill had not passed. But, though the most obvious views of policy would dictate precisely the same remedy for the separation between guineas and bank notes, whether it arose from excessive issues of paper, or from a deficient supply of gold, yet it cannot but be a matter of considerable interest and utility, to ascertain which of these two causes has actually produced the effect in question. And here we feel no doubt in pronouncing, that all the circumstances attending the peculiar state of our currency, conspire to point clearly and unequivocally to an excessive issue of paper as its main, and indeed almost sole, cause.

In the first place, if a rise in the price of gold, compared with the mass of commodities to the amount of 17 per cent., had taken place throughout Europe during the last three years, it is scarcely possible that such an event, so contrary to the general course of prices for many years past, should not have awakened a very marked degree of notice and attention among foreigners.

Secondly, if the gold had left the paper, and not the paper the gold, as bank notes would then be of the same value, compared with commodities, as they were before, the paper prices of our goods of home consumption would have remained stationary, while a fall would have taken place in their bullion prices to the amount of 17 per cent.

Thirdly, if the change had been confined to the gold, and

the paper had retained its value, it is not probable that there should have been any very marked and unusual increase in the amount of bank notes during the three years in question.

These, we conceive, would have been the circumstances attending an exclusive rise in the value of gold. Now, what are the actual circumstances?

First, no striking exception has been remarked on the Continent during the last three years, to that gradual and general fall in the value of the precious metals which has been long the subject of notice.

Secondly, almost all British commodities, the vent of which has not been impeded by the shutting of the Continental ports; that is, commodities of home growth and consumption, such as wheat, butcher's meat, butter, &c. &c. have experienced a very marked rise, which, if not fully equal to 17 per cent., falls very little short of it.

And lastly, the paper issues of the Bank of England have, during the short space of the last three years, received an addition of more than one third of their amount in 1808; * while, for the whole course of six years before, that is, from 1802 to the latter end of 1808, † the average amount had been nearly stationary.

One of the causes which peculiarly fits the precious metals for being used as a measure of value, is, that the variations to which they are subject are comparatively slow and inconsiderable. A person aware of this quality, who was told that the paper currency of a particular country had suddenly, and to a considerable extent, separated from the metallic standard to which it had been usually compared, would undoubtedly be inclined at once to pronounce that, according to all probability, the change was in the paper, not the gold; and he would require pretty strong proofs to convince him of the contrary. But if, instead of such proofs, he found that his first natural presumption was supported by stationary bullion prices in other countries, a marked rise of paper prices at home, and an increased issue of notes equal to one third of their former amount, we conceive that no additional evidence could possibly strengthen his conviction. And we really believe that no person of common candour and impartiality, who is in any degree acquainted with the subject, can advert to these circumstances, and yet

---

* See Mushet's Tables.

† According to a return made to the House of Commons, the average amount of notes in circulation in 1802 was 17,054,451. Appendix to Bullion Report, p. 109.

continue to doubt whether, in this country, the paper has quitted the gold, or the gold the paper.

All the circumstances attending the state of our currency, in relation to our foreign trade, will show with the same conclusive evidence, that our unfavourable exchanges with the countries connected with France, are mainly nominal, and not real; if, indeed, we can so far admit the strange and improbable supposition of a real exchange of 30 per cent. against us, as to think it worth examination.

One of the certain effects of a really unfavourable exchange; and the precise cause which prevents the possibility of its permanence, is its tendency to raise the price of foreign commodities, and lower the price of home commodities; and an exchange to an amount here supposed, must, in a very moderate time, produce this effect in a considerable degree. We ought therefore to see a very marked fall in the price of our home produce, and a marked rise in the price of foreign commodities; instead of which, our home produce has experienced a marked advance in price, and our imported commodities are stationary. Nothing, we conceive, could have produced effects so opposite to those which were to be expected, and of the duration and extent actually observed, except an issue of notes not only insufficient to prevent that compression of the currency, which is at once the natural effect and natural remedy of an unfavourable exchange, but greatly to enlarge the medium of circulation, at the very moment when circumstances required it to be contracted.

Another effect of a very unfavourable real exchange with one country, or set of countries, is a very favourable exchange with others. This has been exemplified in the case of our great exports of silver to India and China, which, it is generally acknowledged, greatly contributed to render our exchanges with Europe more favourable than they otherwise would have been. We might expect therefore to see unusually favourable exchanges with all the countries not connected with France. Instead of which, there is, we believe, no one country with which the computed exchange, when correctly estimated, is favourable to us, although there are countries from which we are actually receiving bullion, and with which, therefore, the real exchange is favourable. A more than usual quantity of silver bullion has lately, we believe, been imported from Jamaica; which shows, that what is called the balance of payments is more than usually favourable to us with that country: and yet the prices of London bills in the Jamaica markets, instead of rising considerably, as we should have expected, have fallen 15 per cent. since 1808. In 1808 they were about 20 per cent. premium, and now they are only five,—a fall of price perfectly unaccountable, under such circumstances, upon any other supposition than the continued depreciation of our currency since 1808. The constant premium upon London bills in Jamaica, arises merely from an original incorrect valuation of the par of exchange ; 140*l.* Jamaica currency being reckoned equal to 100*l.* Sterling, although it would require 154*l.* 11s. 6d. to yield the same value of silver as 100*l.* of English silver currency; and 164*l.* 2s. to purchase 100*l.* of the gold currency, which is the English standard, at its present proportion to silver ; consequently, the computed exchange with Jamaica, when correctly estimated, is about 10½ per cent. in favour of Jamaica; and, with this *favourable* exchange, Jamaica exports dollars in considerable numbers !!—an event which could not possibly happen from any other cause than from the real exchange being quite different from the apparent exchange. In fact, it appears from the price at which the dollars thus exported are sold in England, that the real exchange is above 10 per cent. against Jamaica; while the apparent exchange being about 10½ per cent. in her favour, leaves above 20 per cent. for the depreciation of our currency.

Instances of this kind might easily be multiplied ; but we have already said enough to show, that all the circumstances attending the state of our currency, conspire to prove that our unfavourable exchanges cannot possibly be all real, nor the separation between guineas and bank notes be caused principally by a rise in the value of gold. We allowed, in a former article on this subject, that a small rise might possibly have taken place in gold, during the last three years, from the greater use of it in all mercantile transactions ; which might be occasioned by a general failure of confidence. If we ascribe to this cause half the variation which has taken place between gold and silver, we shall probably allow more than we are warranted in doing. This allowance would contribute to account for those instances where some of our home commodities have not risen in price quite in the proportion of gold ; and it should be recollected besides, that the effects of a depreciated currency are always rather slow in showing themselves, and are generally at first partial.

In what we have hitherto said, we have purposely confined ourselves to the last two years and a half, or three years—because the great difference between the value of gold and paper has taken place since the latter end of the year 1808 ; but if we survey the whole period since the restriction, we shall find the same conclusions constantly forcing themselves upon us. We have already stated, that during the last three years, while the excess of the market price above the mint price of gold, and the unfavourable foreign exchanges, have very far exceeded all former experience, no less an addition has been made to the quantity of bank notes in circulation than one full third of their former amount—an addition equally exceeding all former experience: And if we look at the other period, in which the same kind of excess, and the same unfavourable exchanges were remarkable, though not in the same degree, that is, from the end of 1799 to the middle of 1802, we shall find that an addition of about one fifth of the previous amount of bank notes was made in that short time—an addition coinciding very remarkably with the degree of depreciation which then took place. The only instance in which an approach to a similar addition was made to the amount of bank notes without producing similar effects, was in the period from the Bank Restriction bill, in 1797, till towards the end of 1799, when it is well known that a very great previous compression of the currency had taken place ; when the demand for guineas arose from the practice of hoarding, and not from an unfavourable exchange ; and when there was every reason to believe from the unusual quantity of gold collected by the Bank during these two years, that the addition to the notes in circulation was scarcely equal to the guineas which had been withdrawn.

With regard to the other period, from the middle of 1802 to near the end of 1808, which has sometimes been very strangely brought forward, as a proof that the currency recovered itself after the depreciation of 1801, under the very same regimen which was said to have brought it so low, * the facts appear to us to prove directly the contrary. According to returns published in the Appendix to the Bullion report, the average amount of bank notes in circulation for the year 1802, was 17,054,454; and in November 1808, the amount was 17,467,070; that is, during the course of above six years, while the price of gold remained at 4l. an ounce, the amount of notes in circulation was not increased so much as 500,000. If, indeed, we were to advert solely to the notes above five pounds, we should find them, in the year 1802, 13,917,977, and in November 1808, 13,255,460 ; by which it appears, that an actual *dimi-*

---

* Lord Harrowby used a metaphor of this kind in his speech on Lord Stanhope's bill; and particularly, insisted upon the period subsequent to the unfavourable exchanges of 1800 and 1801, as adverse to the principles of the Bullion Committee.

nution of notes above five pounds took place during these six years, while the price of gold remained stationary. A further inquiry into the amount of notes in circulation would also show us, that there was a very considerable diminution of them during the year 1803, when the exchanges began to recover themselves ; * and if, in addition to this, we take into consideration the quantity of guineas which had been withdrawn from circulation, during the very unfavourable exchanges of 1800 and 1801, aud recollect, at the same time, the usual tendencies of this country to maintain a favourable exchange with the greatest part of the Continent, unless very powerfully counteracted ; and further, that the currency was not, after all, restored to its usual and proper state ; we shall be compelled to acknowledge, that the period from 1802 to the end of 1808, affords as striking an illustration of the principles of the Bullion Committee, as any period that can be named either before or after the Restriction bill.

We do not mean to say, that our late unfavourable exchanges have always exclusively *originated* in the increased issues of the Bank. On the contrary, we are inclined to believe, that, both at the end of the year 1799, and, still more strikingly, at the end of 1808, a greater and more sudden fall of the exchange took place, than could possibly be accounted for by the increase of notes that had been thrown into the circulation. But we mean to say, that when the turn had taken place from causes which might originally be but little connected with the issues of notes, the Bank, upon the pretence, perhaps, of supplying the place of the guineas exported, or some other pretence, not only issued notes to the amount of the guineas withdrawn, which alone would have prevented the return to a favourable exchange at its natural time ; but issued them in such numbers, as greatly to increase the whole mass of the circulation, and, as a natural consequence, so to depreciate it, as to render our unfavourable exchanges necessarily permanent, and to expel all the gold from our circulation.

The fact seems to be, that it is generally on occasion of an unfavourable state of the exchange, arising from the failure of

---

* According to a paper delivered to the House of Commons, entitled ' Bank of England Accounts, ' the average of the two returns given for the 1st of January and 1st of July 1802, exceed the two returns for the 1st of January and 1st of July 1803, by three millions ; and these are the only returns given for these years in the paper in question. They do not certainly quite agree with Mr Mushet's Tables.

crops, or from shocks to commercial intercourse and confidence, that the Bank is most beset with borrowers. Unfortunately, these applications for discounts, which merely imply an increased desire of individual merchants to get money at five per cent.; either to make foreign purchases; to supply funds which have been lost, or are slow in coming in; or to enter into new speculations on the failure of the old; are mistaken by the Bank for an indication, that the currency is insufficient for the purposes of trade; and the country is thus inundated with paper at the very moment when it ought to be diminished.

We consider it as a point susceptible of complete demonstration, that an increase in the issue of Bank of England notes is attended with a proportionate increase in the issue of country bank notes, provided they continue to occupy nearly the same districts as before, and neither essentially displaces the notes of the other. As the great object of the country banker is to keep as many of his notes in circulation as possible, and the precise limitation of his power in this respect, is the obligation he is under of giving Bank of England notes in exchange for his own, when they are returned upon him; it is not conceivable that he should not eagerly seize the opportunity of issuing more of his notes, whenever a depreciation of bank notes, from an excessive issue, would prevent such a return, and enable him to do it with perfect security. If he did not do it, the notes of other country banks would quickly do it for him, to his great loss. We cannot, indeed, without the most gross violation of all the principles of supply and demand, suppose it possible, that while bank notes and country notes are constantly interchangeable, any marked alteration in the proportion between currency and commodities could take place in the districts chiefly occupied by Bank of England notes, and not be accompanied by a similar alteration in the proportion between currency and commodities in the districts chiefly occupied by country notes. But this necessary equality in the proportion between currency and commodities throughout the country, before and after an increased issue of Bank of England notes, could not of course take place, unless such issue was followed by a proportionate increase of country bank paper.

We are now supposing, that the districts chiefly occupied by Bank of England and country notes are nearly the same, before and after the new issues. But instances may occur, as in the case of discredited country notes, in which Bank of England notes will be required as a substitute for them. An instance of this kind occurred during the summer of 1810, when the failure of the Western Banks took place; and this period has been brought forward triumphantly, to show the failure of the general principle. But it is plain that the principle always presupposes, that the Bank of England and country notes do not materially encroach on each other's provinces ; and as the instances in which the Bank of England notes enlarge their sphere of circulation, are confined almost exclusively to the failure of country banks, and are of course completely obvious, the principle may be considered as established on all ordinary occasions. Of late years, indeed, the increased number of country banks, and their nearer approach to the metropolis, seem to imply, that the increase of country bank paper has been even greater, in proportion, than that of the paper of the Bank of England ; and we cannot be wrong in assuming it to be at least as great.

We may fairly, therefore, consider an increase of Bank of England notes, in any particular proportion, as an increase of the whole currency of the country in the same proportion, with the exception of the guineas which may be withdrawn from the circulation. What may be the amount of these, it must of course be very difficult to ascertain. There is reason to believe, from the great influx of gold, and the unusual coinage of guineas for two years immediately subsequent to the Bank Restriction bill in 1797, that the unfavourable exchanges of 1800 and 1801 were accompanied by a great exportation of coin. But there is by no means the same reason to believe, that our late very unfavourable exchanges have had the same consequences. According to Mr H. Thornton, most of our gold left us in 1801, and but little flowed into the country during the six years from 1802 to 1808. The probability, therefore, seems to be, that the notes under 5*l.*, added to the circulation by the Bank of England since 1808, have more than covered the quantity of guineas withdrawn during the last three years ; and that a portion even of these notes—perhaps not an inconsiderable portion— ought to be looked upon as a permanent addition to the currency. But, to be quite sure that we do not err on our own side, in the estimate which we are about to make of the proportion in which our whole currency has been increased during the last three years, we will take only the notes above 5*l.*

According to a return to the House of Commons, of the amount of Bank of England notes in circulation on the first days of January and July from 1790 to 1810, * it appears that the average of the two returns in July 1797 and January 1798, was 11,700,000 ;

* See a paper before referred to, entitled, ' Bank of England Accounts, ' ordered by the House of Commons to be printed, 22d of February, 1811.

11,700,000 ; and, according to another return in the same pa‑
per, of the weekly amount of bank notes in circulation from
the 9th of March 1810 to the 15th of February 1811, it ap‑
pears that the seven returns for January and February 1811
give an average of about 15,300,000. By comparing these a‑
mounts at the beginning of 1808 and the beginning of 1811, it
will appear that the amount of Bank of England notes, exclu‑
sive of bank post-bills, and notes under 5*l.*, must have increas‑
ed, in the course of three years, in a proportion much nearer
to one third than one fourth ; and if we assume, as we are en‑
titled to do, that the country bank notes must have increased,
soon after, in the same proportion, we may fairly conclude, that
the increase of the whole circulation cannot be overstated at one
fourth. Now, we would ask, whether an increase of one fourth,
in the short space of three years, is not sufficient to account for
a depreciation of the currency in the same time, amounting to
17 per cent., or a little more than one sixth, after making every
allowance for the increased quantity of circulating medium that
can be supposed to have been required by increased produce and
increased taxation ;—particularly when we recollect, that, dur‑
ing the six previous years of nearly equal taxation and expendi‑
ture, and much greater prosperity and produce, scarcely any
perceptible addition was made to the amount of the circulation.

We entirely agree with those who are of opinion, that no po‑
sitive conclusions are to be drawn respecting an excess of cur‑
rency, from the mere quantity of notes in circulation, inde‑
pendently of other circumstances; and think, that the mar‑
ket price of bullion, and the state of the exchanges, are the on‑
ly certain criterions of depreciation. But as the opposers of the
Bullion Report have been very fond of insisting upon the small
addition that has been made to the currency of late years, com‑
pared to the increased scale of our expenditure, we have thought
it right to set this argument in what appears to us to be its true
light. And when, instead of talking of the mere numerical in‑
crease of bank notes, compared with our prodigious expendi‑
ture and debt, we advert to the *proportion* in which the whole
currency has been enlarged ; and instead of spreading this nu‑
merical increase over fourteen years, we confine it to the peri‑
ods in which the increase really took place ; and, above all, when
we advert to a period of six years of great taxation and expen‑
diture, and great increase of the national debt, unaccompanied
by any increase of Bank of England notes above 5*l.*, or any
increase in the market price of gold ;—the facts will appear to
prove directly the reverse of what they are intended to prove ;
and our only astonishment will be, that the rapid increase of

currency which has taken place during the last three years, has not been accompanied by a still greater depreciation.

If then it appears, beyond all possibility of doubt, that a comparatively excessive issue of paper has taken place since the Bank Restriction bill, and most especially during the last three years; and if, even according to the concessions of those who oppose the Bullion Report, an excess of paper is in its nature calculated to expel the precious metals from the circulation of the country where such excess exists, What pretence have we to complain of our inability to obtain gold ? What pretence have we to attribute this inability to the untoward circumstances attending the state of the Continent ; when, under *any circumstances* the most favourable, the conduct which we have adopted could not fail to deprive us of all our guineas ?

We are far from meaning to deny the tendency of the present unnatural state of the Continent, to throw difficulties in the way of all sorts of commercial transactions, and that of obtaining gold among others ; but we have no hesitation in saying, that the measures we have resorted to, are of all others the most calculated to aggravate and extend those difficulties.—What has, in fact, been our situation ?—We have had to contend with an enemy whose power extends over so large a portion of the Continent, that he has been able to exclude our produce and manufactures from almost all the principal ports of Europe ; and we have had to support a great foreign expenditure, without the same facilities as formerly of defraying it by the export of our commodities. In this situation, what is the line of conduct that common sense and sound policy would seem to dictate ? In the first place, we conceive it would be, so to proportion our manufactures for foreign sale to the confined vent for them, as not to have immense quantities returned upon our hands, to involve our merchants in ruin ; and, in the next place, to be very careful not to take any steps respecting our currency, which would tend to deprive us of the precious metals, and prevent the country from having a considerable store of them to resort to, and a steady supply of them coming in, whenever they were found to be the most convenient remittances for our foreign expenditure. Instead of this, however, what has actually been our conduct ? By means of the profuse and unusual accommodations afforded by the Bank of England to our merchants, they have been encouraged, and enabled, to work an unusual quantity of manufactures, at high prices, for foreign sale, at the very time when the vent for them was unusually diminished ; and, by means of the same profuse issues, all our gold

117

has been driven from the circulation, and its return effectually prevented.

The consequences are such as might have been 'anticipated. The period to which we principally allude, and during which the great issues of paper have taken place, has been marked by the most extensive failures in the mercantile world, and by the most wide-spreading poverty and misery among the manfacturing classes, ever witnessed ; and our armies and expenditure abroad, have been maintained not only at a disadvantage, and expense unheard of before, but the Government has been put to the greatest difficulties to obtain the means of supporting them, even while it consented to purchase these means at the most extravagant prices.

There cannot, we conceive, be a grosser error than to suppose, that the Government will have a greater command of bullion for its foreign expenditure, if the domestic circulation be confined almost exclusively to paper. The actual store of the precious metals which a country may possess, though of the greatest use and advantage in any sudden demand occasioned by an unfavourable balance of payments, can never be sufficient to supply a continued foreign expenditure of any magnitude. The means of this expenditure, if we suppose that bullion must form a part of it, can only be abundant, when, as fast as the precious metals are sent out in one quarter, a steady supply of them flows in from other quarters. But this, of course, can only happen, when bank notes and guineas are precisely of the same value ; and when, instead of the scanty influx occasioned by the precarious and uncertain wants of Government, a large and steady demand for bullion, to maintain the accustomed circulation, produces its invariable concomitant, a large and steady supply. But there is yet a much more fatal error prevailing among the supporters of the present system of paper circulation, the consequences of which, it is to be feared, we shall long have reason to lament. This is, that the profuse issues of the Bank of England, and the accommodations which the Government receives from them in their general expenditure, form so essential a resource for carrying on the present expensive war, that our efforts would be immediately paralysed if this resource were to fail.

It is certainly true, that a paper circulation issued by a Government, and increased according to its wants, has often been found, in other countries, and undoubtedly would be found in this, a very powerful temporary resource. Such a mode of obtaining resources has, however, always been reprobated, not only as adapted exclusively to a tyrannical, or a revolutionary

Government, from the unlimited extent to which it may be pushed ; but as extremely oppressive and unequal in the manner of its operation ; and as giving a most unfair advantage to the profuse debtor over the thrifty creditor. Whatever objections, however, may be made to it on these grounds, it is, beyond all doubt, a system of *taxation* (for this is its true character) calculated to afford, for a short time, very powerful and effective resources. But there never was, we conceive, so mistaken and puerile an imitation of it, as that of supporting the present profuse issues of the Bank, under the idea that they furnish similar resources to the Government for carrying on the present expensive contest. They press, indeed, in proportion to their extent, with the same severity and the same inequality upon the subject ; and give the same unjust advantage to the debtor, at the expense of the creditor. But in this violent and unfair transfer of property, the Bank proprietors and the debtors are the gainers,—not the Government. The Government, by the sanction and support which it has given to the present system of circulation, almost avowedly for the express purpose of enabling it to carry on the war, may fairly be said, in addition to all its direct taxes, to have laid an indirect tax upon the people during the last three years, to an amount approaching towards a *double income tax ;* and yet we will venture to say, that the advantages which it has derived from the profuse issues of the Bank, do not exceed a few hundred thousands. They appear to us, indeed, to be confined (in all cases, where a manifest injustice is not committed towards a public servant or public creditor) to the circulation of a few Exchequer and Navy bills at rather a better price, and a few temporary advances to Government, which, in such a country as this, might always be obtained without such unnatural aids. We really believe, that no instance can be found of so great a change being produced in the property of a country, through the medium of its Government, from which that Government derived so little advantage, either immediate or prospective.

We are fully aware, that the system of indirect taxation to which we are now alluding, is of the nature of a transfer of property from one set of people to another, and not an actual consumption of it by the Government. But so are the taxes which are imposed for the purpose of paying the interest of the national debt. Yet these taxes occasion a very severe pressure upon individuals. And such a pressure as this, ought surely to be reserved to maintain a great national expenditure, and not be wantonly inflicted for the most trifling accommodations.

We are also fully aware, that the transfer of property occasioned by a rise of prices, has a tendency to give a stimulus to

119

industry. To this principle we gave its full weight in a former Number. It appears to us, indeed, a very important one; as explaining the reason why severe taxation is not so prejudicial to the resources of a state, as might naturally be expected; and why great public prosperity is not incompatible with much individual distress. But, independently of the great injustice of ever calling such a principle into action unnecessarily, the principle itself cannot safely be received without considerable limitation.

If those who have triumphantly brought forward the very just observations of Hume, on the good effects of an increasing circulating medium, had studied with attention the former part of the same admirable essay from which these observations are taken, they would have found, that, in the opinion of the author, the natural check to the continuance of great commercial prosperity in any one country, is the rise of corn and labour, necessarily occasioned by that prosperity itself; and that, for fear of accelerating the period of this check, he entertains great doubt of the benefit of banks, even without reference to any depreciation of their paper below the value of bullion. And when the same persons, in order to deprecate the return of the Bank to payments in specie, dilate with satisfaction on the poverty, beggary and sloth which are the consequences, according to Hume, of a decreasing circulating medium ; let them read the whole essay, and then say whether it is not clearly Hume's opinon, that the most certain way of producing that poverty, beggary and sloth which he describes, is a profuse issue of bank paper,—an intemperate use of an excessive stimulus, which, from its very nature, cannot admit of being continued. We have increased the circulating medium at least one fourth during the last three years. Is it meant to be asserted, that we ought to go on at this rate, in order to avoid the check we so much dread? If we were to make the attempt, is it not certain, that the disease would overtake us even during the time that we were applying what we conceived to be the remedy? Has it not, in fact, already overtaken us? Is not that period, contemplated by Hume as so unfavourable to industry, already arrived? And do not our ruined merchants, our impoverished manufacturers, and the severe check that our capital and revenue have of late suffered, amply testify, that, even in the first application of the stimulus, it was administered in much too large a dose?

Yet, under all these circumstances, and under the moral certainty of rendering a return to a wholesome state of the circulation more and more difficult, the longer we continue the present system, we are taking further steps in the same career, with

120

a confidence that is perfectly inconceivable. By the late act, we have done nearly all that is possible, short of making bank notes a legal tender, to force the people of this country to consider bank notes and guineas as of equal value. And if this act should not be sufficient for the purpose, that is, if the public should obstinately persevere in giving the preference to that commodity, which, in any fair and open market, will sell for 20 per cent. more than the other, the ulterior measure, of making bank notes a legal tender, is openly and distinctly threatened. The immediate and avowed causes which, in the opinion of ministers, rendered this act, and the accompanying threat necessary, were, the conduct of a noble Lord respecting his rents, and the decision of the Judges in the case of De Yonge.

We confess, that when we first heard of the notice which Lord King's requisition to his tenants had excited, we were disposed to regret that the event had happened;—not because we did not think that the proceeding was perfectly equitable and honourable, but because we thought that, in the actual state of the knowledge and temper of the administration, it would lead immediately to the making of bank notes a legal tender. But though it has, in fact, led to something as nearly as possible approaching to this, yet further reflection has convinced us, that, in spite of this consequence, the discussion which it has occasioned, and the manner in which it has brought the subject home to the public feeling, cannot fail to be of the highest use in explaining the true state of the circulation. It must be acknowledged, indeed, that the period at which the noble Lord determined to stand forward upon this occasion, was, in every point of view, most correctly and happily chosen. It was not very wisely urged, in the debates upon this subject, that as, for the whole course of the fourteen years since the Restriction bill, no landholder in England had been known to demand his rents in the legal coin of the realm, it might fairly have been presumed that none would in future do so, and that it would not be necessary to provide against such a case by law. But we would ask, whether, at any former period, there was the same reason for demanding gold? or, whether, because a person submits to a loss of 5 or 10 per cent., rather than revert to the remedy which the law allows, it follows, that he ought to submit to a loss of 20 per cent. without any effort to avoid it? For more than two years after the Restriction, bank notes and guineas were precisely of the same value, and, of course, no person could feel any preference of the one above the other. For the next three years, there was a difference between them, which varied from 5 to 10 per cent. This difference excited, as might be expected, considerable attention and discussion, which, there was reason to believe, produced a greater degree of caution on the part of the Bank; and the period of so great a depreciation as 10 per cent. was but of very short duration. For the next six years, the price of gold remained stationary, and the exchanges returned nearly to their accustomed state. This price was, indeed, between 2 and 3 per cent. above the mint price; but it was not to be expected, that any person, for so slight a difference, should incur the trouble and odium of an appeal to the law. It was, however, quite a different thing, when, instead of 3 per cent., 5 per cent., or 10 per cent., the depreciation during the next three years amounted to more than 20 per cent.; and when, above all, the fact of this depreciation was formally denied by the party who alone had the means of checking it, and when, of course, there was every reason to believe. that it would be continually progressive. We must say, therefore, that, whether with a view to the mere question of property, or that which probably might influence the noble Lord still more, a desire to make a practical protest against a system subversive of some of the most sacred and fundamental laws of his country, he could not have chosen a more happy time for another appeal to the good sense of the country. and we really think that those who feel with the noble Baron on this subject, and on such fundamental and constitutional questions, are ready to say with the Barons of old, *Nolumus leges Angliæ mutari*—must consider him as entitled to great praise for the manly and able manner in which he has conducted this appeal, both in his private and legislative capacity, undeterred by the clamours of ignorance and folly.

The laws to which Lord King had the power of appealing, in order to enforce the performance of the contracts into which he had entered with his tenants, according to their true and legitimate meaning, afford the most unquestionable proofs, that the spirit in which the Restriction act was conceived and brought forward as a temporary measure in 1797, was totally different from that in which it has been lately continued. And it appears to us, we confess, a most cruel calumny on the character of Mr Pitt, to insinuate that he would have been ready, at any time, to sanction the late unjust transfers of property, and wanton and useless pressure upon the people, which have been occasioned by the present excessive depreciation of the currency. On this point, without the most direct proofs of intentions which were not executed, it is but candid to judge from the measures to which he actually did give his support; and in these, it must be allowed, there was a very marked attention to the protection of private property. While it was thought necessary temporarily to suspend the cash payments of the Bank, which, of course, prevented individuals from converting their property immediately into a legal tender for a debt; it was justly thought proper to suspend the power of arrest in mesne process, for fear such a power, against which no one who was indebted to another could be immediately prepared, might be exercised wantonly and capriciously, when there was no essential difference between bank notes and guineas. But in order, at the same time, effectually to protect the property of the subject from the chance of loss from a paper currency not immediately convertible into specie, all the other processes for recovering a debt in the legal coin of the realm were left open; which was, in our opinion, clearly and distinctly to point out the precise remedies which the Legislature intended should be taken, if at any time the currency really became depreciated, and the debtor proposed to pay his creditor in a medium decidedly of less value than that in which he had contracted to pay him.

And yet it is because an individual has resorted to a remedy thus left open by the Legislature for the most just and obvious purpose; and because it has been determined by the judges that the laws of England as hitherto constituted, will not sanction the degradation of the legal coin of the realm to whatever value in exchange a banking company may choose to give to their notes, that the late act to make bank notes equivalent to guineas has been passed, and that the further measure is threatened of making bank notes a legal tender!

But what is still more extraordinary than the act itself, is, that such a measure should have been brought forward for the avowed purpose of protecting the property of the public creditor. Now, of all the descriptions of persons in the state, the public creditor appears to us to be the most deeply and cruelly injured by it. The mercantile classes, it is well known, do not suffer from a depreciated currency, as long as confidence remains unimpaired. The landholder, though he will undoubtedly have that proportion of the produce of his land which he stipulated to retain, when he consigned the temporary possession of it to a tenant, very unjustly diminished during the time that his leases have to run, will always have the opportunity, at the expiration of these leases, of recovering the genuine value of his property. The public servants of the state, and all other descriptions of servants who live on the wages of labour, though they may suffer very cruelly for a time, must ultimately have their wages raised in proportion to the depreciation of that

123

medium in which they are paid. But the public creditor has
no remedy, either immediate or prospective. He is utterly at
the mercy of the circulating medium ; and if the 20 millions,
which now form the revenues of so many British families, were
not equal in value, and the command of the necessaries of life,
to the bullion contained in a single million of the legal coin of
the realm, the condition of these families must inevitably sink
in this frightful proportion. We do not mean to assert it as
our opinion that this extreme case will probably occur ; but we
mean distinctly to assert, that if bank notes be made a legal
tender, and they are virtually so even at present, the Legislature will deliver to the Bank Directors the full and complete
power of producing such a case. And whatever may be the
result, whether the currency becomes depreciated 40 or 50 per
cent., or remains nearly stationary at 20 per cent. ; or whether,
from the individual good conduct of the Directors, it recovers
a part or the whole of its lost value ; we do not hesitate to say,
that in the whole course of English history no act can be pointed out which can be more properly designated by the term un-
constitutional, or which more directly contradicts the general
spirit of British legislation in the best times, than that which
thus gives up 20 millions worth of revenue belonging to British
subjects, to be regulated in its value according to the will and
pleasure of 24 individual merchants, whose interests are in reality different from those of the owners of such revenue.

It was asked, in the debates on the late act, whether the state
ought to allow of guineas being demanded in discharge of other
debts, while it continued to pay its own debts in paper ? We
should undoubtedly say that it ought ; and that if it did so, it
would give the surest pledge possible that the public dividends
would not long continue to be paid in a depreciated currency.
It seldom falls to the lot of a fraternity of reviewers to possess
money in the stocks; but it is well known that we are richer than many of our brethren ; and the report of our having accumulated above a hundred pounds in the three per
cents. (though we did not mean to boast of it) is really true.
For this little nest egg, it may be supposed that we are
proportionably anxious ; and with a view to its safety, and
the value of the yearly income we derive from it, what of
all other things we should most like to see, is a fair and
open discount upon paper, and a free circulation of guineas at
their market price. We should then submit to our present diminution of income, in the full confidence that it would be
temporary ; and that when the injustice which the public creditor was suffering was daily and hourly brought before the

view of the Legislature, a British Parliament would infallibly interfere to prevent it. But we confess that we are most seriously alarmed for our property, when the Government, under the insidious pretext of supporting the interests of its creditors, does every thing that is possible to conceal their losses from the public ; and by solemnly declaring bank notes to be equivalent to guineas, furnishes to the interested and unthinking the pretence of saying, that the ruin which crushes the public creditors, while other classes find the means of escaping from it, is owing to a rise of profits, a rise of rents, and a rise of wages, and not to its true cause, a depreciated currency.

One of the principal arguments urged in favour of the ever memorable act for making bank notes equivalent to guineas in public estimation, when they were not equivalent in the market, was, that however it might be lamented by some, that the measures which had led to the present state of our currency had ever been adopted, it was evidently impossible to retract, or even not to go on with them at present. This, it must be confessed, is a most fearful argument; and if it be really intended to go on in the same spirit which has marked the last three years, there are no limits to the degree of depreciation which may be expected. All that has yet happened is in exact conformity with the general principles which have been laid down on this subject by those who are called theorists ; and the experience of the past enables us, with the utmost certainty, to predict, that an excessive issue of paper in England will be accompanied with precisely the same results which have invariably attended it in other countries,— with the same unavailing endeavours to prop the falling value of the paper—the same failure of confidence and check to all regular commercial dealings—and the same wide-wasting convulsion of private property.

We cannot, however, bring ourselves to believe that we shall continue to proceed in this destructive career. We cannot believe that, though the Legislature appears to be blind to a depreciation of 20 per cent., it will not open its eyes to a depreciation of 30, 40, or 50 per cent. We have even some hope in the Bank Directors themselves, and in the natural repugnance which men of character and respectability must feel to be considered as the instruments of so much mischief to their country. One of the most cheering gleams that has reached our northern hemisphere, was the statement of Mr Manning, a Bank Director, in the House of Commons, that the issues of bank notes had been diminished three millions,— that they had, at one period, been twenty-five millions, and were then twenty-two millions. Let three more millions be withdrawn gradually from the circulation, and then let the Bank rest a while upon its oars. The effect of a diminished circulation on prices cannot be expected to be immediate and universal; but we are certain that no long time would elapse, before a marked change would be perceived in the price of gold, and the state of our foreign exchanges.

The diminution of the issues of paper is the grand point to be accomplished; and, from whatever quarter it may come, or from whatever motive it may be prompted, we shall hail it with joy and gladness as the only specific for the present disordered state of the currency. The next remedy we should recommend, is one which ought certainly to accompany the first, and would be the surest pledge of its continued application. This is the immediate repeal of the late act for regulating public estimation, and the free permission to the legal coin of the realm to circulate with paper at its real value in exchange. We can readily understand why the Bank Directors, and perhaps the Government, should object to this measure, as it would undoubtedly be a standing reproach to them, that any difference should remain, in public estimation, between guineas and bank notes; but that any of the other members of the state, who are not, or at least do not think themselves personally interested in the continuance of the present system, should contemplate such an event with fear, as a dangerous and alarming crisis, is what we cannot comprehend. An open discount upon paper has taken place in all the continental countries, where an excess of paper has been issued, without any difficulty or convulsion. It is, in reality, the natural effect of a depreciated currency; and is, at the same time, the best immediate remedy that can possibly be applied, and the best preparative for a return to payments in specie. Care should be taken, and such care may always be taken, equitably to settle past contracts; and the reference to gold, which would then always be made, would at once settle all future contracts upon the most solid foundations. We should then again see guineas in our circulation; and the Government would no longer be driven to the same difficulties, and the same extravagant means in the support of its foreign expenditure.

With regard to the gold which ought gradually to be collected, to enable the Bank, after a moderate time, to resume its payments in specie, and render the cure complete, nothing would of course facilitate it so much, as the taking off the present bounty of 20 per cent. on the melting or exportation of guineas; and we really think, that if the legal coin of the realm were allowed to pass for what it is worth, no great scarcity of it would long be felt, notwithstanding the present convulsed state of the mercantile world. But as the Bank Directors seem to consider the collection of a sufficient quantity of gold for a return to cash payments, as a labour absolutely herculean, in the present state of things, let the Government so far indulge them, as to adopt the valuable suggestion of Mr Ricardo, and merely compel them, at the expiration of two years, to pay their notes above 20*l.*, and no other, in guineas, standard gold in bars, or foreign gold of the same value, at their option. This plan (for the further explanation of which we refer to the Appendix of the 4th edition of Mr Ricardo's first pamphlet, p. 94.) would preclude the necessity of providing, at first, such a quantity of gold as would be required to fill the smaller channels of circulation with guineas; and, while it was continued, would protect the Bank from the dangers to which it might be exposed, on the resumption of its payments in cash,—from the effects of small hoarding, or the pressing demand for guineas, or the failure of country banks. It would only be necessary to provide such a quantity of bullion as would be sufficient completely to secure it against an unfavourable balance of payments, occasioned either by its own imprudent issues, or the natural inequalities which must occasionally occur in the wants and supplies of different nations; which last cause can never be of serious magnitude and continuance, unless aggravated and prolonged by the former.

How long such a plan should be allowed to continue, or whether it might be advantageously made permanent, would of course be the subject of future consideration. Its great object is to maintain, steadily, the bullion value of our paper currency, at a very small expense of the precious metals; and this object it seems calculated to answer.

From *Edinburgh Review*,
July 1821

ART. VI. *An Inquiry concerning the Power of Increase in the Numbers of Mankind. Being an Answer to Mr Malthus's Essay on that Subject.'* By WILLIAM GODWIN. London, 1821.

WE are surprised at this publication of Mr Godwin. Notwithstanding the prejudices which have prevailed against him on account of his moral and political theories, we have always felt a respect for his talents; and have thought that his reputation has been as much too low of late years, as it was too high soon after he wrote his Political Justice. The present work proves, either that we were wrong in our estimate of his powers, or that they are now greatly impaired by time. It appears to us, we confess, to be the poorest and most old-womanish performance that has fallen from the pen of any writer of name, since we first commenced our critical career. So long

---

For Semmel's commentary on this article by Malthus, see especially pp. 21-22 *supra*. (*Publisher*).

as Mr Godwin's judgment remained in sufficient vigour to repress useless ebullitions of anger against Mr Malthus, he seems to have bit his lips in silence; and this laudable restraint lasted twenty years. But the sight of a fifth edition of the Essay on Population, operating, as we must suppose, upon an enfeebled judgment, was at length too much for him. As he says himself, he could refrain no longer: * he determined, at all events, to take the field; and, not being well prepared with the weapons of sound argument, he, like an old scold, ' unpacks his heart in words. ' Though he professes a personal respect for Mr Malthus, there is no kind or degree of abuse which he does not pour out upon his doctrines. He regards them with inexpressible abhorrence. They are portentous; they are calamitous; they are appalling; they are disgusting; they are atrocious; they are cabalistical, &c. &c. &c. He says he is full of matter, and that the spirit within constraineth him; † and this is the kind of stuff which he pours forth.

Now, we really think that this mode of treating a subject, on which a just decision is confessedly of great importance to the happiness of society, is utterly disgraceful to any writer of character and ability. If the arguments which Mr Godwin can advance against Mr Malthus's theory be just, there can be little doubt of its being overthrown without the aid of abuse. If, on the other hand, Mr Malthus be correct in the view which he has taken of the law of population, abuse cannot possibly do any good, though it may obviously do some harm.

We confess that we have, for many years, been in the habit of considering the question of the principle of population as set at rest by Mr Malthus. We should not, however, in any degree, have objected to see the view which he has taken of it *proved* to be fundamentally erroneous; but we really think that it would be a serious misfortune to society, and to the labouring classes in particular, that it should be believed to be erroneous, when it is not.

On first looking over Mr Godwin's work, we were certainly not disposed to pay such a compliment to his eloquence, aided even by the zest of abuse, as to think that it would make what was true appear to be false; and, as the book was dear, and not likely to fall into the hands of the labouring classes, unless brought forward and quoted by others, which, from the manner in which the subject is treated, could not have been expected, we had no thoughts of noticing it. To our great surprise, however, we heard that it had made some impression in London upon a certain class of readers; and, to our still greater

---

* Preface, p. vi.   † Ibid. p. vi.

surprise, we learned from the papers, that, upon occasion of a late discussion on the Poor-Laws Amendment Bill, it had been referred to by a member of the House of Commons as an elaborate work, which, in the opinion of good judges, had shown that Mr Malthus's statements respecting the rate of the increase of population were quite unfounded. This set us upon looking again at the work which we had thrown aside; and, having convinced ourselves that the tables, and remarks upon them, brought forward by Mr Godwin and his friend Mr Booth, instead of weakening the statements of Mr Malthus, tend to establish them on firmer foundations than ever, we think it may be of use, in reference to the subject generally, to state the grounds of this conviction.

It would be quite a waste of time to follow Mr Godwin through the mass of abuse, repetition, and irrelevant matter, of which the different divisions of his work consist. We shall hasten at once to the latter part of the third book, which contains the only argument which has any appearance of shaking, by an appeal to facts, the ratios of the natural increase of population laid down by Mr Malthus.

In this part of the work, which appears to be written by a Mr Booth, after many pages of the most solemn and absurd trifling which we have ever witnessed, * the following useful observation occurs.

' When enumerations are taken every ten years, it is obvious, exclusive of immigration, that in any particular census the persons living above ten years of age must have all existed in the census immediately preceding. In that of 1810, for instance, all above ten years formed part of the population of 1800; and are in reality the same, except inasmuch as they are diminished by death. Those under ten have all been born in the interval between the censuses. '

This observation may serve to form a rule by which to judge of the amount of immigration in any country where such censuses are taken; because the excess of the population above ten years of age in the second census, after a proper allowance has been made for the mortality in the interval, must consist of persons who have emigrated from other countries.

We are disposed to give Mr Booth some credit for this rule, which, though obvious, has not, that we are aware of, been sug-

---

* Mr Booth gravely informs us, that *in fact* the Swedish children are brought into the world by the child-bearing females, p. 270. He takes a world of pains to prove, that population can never increase in a geometrical progression, *strictly regular*. In this attempt he fails ; but, if he had succeeded, of what possible consequence would it be to the general argument ?

gested before. But we cannot give him credit for the manner in which he applies it. Here his general want of information shows itself, and leads him into gross errors, which render his conclusion quite wide of the truth. A very slight consideration will be sufficient to show the nature and effect of those errors.

Before we can ascertain the amount of immigration from the numbers above ten years old in the second census, it is obvious that we must make a proper allowance for the mortality of the population of the first census in the ten years between the first and second. Mr Booth, proceeding, we suppose, upon the supposition that the mortality in the United States is 1 in 40, imagines that he shall obtain the mortality of the ten years in question, by multiplying the mortality of one year by ten; and so infers, that the population of the first census would, in ten years, be diminished by $\frac{10}{40}$ or $\frac{1}{4}$. He forgets, or perhaps he never knew, that the very early years of life are the greatest contributors to the annual mortality. In a table of the numbers in different ages dying annually in Sweden, brought forward by Dr Price, ‡ it appears, that the mortality of the male children under one year of age was 1 in $3\frac{1}{2}$, while the mortality between the ages of 5 and 10 was 1 in 68; between the ages of 10 and 15, 1 in 131; and between the ages of 15 and 20, 1 in 139. It is quite obvious, therefore, that the ten years' mortality of a population which is rising into the healthiest stages of life, and is not affected by fresh births, and the frail tenure of existence in its earliest periods, must be essentially different from the annual mortality of the whole population multiplied by ten.

According to Dr Price's table, before adverted to, the annual mortality of the male population of Sweden for 21 years, from 1755 to 1776, was 1 in $33\frac{1}{4}$, and of the male and female taken together, 1 in 34.6; but, if a calculation be made from this, and the table immediately preceding it, with a view to ascertain the loss in ten years on a population, none of which had been born during that time, it will appear that this loss will be 1 in 52.89, or nearly 1 in 53.; while, if the annual mortality had been multiplied by ten, the loss would have been as much as 1 in 34.6.

On the annual mortality of the population of the United States, writers have differed. Mr Barton, in the Transactions of the Society at Philadelphia (Vol. iii. No. 7.), has stated it to be 1 in 45; while Mr Winter and others, without referring to any documents of authority, have made it as high as 1 in 40. We should suppose, from the peculiar structure of the American population, and the great excess of the births above the deaths, that it was less than Mr Barton's estimate, as, even upon

---

† Observations on Reversionary Payments, vol. ii. p. 124.

his estimate, the expectation of life would not be so high as in Sweden; which, considering the numbers which must die in the latter country, from the consequences of scarcity and bad food, is making a large allowance for the greater natural unhealthiness of America. It is comfortable, however, to get rid of these sweeping and conjectural estimates, by an appeal to recorded facts; and we find that the mortality of Philadelphia, according to bills published by the Board of Health for eight years, from 1807 to 1814 inclusive, was found to be no more than 1 in 43, as stated in the valuable work of Dr Seybert. * And if the mortality of the greatest towns in America be less than 1 in 40, we should expect that the mortality of the whole country would be less than 1 in 50; and this is the conjecture of Dr Price. We should be aware that a mortality of 1 in 50 in America, where the increase is so rapid, does not imply a greater degree of healthiness than 1 in 34.6 in Sweden, where the population increases very slowly.

Adopting, however, the estimate of Mr Barton, if we apply the calculated proportion of loss in ten years which would take place in Sweden, where the general mortality is 1 in 34.6 to America, where the general mortality is 1 in 45, we shall find that the population existing at the time of any one census, would have lost in ten years, or at the next census, $\frac{1}{6.878}$, or nearly $\frac{1}{7}$.

Instead, therefore, of subtracting $\frac{1}{4}$ for the loss of a given population in the course of ten years in America, we must subtract only $\frac{1}{6.878}$; and it will be found that this correction will make a very great difference in the appearance of immigration.

According to the American tables, as stated in Mr Godwin's work, it appears that the white population of 1800 was 4,305,971. If, from this number, we subtract the $\frac{1}{6.878}$ part for the diminution of the population in ten years, the population of 1800, which should be found living in 1810, will be 3,679,971, instead of 3,200,000, as stated by Mr Booth; and, subtracting 3,679,971 from 3,845,389, the population above ten years of age actually found living in the census of 1810, we shall have 165,418 for the amount of immigration in ten years, instead of 645,389, as

---

* Statistical Annals of the United States, p. 50. This work appears to be sanctioned by the Congress, and contains, we believe, all the authentic materials which are to be found on the subject of population in that country.

stated by Mr Booth. If we then proceed to deduct the amount of immigration so found from 5,862,093, the whole white population of 1810, the remainder will be 5,696,623; and the difference between 4,305,971, the population of 1800, and the number 5,696,623 will express the increase of population between 1800 and 1810, independently of immigration, or by procreation only.

To ascertain the period of doubling which would result from this increase in ten years, we have only to apply the formula given by Dr Price (in vol. i. p. 285.), or the rules relating to compound interest or geometrical progression to be found in most books of arithmetic; and it will appear, that when a population of 4,305,971 increases to 5,696,675 in ten years, the annual ratio of increase will be rather above the decimal .0283, or rather less than the vulgar fraction $\frac{1}{35}$; and, if continued, will occasion a doubling of the population in about 24 years and 10 months.

It will be observed, that the amount allowed for immigration after the proposed correction has been applied, is 165,418 in the ten years, or above 16,000 a year. This, however, is considerably more than is allowed by any of the American Statistical writers; and is probably beyond the truth. We have already stated our reasons for believing, that 1 in 45 is greater than the true mortality of the United States taken throughout; and if so, the amount to be subtracted for the mortality during the ten years, would be diminished. But this amount would be much more diminished from another cause. The proportion of the births, and consequently of the population under one, two, and three years of age, must be much greater in America than in Sweden; and consequently, after the first three years of the ten had passed, the diminution of the annual mortality would be more considerable. If we had American tables, formed like those of Dr Price for Sweden, we should expect, that, on account of the peculiar structure of the American population, arising from the great excess of births above deaths, it would turn out, that the proportion which a given population, without any fresh accession of births, would lose in ten years, instead of being rather more than $\frac{1}{7}$, would not be more than $\frac{1}{8}$; in which case, the amount of immigration annually would, by Mr Booth's own rule, be only between seven and eight thousand, instead of above sixteen thousand; and the period of doubling would come near to the calculation of Dr Seybert.

It appears, then, that, as far as we can judge of the increase of the population of the United States during the period to which Mr Godwin refers, and the particulars of which are best known, Mr Malthus's statements, taking the Eastern and Western States together, are most amply justified. But, in reality, the condition of the *Eastern* States does not now apply to Mr Malthus's proposition. His proposition, as we understand it, is this; that if the obvious causes which check marriage, and occasion premature mortality, were removed in such a way as they are actually found to be removed in some countries for short periods, the population would go on increasing at a rate which would double the numbers in less than twenty-five years. But, in the Eastern States, the towns are now large, and some of them so unhealthy as scarcely to keep up their numbers. It is known that they are subject to the yellow fever, which seems to prevail only in towns of some size, and not to extend itself into the country. And further, there is reason to believe, that these portions of the American population are not exempt from those vices which tend to render marriage less frequent, less early, and less fruitful than in the country. The Western States, therefore, alone answer the conditions of Mr Malthus's proposition, and alone furnish a practical illustration of the rate at which population may increase when unchecked. But what is this rate of increase? Mr Booth has kindly furnished us with the means of ascertaining it with little trouble. He has given a table of the population and progress of some of the Western States, separated from the others. * According to this table, the white population of the States of Kentucky, Tenessee, Mississippi, and Indiana, was, in 1800, 281,341; and in 1810 it had increased to 587,026. Proceeding upon the same principle as before in the application of Mr Booth's rule, the amount of immigration will appear to have been 116,665 in the ten years; and, upon calculating the *rate* of increase, it will be found to be such as would double the population in a little more than thirteen years and a half. Mr Malthus has mentioned, on the authority of Dr Styles and Dr Price, fifteen years as the period in which it was supposed that some of the back settlements had doubled; but he lays no stress upon it in his argument; yet in so large a district of America as that included in the table produced by Mr Booth, a still greater rate of increase appears to have taken place, after making a full allowance for immigration.

That the proofs which have been adduced of the very rapid increase of the population of the United States, from procreation only, are of a kind which may safely be relied on, cannot admit of a doubt. In estimating the *progress* of population in any

---

* P. 280.

country, the first and main object is to ascertain the actual number of the people at different periods. The next is, if there be an increase, to determine what portion of this increase is attributable to immigration, and what portion may be considered as arising from procreation only. If we can ascertain these two points, all other information is quite of a subordinate kind in reference to the main question.

On the first of these points, the different censuses which have been taken in the United States are allowed to be quite satisfactory. Their general accuracy has not been attempted to be impeached even by Mr Godwin.

With regard to the second point, all the accounts agree, that the influence of immigration upon the population of the United States, particularly in the intervals of the two censuses of 1790 and 1810, has been quite inconsiderable. On this subject we would refer to Dr Seybert's chapter on Emigration. * After reviewing what had been stated by other writers, and producing an authentic estimate of the number of passengers, *citizens* as well as aliens, who arrived at the different ports of the United States in the extraordinary year 1817, which amounted to 22,240, he calculates, that no more than 6000 could have arrived annually from 1790 to 1810; and, allowing for their increase at the very high rate of 5 per cent., he concludes by stating, that the duplication of the free inhabitants, independently of immigration, would require only $\frac{4}{5}$ of a year more than when the immigrants were added. When to these accounts of the writers on the United States, we add the useful rule laid down by Mr Booth, and apply it correctly according to the analogy of the tables of mortality in other countries, there is little reason to fear any essential error; and we may safely assert, that the information which we possess on these two points is not only much more important with a view to the main question, but much more to be depended upon than any we are likely to obtain on the ulterior and more difficult question of the proportion of births to marriages.

On this latter point, indeed, there is nothing which can be called evidence. No public documents which we have seen or heard of, give the marriages of the United States; and private estimates are generally so confined, that no safe inferences can be drawn from them. Mr Barton, whose authority on this particular point Mr Godwin is so eager to adopt, † expressly says, that his estimate was formed from a single village; and the few accounts which Mr Godwin says he procured himself, are from

---

* Statistical Annals, p. 28.   † P. 421.

towns which form no rule for the general population.   To these
very insufficient estimates, we may fairly oppose the authority of
Mr Bristed, who says, that, in the United States, the marriages
average six births, of which four are reared. *   Allowing these
opposing statements to neutralize each other, if we add, that
Dr Seybert, who has collected with care all the public documents relating to the population of the United States, is quite
silent with regard to the marriages, it may safely be concluded,
that, as yet, we have no information on the subject which can in
the slightest degree be depended upon.   We cannot, therefore,
be warranted in stating, even as a conjecture, that the proportion
of births to marriages in the United States is nearly the same as
in Europe.   Still less are we entitled to bring forward such a
statement, with a view to invalidate other information of which
there is good evidence.

But, independently of the proportion of births and marriages
deduced from Mr Barton's account, though seemingly against
his own belief, all the other appearances and proportions in the
structure of the American population, most strongly imply a
very rapid increase from procreation.   Dr Price has shown,
that, in towns or districts recruited constantly by grown persons,
the numbers in the higher ages of life exceed the usual proportion to the numbers in the lower.   Consequently, if the increase
of the American population were chiefly occasioned by immigration, we should find the proportion of persons above forty-
five unusually large; instead of which, every American census
shows it to be unusually small.

Mr Booth observes, that in an *indigenous* society there are
nearly a fourth of its members above forty-five years of age, †
while, in none of the United States, is the number of persons
above forty-five more than from 16 to 17 per cent. of the population; and in some of the newly settled districts, they do not
exceed 7 or 8.   Now, we apprehend, that a large proportion of
persons above the age of forty-five has no more necessary connexion with an *indigenous* than it has with a *vertigenous* society.
If an indigenous population be nearly stationary, the proportion
of one-fourth for the numbers above the age of forty-five, will
probably be near the truth; and this we believe to be not an
unfrequent proportion in the States of Europe.   But if an indigenous population be increasing rapidly, it must of necessity
have a much smaller part of the population in the advanced stages
of life; and this is the case with the United States.   The table of

---

* Resources of the United States, p. 453.
† Page 278.

135

a fifteen years colony which Mr Booth has taken the trouble to calculate, * is not in the slightest degree applicable. It is true, that if you suppose emigrant breeders coming into a country in large bodies at the age of twenty or twenty-five, and then make a single enumeration of the population before the end of fifteen years, and consequently before any of these breeders have reached the age of forty-five, you will find a small proportion of the people in the more advanced stages of life. But has this case any relation to the whole of the United States, where the emigrations, to whatever amount they arise, have been going on for above 150 years? We conceive that it is hardly possible to state a proposition which carries truth more clearly in the face of it, than to say, that if a country increases for a considerable time principally by a yearly supply of grown persons, it will contain a much larger proportion of the population *above* forty-five, than if it increase at the same rate from procreation. Mr Booth, in his remarks on this subject, shows so extraordinary a want of general information, that none but his friend can be his parallel. But, to be sure, his friend Mr Godwin more than equals him.

Dr Price, after having stated that the number of persons in New Jersey had been taken, by order of the Government, in 1738, and in the next seven years had been found to increase, by procreation only, at a rate which would double the population in twenty-two years, † remarks, as a peculiarity confirming the fact, that the number under sixteen years of age was nearly the half of the population, while in Dr Halley's table it amounted to little more than one-third. Dr Price, though he did not carry forward his views to all the important consequences of the laws of population, was thoroughly conversant with the scientific part of the question; and, possessing this kind of knowledge in an eminent degree, he mentions this proportion of the population under sixteen as a natural consequence, and additional proof of a very rapid increase by procreation. Yet Mr Godwin produces this very fact as a proof of a result exactly the reverse! From this fact he says ' it inevitably follows, that, throughout the Union, the population, as far as depends on procreation, is at a stand.' ‡ This *sage* conclusion would make it appear, that the population of all the States in Europe is diminishing most rapidly, and that Sweden, which Mr Godwin himself asserts is increasing, must soon be a desert.

Upon the inspection of the American census it appears, that

---

* Page 276.
† Observations on Reversionary Payments, Vol. I. p. 283.
‡ Page 441.

about one half of the population is under sixteen years of age, and one-eighth above forty-five; while, in many of the States of Europe, the proportion of the population under sixteen is about one-third, and above forty-five about one-fourth. These different proportions in the American tables, compared with those of Europe, supposing the expectation of life to be in any degree alike, must, to every person conversant with the subject, afford the clearest and most intelligible proofs of a very rapid increase of population in the United States from procreation. What, then, must we think of the knowledge of Mr Godwin and Mr Booth, who have chosen these proportions to prove, that almost the whole of the American increase arises from emigration? We did not think that such an instance of false reasoning could have occurred in the nineteenth century.

Nor does Mr Godwin's knowledge appear to greater advantage when he talks about the proportion of births to marriages, which he thinks necessary to occasion a doubling of the population in twenty-five years. He insists upon it, over and over again, that for this purpose there must be eight births to a marriage. On this subject we would recommend him to read, with more attention than he appears yet to have done, Mr Malthus's chapter on the Fruitfulness of Marriages. He will there see, that the rate of the increase of population is powerfully affected by two other causes besides the fruitfulness of marriages, namely, the proportion of the born which lives to marry, and the interval between the average age of marriage and the average age of death; and that, taking these circumstances into consideration, and the effects produced on registers by second and third marriages, the population in the United States might double itself by procreation only every twenty-five years, with a proportion in the registers of only *five* births to a marriage. But on all these matters Mr Godwin seems to be as profoundly in the dark as if he had never opened a book on the subject, or heard of a parish register. If he is determined to receive no information from Mr Malthus, we recommend him to study diligently Dr Price's two volumes on Reversionary Payments, before he ventures again to discuss the principles of population.

Among the many instances of Mr Godwin's curious mode of illustrating his subject, it is difficult not to notice the strange absurdity of choosing Sweden as a specimen of the natural increase of population. * Mr Malthus had stated, that when the labouring classes of society are amply supplied with necessaries, the increase of population is always very rapid. To show that

----

* Page 352.

this cannot be, true, Mr Godwin instances the case of Sweden, where it is well known that the labouring classes are very scantily, instead of very amply supplied. He asks, Why the United States double their numbers in twenty-five years, while the increase of Sweden is so inconsiderable? † We answer, that the American labourer is able, with ease, to support a family of ten or twelve children, while the Swedish labourer can with difficulty support three or four. Surely this is a broad, glaring, and sufficient reason for the difference in the rates of increase, without entering into further particulars. But if we want some of these particulars, it is obvious that, when the wages of labour can only support tolerably well a small family, some will be entirely deterred from marrying, and others will marry later than they otherwise would do; while those who marry early in spite of all difficulties, if they happen to have large families, will not be able to support them in such a way as to prevent the diseases and premature mortality arising from poverty and bad nourishment. On the other hand, when the labouring classes, as in America, never find the least difficulty in the support of the largest families, they will not only be tempted to marry early, by which means each generation, by marriage and birth, will be shortened, but they will be able to maintain the largest families in such a way as not to be subject to any of the diseases arising from insufficient nourishment. In the one case, both the preventive and positive checks to population will be actively in operation: in the other they will, comparatively, have no influence. The measure of the encouragement to population is the facility of supporting a family, determined by the actual earnings of the labourer, combined with those of his wife and children, throughout the year. These earnings will be regulated, according to Adam Smith, by the rapidity with which the funds for the maintenance of labour continue to increase; and it is a physical impossibility that these funds should continue to increase as fast in Sweden or in Switzerland, the countries to which Mr Godwin refers, as in the United States. Consequently in such countries, though we may not know precisely *all* the modes in which the checks to population operate, we may be quite certain of their existence, and that to a considerable extent.

    Hitherto we have been inclined to consider the gross mistakes which Mr Godwin has made, as arising chiefly from a total want of knowledge of his subject. There are many, however, which do not admit of so favourable an interpretation, and seem as if

---

† Page 357.

they could only have arisen from wilful misrepresentation. Mr Malthus has limited his term, *moral* restraint, to a temporary or final abstinence from marriage on prudential considerations, with strict chastity during the single state. Taken exclusively in this sense, and in reference to one half of society, he is not perhaps wrong in supposing, that its operation has not hitherto been very powerful. But whether right or wrong in this observation, it is quite certain that, throughout the whole of his work, he lays the greatest stress upon the preventive checks generally; and there is scarcely a country which he has examined, particularly in Europe, where he does not consider the checks of this kind as having had a very great effect in diminishing the number of births. It is inconceivable, therefore, that any degree of innocent misconception should have suggested the following passage. ' It is clearly Mr Malthus's doctrine, that population is kept down in the old world, not by a smaller number of children being born among us, but by the excessive number of children which perish in their nonage, through the instrumentality of vice and misery. ' * This could only be said with a view to the prejudice which might be excited against Mr Malthus's doctrines, by representing the excessive mortality, or ' universe of death, ' which, Mr Godwin observes, would thus be occasioned for the benefit of the geometrical ratio.

Another still more glaring misrepresentation, which cannot be otherwise than wilful, is contained in the following passage. ' Upon the principles here explained, and with the most perfect consistency, Mr Malthus is, upon all occasions, an advocate for low wages. ' † Now, if there be one point more than another which Mr Malthus has laboured in all his works, even to tiresome repetition, it is to show the labouring classes how they may raise their wages effectively and permanently, and become more independent of the rich. On this subject, the tendency of his principles, and the tenor of his language, cannot be mistaken by the meanest capacity. When Mr Godwin, therefore, asserts, that Mr Malthus is on all occasions an advocate for low wages, it is quite impossible that he can believe what he says; but he chooses to say it, for the chance of its making an impression upon those who, from indolence, ignorance, or prejudice, are disposed to take bold assertions for proofs.

But it would be endless to follow Mr Godwin through his numerous misrepresentations; particularly as it may be fairly said that his whole work is founded on the grand misrepresentation of asserting, that the misery and vice which Mr Malthus

---

* Page 32.   † Page 598.

has stated to be the *consequences* of an excessive population, have been proposed by him as its *remedies,* and of representing him, consequently, as a friend to misery and vice; * while the letter and spirit of his work clearly show that he is their greatest enemy, and that his whole aim and object is to diminish their amount.   Mr Godwin has followed Mr Graham and others, in accusing Mr Malthus of the ingenious expedient of proposing misery as a remedy for want.

On the whole, we cannot but think that this performance of Mr Godwin is extremely discreditable to him, both as to matter and manner.   It contains more nonsense, and more abuse, than any other answer to Mr Malthus which we have met with; and, whatever impression it may chance to make, for a short time, from the virulence of its language and the boldness of its assertions, the only permanent effect of it will be, to establish more firmly the doctrines of the Essay on Population.

As a strong presumption of this, we will notice one more passage in Mr Godwin's work, in which, with great rashness, he reduces the question to a very narrow compass; and makes an avowal which leaves him quite without excuse for the language he has used.   In page 402, he distinctly acknowledges that there is great difficulty in accounting for the rapid increase of population which appears in the American censuses; and then goes on to say—' We have no choice in the solution of this difficulty, but either to refer it to an inherent, rapid, and incessant power in the human species to multiply its numbers, or to emigration.'   Now we think we have clearly shown, that it is not owing to emigration. †   Consequently it follows, from Mr Godwin's own statement, that there is *an inherent, rapid, and incessant power in the human species to multiply its numbers.*   ' And that there is, all nature cries aloud.'   The United States of America afford a specimen of the most rapid increase with which we are acquainted; only because, from peculiar circumstances, the demand for labour, and the real reward of labour, have been there the greatest.   But there is hardly a country in

---

* This is Mr Godwin's constant language ; and he sums up by saying, ' He who has written three volumes, expressly to point out the advantages we obtain from the presence of vice and misery, ' &c. &c.!!!   The extreme absurdity of such accusations must of course blunt the effects of their malice. p. 524.

† Mr Godwin himself speaks of the passage over of 165,000, or even 90,000 persons yearly, to America, as an *astounding conception,* (p. 403).   It is indeed so astounding as to be utterly incredible ; and from 1800 to 1810, when scarcely a rumour of emigration was heard, morally impossible.

Europe where, under similar circumstances, the increase of population would not have been as rapid: And if America had
never been known, we should not have wanted ample testimo-
nies to the truth of that great law by which the progress of population is regulated. Russia, Ireland, and some of the parts
of Germany referred to by Lusmilet, with the wages of labour
much inferior to those of America, have increased with a rapidity quite sufficient to establish the principle, if not the exact
rate. Ample proofs of the principle are indeed at our very
doors. In many of the country parishes of England, the number of births is nearly double the number of deaths. And
throughout the whole country, in the interval between the first
and second enumerations in 1800 and 1810, the rate of increase
was such as would double the population in 56 years, notwithstanding the number of persons in England who do not marry,
the number who delay marriage till late, and the mortality occasioned by our large towns and manufactories. There cannot, then, be the slightest doubt that, if nearly all our population lived in the country, and the labouring classes could have
as great a command of necessaries and conveniences as they
have had in the United States, the population of England would
double, from procreation only, in considerably less than twenty-
five years.

But, supposing this to be true (and in reality there can be
no reasonable question of its truth), it becomes those who are
continually declaiming against the doctrines of Mr Malthus to
consider, that their declamations must all tend, as far as they go,
to lower the wages of labour, and depress the condition of the
poor. If the tendency to increase be such as has been stated,
it is not only an act of folly, but an act of injustice and cruelty
to the labouring classes, publicly to deny it. And those who,
in the House of Commons, hold a language calculated to make
the poor believe that there is no kind of reason for any prudential restraint on marriage, because all that are born have a mortgage upon the land, and a claim of right to be furnished with
work and subsistence, certainly take upon themselves a most
perilous responsibility. They are not only doing all they can to
make the Poor-rates absorb the whole rental of the kingdom;
but, what is of infinitely more consequence, they are contribut-
ing, by all the means in their power, to plunge the labouring
classes into irretrievable poverty, dependence, and distress.
What cannot be done, will not be done. We may *promise* to
maintain the poor adequately; but we shall deceive them, and
shall not do it; and the main consequence of our inconsiderate
promises will be, to enlarge the circle of misery, and to force
many into it, who, if they had not been deprived of the proper

motives to exertion, by being led into an error, would have a-
voided it. If the law of population be such as has been stated,
it is a truth which it particularly concerns the poor to know:
And, in fact, the general circulation of this truth must be the
foundation of all essential improvement in their condition. We
quite agree with Mr Malthus in reprobating any positive laws
against early marriages: But without any such laws, we think
that something very important would be done, if the poor were
fully convinced that population has a powerful tendency to increase; that the main cause of low wages is the abundance of
hands, compared with the work to be done; and that the only
mode of raising them effectively and permanently, is to proportion more nearly the supply of labour to the demand for it.

With regard to the general question of the Poor Laws, we
have obviously left ourselves no room to enter upon it. We
will only therefore add, that, even should the Legislature determine, under all circumstances, to make no very essential alteration in them; yet if, instead of asserting that the poor have a
mortgage to an indefinite extent on the land, and a full claim
of right to support, the Poor-rates were called a compulsory
charity, limited by the necessity of the case, and the discretion
and resources of the society; and if they were administered under the constant conviction of the great truth above referred to,
we cannot but think that the present evils arising from them
might not only be prevented from increasing, but might be gradually diminished; and that, after the present season of difficulty was over, we might look forward, with some hope, to a
positive improvement in the condition of the labouring classes
—to higher wages and greater independence.

PART III

Articles by
MALTHUS
in the Quarterly Review

From The *Quarterly Review,*
April 1823

For Semmel's commentary on this article by Malthus, see especially pp. 24-27. (*Publisher*).

ART. VIII.—*Thoughts and Details on the High and Low Prices of the last Thirty Years.* By Thomas Tooke, F.R.S. London. 1823.

WE look upon this work of Mr. Tooke as a very valuable contribution to the science of political economy. It is an inquiry into the causes of the fluctuations which have occurred during the last thirty years in the prices of corn and other commodities; and in the pursuit of it he adduces a large and interesting collection of facts. This mode of treating his subject we consider as peculiarly judicious. At all times an extensive collection of facts relative to the interchange of the various commodities of the commercial world, which is more within the reach of intelligent merchants than any other class of men, cannot but be of great importance to the science of political economy; but it is more particularly required at the present moment, when it must be acknowledged that some of our ablest writers in this science have been deficient in that constant reference to facts and experience, on which alone it can be safely founded, or further improved.

Mr. Tooke's work is divided into four *Parts*. The principal causes of the variations in the prices of commodities, he thinks, may be classed under three general heads: 1st. Alterations in the value of the currency. 2d. War, with its attendant taxes, and the return to peace. 3d. Varieties of the seasons. (i. p. 4.) The effects of these causes on prices he considers in the three first *Parts*, according to the order named; and to these he has added a fourth, consisting of valuable tables of prices from 1782 to 1822.

Before he begins his inquiry into the influence to be ascribed to alterations in our currency, he very properly defines the meaning which he attaches to the terms depreciation of money and currency, excess or over issue of paper.

By depreciation of money, when applied generally, he understands the diminished value of the precious metals in the commercial world.

By depreciation of the currency, he means that state of it in which the coin is of less value in the market than by the Mint regulations it purports to be, or in which the paper that is compulsorily current is of less value than the coin in which it promises to be payable.—*Part* i. p. 8.

We quite agree with Mr. Tooke in the propriety and utility of the definitions which he has adopted with regard to coin and currency; and although a more general meaning has frequently been given to depreciation, and writers consequently appear to be warranted in so using it, yet we are persuaded that it would greatly

145

contribute to clear ideas on the subject, if we were to confine the term depreciation exclusively to a deviation in defect from the standard which the coin or paper currency professes to represent; and denominate exclusively a *fall* or *rise* in the *value* of money or bullion any change which affects the standard itself, whether in any particular country, or generally. We cannot therefore agree with Mr. Tooke in his application of the term depreciation of money to a diminished value of the precious metals in the commercial world; and we were not a little surprized to find, that among his definitions there was no reference whatever to the alterations in the value of money and bullion in particular coun‑ tries, alterations which have been acknowledged by all econo‑ mists, and must be allowed to be especially connected with Mr. Tooke's subject.

Having thus, however, cleared the way by defining his terms; he proceeds with his facts and reasonings; and the conclusions at which he arrives are, in substance, that prices have been no fur‑ ther affected by the alterations in the value of the currency, (or only in the slightest degree further,) than to the extent of the dif‑ ference between gold and paper; that, with the exception of commodities particularly taxed, or increased by charges on im‑ portation, or extra demand for government, there is no observable coincidence between a rise of price during war, and a fall during peace; and that the fluctuations of prices which have taken place during the last thirty years are, with the exception of the diffe‑ rence between paper and bullion, and the few exceptions noticed before, almost exclusively attributable to the variations of the sea‑ sons.

We cannot say that we are able to accompany Mr. Tooke to the full extent of these conclusions; but the excellency of his mode of treating the subject is, that he has put his reader in possession of so large a range of facts applicable to the questions treated of, that he is not only enabled to judge whether Mr. Tooke's con‑ clusions are well founded, but furnished with the means of draw‑ ing other conclusions interesting to the science of political eco‑ nomy, which seem strictly and legitimately to follow from the facts advanced.

From a careful attention to these facts, we should say that Mr. Tooke's work distinctly proves the four following propositions:—

First, that all exchangeable value, and consequently the prices of all commodities, depend entirely upon the supply compared with the demand, and are no further affected by the labour re‑ quired to produce them, than as this labour is the main condition of their supply.

2d. That the supply of commodities, as compared with the

demand, is much more affected, and for a longer period, by the variations in the seasons, than has hitherto generally been supposed.

3d. That when the supply of commodities is in some degree deficient compared with the demand, whether this arises from the increase of demand, or the diminution of supply, the state of trade is brisk, profits are high, and mercantile speculations are greatly encouraged; and on the other hand, when the supply is abundant compared with the demand, there is a period of comparative stagnation, with low profits, and very little encouragement to mercantile speculation.

4th. That when these periods of deficient or abundant supply compared with the demand, are of considerable duration, which is found by experience to be frequently the case, they are necessarily accompanied by a fall or rise in the value of the precious metals in the country where they take place, according to any mode of estimating their value, which has ever been considered as approximating to the truth.

Each of these propositions appears to us to be of fundamental importance to the science of political economy; and the inquiry into the proofs of them, contained in Mr. Tooke's work, will show us at the same time to what extent he may be considered as having established his own conclusions.

In reference to the first proposition, or the universal influence of supply and demand on prices, both temporarily and permanently, we should say that the facts of all the four *Parts* of Mr. Tooke's work, and the reasonings of the first three, conspire to place the effects of demand and supply in such a light as to leave the truth of the proposition beyond the reach of any reasonable doubt. In the first *Part,* all that rise of prices beyond the difference between paper and gold, which was coincident in time with the Bank restrictions, Mr. Tooke uniformly and distinctly attributes to the state of the supply compared with the demand. He is indeed disposed to think that this rise was neither so great nor so general as has been usually supposed; but the facts which he adduces do not bear him out in this opinion: he observes,

It has further been asserted, that labour as well as necessaries experienced a progressive advance during the period referred to. I have already suggested grounds of objection to the admission of the wages of carpenters in and near London as affording a sufficient ground of inference with respect to the general rate of wages in the country; and the same objection applies, in point of principle, to the admission of the higher price paid for some other descriptions of labour, which happened to be in great relative demand. It is clear that, during the progress of a war on such a scale as the last, there must have been an unusual demand for full grown able bodied men; and the encouragement held out to a great extension of tillage, during the same period, might be supposed to have added to the demand; and as the supply could barely within the period keep pace with the extra demand, a considerable portion of that description of persons might naturally be expected to command a high rate of wages. Of this description were soldiers, sailors, labourers in husbandry, carpenters, bricklayers, domestic men-servants, and many others.'—*Part* i. p. 76.

Now we confess that we should, without hesitation, call this a general rise in the money price of labour; nor do we think that the propriety of the term would be impeached by the instances which Mr. Tooke produces (I. pp. 81. 83.) of a low price of manufacturing labour in some of the years between 1808 and 1812, in which it is well known that anti-commercial decrees, by obstructing the vent for our exportable products, had thrown our manufacturers into a state of great distress. It was not surely that the demand for able bodied men was peculiar and unusual, in reference to a period of considerable length, but that the want of demand for manufacturing labour was peculiar and unusual, in reference to certain portions of that period.

On the same principle we cannot consider the instances which Mr. Tooke produces of an occasional low price of corn and butcher's meat (pp. 72. 75.), after the Bank restriction, and before the termination of the war, as invalidating the proofs of a great and general increase in the prices of provisions. The mass of facts brought forward, after allowing all due weight to the exceptions referred to, show, in our opinion, a decided rise in the average price both of necessaries and labour, beyond the difference between paper and gold.

But though we cannot attach so much importance to these exceptions as Mr. Tooke is disposed to do, we are persuaded that he would fully agree with us in attributing both the general rise and the temporary fall of prices during the war to the state of the demand and the supply. And after the termination of the war, Mr. Tooke's opinion is expressed as strongly as possible, that the fall of prices was owing exclusively to the abundance of the supply compared with the demand. After producing numerous proofs of this in the earlier periods of the peace, he remarks, with regard to a later period, (*Part* i. p. 191.)—

' Of the fact of the abundance of supply of the leading articles of consumption, there cannot, I should think, be any reasonable doubt. Let any cornfactor be asked whether the supplies of wheat and flour in Mark Lane, at the close of 1821, and through the first half of 1822, were not quite sufficient to have produced the fall of prices, and the apparent tendency to a further depression, as long as there was no security against the continuance of so overwhelming a supply, and whether there is any appearance of a want of funds, or of inclination on the part of buyers to speculate, if they could be satisfied of an inadequateness of the stock of the country?

' The extremely low price of cattle has of late attracted so much attention that I insert a statement of the numbers sold at Smithfield for the last four years.

	Neat Cattle.	Sheep and Lambs.
1819	135,226	949,900
1820	132,933	947,990
1821	142,133	1,107,230
1822	143,830	1,353,043

' The comparative increase has been equally great at Liverpool and Hull, and I am told that the supplies at the other markets in England have been no less superabundant. How then can there be any difficulty in accounting for the very low prices of meat during the last twelve months?'

In the second *Part* of Mr. Tooke's work, which relates to the effects of war on prices, he is disposed altogether to deny its tendency to occasion an increase of demand; although he readily allows that it is capable of raising prices by the diminution of supply. We should be inclined to admit that the latter cause is generally more powerful than the former, particularly at first; but we think that the former is by no means inefficient; and for this we shall give our reasons in a subsequent part of our examination. In the mean time it may be observed, that both when Mr. Tooke denies the effect of war on prices from increased demand, and admits it from diminished supply, his criterion uniformly is the degree in which it may affect the proportion between the two; and it is only because he thinks that the actual proportion of the supply to the demand during the years in question was determined by other causes, that he considers the war as having had little to do with the high prices, thus referring every thing to the state of the supply and demand.

In that part of the work which considers the effects of the variations of the seasons, and refers the high and low prices of the last thirty years almost exclusively to these variations, it is obvious that every thing must be attributed to supply and demand, as the seasons can operate in no other way. And the great fluctuations of prices which appear in the tables of the last Part, without the possibility of their being accompanied by *proportionate* alterations in the costs of production, can only be attributed to the same overpowering cause. It may be safely said, therefore, that every *Part* of Mr. Tooke's work conspires to prove that all prices depend upon the state of the demand and the supply, and that labour and the costs of production only influence prices as they are the necessary conditions of the supply.

149

For the proofs of the second important proposition which we consider as established in Mr. Tooke's work, namely, that the supply of commodities as compared with the demand is much more affected and for a much longer period by the variations in the seasons than has hitherto generally been supposed, we must refer to his *Third Part.* He there enters into a detailed and interesting account of the character of the seasons from 1788 to 1792, and from 1793 to 1821 inclusive; and having explained very correctly the effect of quantity on price as being always very much greater than in proportion to the deficiency or excess of that quantity, he applies this principle to explain the high prices of corn between 1792 and 1812, and the fall of prices since that period.

Few persons, we conceive, have ever doubted the great effect of scanty crops on the price of grain in the particular years in which they have occurred. In estimating, consequently, the price of corn at distant periods, it has been generally recommended not to include years of scarcity in too short an average; and it has been even sometimes proposed to throw them out entirely. But we have met with no writer who, in considering the causes of a very great rise of prices spreading itself over so large a period as twenty years, has attributed it almost exclusively to the seasons. We cannot, as we have said, go with Mr. Tooke to the full extent of this conclusion : yet we think that the facts which he has produced clearly show not only that, as a general truth, the effects of the seasons extend themselves at times over periods of considerable length, but that in the particular case referred to they had a much greater influence on the rise of prices than had been generally supposed. As a general truth, we think the position would be confirmed by a reference to other parts of our own history besides those examined by Mr. Tooke. In that very valuable table of prices collected by Sir Frederick Morton Eden in his work on the Poor, periods of high and low prices are to be found, of considerable duration, for which it would be very difficult to give any other adequate solution than the comparative abundance or scantiness of the supplies of corn arising from the number of favourable or unfavourable seasons included in such periods.

After the great plague which occurred about the middle of the reign of Edward III. and gave occasion to the first attempt to regulate wages by law, one should naturally have expected that, owing to the great loss of people then sustained, corn would become cheaper rather than dearer; instead of which it appears to have risen from about 5s. 4d. the average of the first twenty-five years of the reign of Edward III. to 11s. 9d., the average of the last twenty-six years, with very little difference in the quantity of silver contained in the same nominal sum. For this great rise of bullion prices, spreading itself over a period of twenty-six years, it would be scarcely possible to assign an adequate cause without resorting to a succession of unfavourable seasons. During the reigns of Richard II. and Henry IV. a period of thirty-four years, the bullion price of corn seems to have fallen rather lower than it was in the first half of the reign of Edward III. In the first twenty-three years it was 5s. 7d. and in the last eleven years 6s. 1d.; and as in the latter half of the reign of Edward III. the pound of silver was coined into 25s. and at the end of the reign of Henry IV. into 30s. the bullion price of this period was rather below what it was in the first half of the reign of Edward III.; and it certainly would be very difficult to explain the low prices of these thirty-four years and the high prices of the preceding twenty-six without the powerful operation of seasons.

In 1444, other statutes regulating the price of labour were passed, probably owing to the high price of corn, which had risen on an average of the ten preceding years to 10s. 8d. without any further alterations in the coin ; and for this rise there seems to be no adequate cause but a succession of comparatively scanty crops, particularly as after this period there was a continuance of low prices for above sixty years. The average price of wheat from 1444 to the end of the reign of Henry VII. in 1509, returned to about 6s. while the pound of silver being coined into £1 : 17s. 6d. instead of £1 : 2s. 6d. as at the time of passing the first statute of labourers in 1350, showed a very decided fall in the bullion price of wheat. This fall, however, was so considerable and lasted for so very long a period that we cannot attribute it wholly to the seasons. Still less are we disposed to attribute it to the cause assigned by Adam Smith—a gradual rise in the value of silver; because, if we refer to his own criterion of value, *labour,* we shall find that while the bullion price of corn had been falling, the bullion price of labour had been rising, and, consequently, silver had been diminishing instead of increasing in value. These prices of corn and labour could only have arisen from a great and continued abundance of corn which was evinced by the very large quantity of it awarded to the labourer ; and this abundance was occasioned probably by the combined operations of favourable seasons with the introduction of a better system of agriculture, before the distribution of property and the habits of the labouring classes had been so far improved as to encourage a proportionate increase of their number.

The rise in the price of corn during the course of the next century may, no doubt, be easily accounted for by the progress of population and the discovery of the American mines, without any aid from unfavourable seasons, although in fact such seasons did combine with the other causes just mentioned, in raising the price of wheat towards the end of the century, from 1594 to 1598. The same cause unquestionably operated for twenty years, about the middle of the subsequent century, from 1646 to 1665 inclusive, when the price of the quarter of wheat was £2 : 10s. —considerably higher than it was either in the earlier or latter part of the century ; and it is somewhat singular, that while during a considerable part of the civil wars between the houses of York and Lancaster, and subsequently, corn was remarkably cheap; during the civil wars under Charles I. and for some time subsequently, it was as remarkably dear—a pretty strong presumptive proof that the seasons had more to do with the prices in both cases, than the civil wars.

All these cases are noticed by Mr. Malthus, in the fourth section of his chapter on the Wages of Labour, in his work on Political Economy, and he has occasionally referred to the influence of the seasons ; but he has not, as we should have expected, from his usual and laudable habits of attending to facts and experience, called the particular attention of his reader to the general conclusion which unavoidably follows from them.

It will be seen, from the slight sketch we have given of the high and low prices of a long period anterior to the period examined by Mr. Tooke, that, as a general truth, we are fully prepared to attach very great importance to the effects of the seasons on prices, for periods of twenty or thirty years together. We further think, that in the particular case in question, the coincidence of the highest prices with the scarcest years shows, incontestably, that a considerable part of these high prices belong to the same cause. The reason why we cannot attribute nearly the whole of them to the seasons is, our firm conviction that the circumstances of the late war, notwithstanding the opinion of Mr. Tooke to the contrary, were such that they must necessarily have occasioned a general rise in the money price of corn, if the seasons had continued to be of the same description, exactly as those which prevailed for ten or twenty years before 1793.

Mr. Tooke has produced documents which show, that during the last century, up to the commencement of the war with France, the prices of corn, meat, and even labour, were as low in the periods of war as in the periods of peace. These documents we consider as containing most useful and important instruction, calculated to remove the impression too common among the producing classes, that war must be favourable to them. They certainly prove, as Mr. Tooke states, that a rise of agricultural produce, wages, and other articles not taxed, or not the immediate objects of war consumption, is not a *necessary* consequence of a state of war. But though in the three subsequent sections he seems to intend to examine all the causes of high price, which especially belonged to the character and circumstances of the late war, yet the most striking peculiarities of it in this respect, he has either omitted to notice, or allowed them a weight in no degree commensurate with their real importance. These peculiarities were the unusually rapid increase of the population, the extraordinary increase in the quantity and value of the exports, and the very important circumstance, that whereas in all the former wars noticed, we grew more corn than our own consumption, in the last, we were obliged to import corn from abroad, in order to make up our habitual supply. We have always considered the very great rise of general prices, which took place in the interval between 1793 and 1814, as mainly occasioned by the rise in the price of corn; and if, independently of the seasons, there are any causes more influential than others on the price of corn, they must be those which we have just named. The obstructions which the war, and high freights, would throw in the way of importing the usual quantity of foreign corn, would, upon every principle stated by Mr. Tooke, necessarily raise the price; and this rise would continue to be proportioned to such freights and obstructions, till the corn of home growth was sufficient for the support of the population; but the great demand for labour and the great increase of the population, would be exactly calculated to throw this event to a distance, while the general rise of prices so occasioned, would be supported by the abundance and value of the exports.

We are disposed to agree with Mr. Tooke, when he says, (*Part* II. p. 57.) 'If it had so happened, that in the last war we had habitually grown as much corn beyond the proportion of our own consumption, as we did between 1740 and 1750, and that the seasons had been equally favourable to the growth, we should have witnessed a totally different set of phenomena connected with prices. The transition from war to peace might, as was the case on many former occasions, have been attended with a rise of the prices of agricultural produce, and nothing would have been heard of the distress of the landed interest as resulting from the peace, nor would war be considered as the source of their prosperity.' But as the actual state of things was quite different; as, instead of growing a considerable average surplus of grain, which we did in all the former wars of the century, our home growth had become insufficient for our consumption, and the population seemed to be outrunning our cultivation, there was evidently a very great and decided cause of a high price, from high freights and insurance, unconnected with the variations of the seasons.

We would intreat our readers to refer to the comparatively stationary population, the comparatively stationary exports, and the comparatively abundant supply of corn of home growth, during the four wars preceding that which commenced in 1793, and then ask themselves, whether the character and circumstances of the late war were not calculated to have a totally different effect on prices from those of the preceding wars? But if when a great rise of prices has been observed to take place, attributable to the seasons and other causes, and the other causes, according to the acknowledged principles of supply and demand, must have had a very powerful influence on these prices, it would be obviously most incorrect to attribute the whole, or nearly the whole effect to the seasons.

We cannot therefore go with Mr. Tooke to the extent of his opinions on the influence of the seasons upon the high and low prices of the last thirty years; but we decidedly think, that the facts which he has referred to, and the reasonings with which they are accompanied, clearly prove, both as a general truth, and in the particular instance considered, the second proposition stated by us, namely, that the supply of commodities as compared with the demand, is much more affected, and for a much longer period, by the variations in the seasons, than has hitherto generally been supposed.

In proceeding to consider the proofs which Mr. Tooke's work affords of the third fundamental proposition, we must previously notice an extraordinary passage with which he commences the 5th section of his Second *Part.* He observes—

' Enough has been said to prove that war cannot operate in raising general prices through the medium of increased demand, *the quantity of money, and its rate of circulation continuing the same.*'

This, we own, appears to us a most strange limitation, and if adhered to, would convert a very interesting practical inquiry into a barren discussion of a suppositious case which, perhaps, it would not be too much to say could never be realized.

It is of the very nature of war, and of the obstructions which it occasions to supply, to influence the quantity of money in a country, and the rate of its circulation. And surely the proper inquiry for us, on the present occasion, is, *the fact,* whether the circumstances of the late war did really create an increase of demand as well as an obstruction to the supply, without precluding the natural means by which such a result would be effected. At any rate, we give our readers notice that our own inquiry is meant to be conducted without any such limitation, thinking, as we certainly do, that it is the only way of making it of the least practical use.

Of the alterations in the proportion between the supply of commodities and the demand for them, during the last war, occasioned partly by obstructions to supply arising from the war, and partly from the unfavourableness of the seasons, there cannot, we believe, be two opinions. Our only question with Mr. Tooke, on this part of the subject, is, whether this state of the proportion between supply and demand does or does not occasion an increase of demand, which may properly be considered as positive as well as relative. This question, it appears to us, that the facts and general reasonings which he has brought forward clearly answer in the affirmative.

In Part I. Section VII. which contains a very able and useful explanation of the causes of the extension and contraction of private paper and credit, Mr. Tooke commences by saying, that—

' The circumstances most conducive to an enlargement and contraction of the circulation of private paper and credit are identical with those which give rise to a spirit of speculation and overtrading on the one hand, and to stagnation and despondency on the other. The circumstances which give rise to a spirit of speculation and overtrading are scarcity, or, in other words, a deficiency in the supply of some important article or articles compared with the average consumption, and the opening of new and extensive markets, or, in general, of any new sources of demand. Agricultural produce, which forms by far the largest portion, as well as the most valuable class of commodities, and which, as it includes the subsistence of the labourer, and supplies the raw materials of some manufactures, affects the value of many other commodities, is that, of which any casual scarcity most powerfully contributes to a temporary increase of the circulation of private paper.'

Further on, he says—

' Independent of the paper created on such occasions by the prevalence of a spirit of speculation, whether arising from deficiency of supply, or from increased demand, there is a further effect produced on prices in both cases by an extended substitution of mere credit in transactions of purchase and sale, in some branches of trade in which it is not usual to deal through the medium of acceptances; and it is clear that an increased use of credit for the purposes of purchase may operate on prices as effectually without, as with the intervention of paper.'

He concludes the section as follows—

' It is evident from this view, that a currency consisting as our's does of a considerable portion issued through the medium of credit, is subject to great variations in that proportion; that those variations

155

originating, in most cases, in a spirit of speculation and the re-action from it, tend to extend the range and accelerate the rate of the consequent fluctuations in price, *supposing that the rest of the currency, as dispensed by the Bank of England, were stationary in amount.* If the Bank of England, under the circumstances described as tending to enlarge the circulation of country and private paper, should simultaneously increase its issues, whether through the medium of discounts or of advances to government, it is clear that the rise of prices would be greater and more rapid, as on the other hand a contraction of its issues, if it should coincide with a return of abundance, and with a re-action from speculation, would aggravate the fall of prices and consequent distress.'

For further information we refer the reader to the whole section, which is well worthy of his attention : but we think that even the very short extracts which we have here given, not only clearly state that a deficiency of supply of some important article, compared with the average consumption, creates an increase of general demand, accompanied by a rise of prices ; but they point out distinctly how this rise of prices may take place, even without an increase either of Bank of England paper or money.

In a subsequent section, which treats of the *Effect of Quantity on Price*, the increase of demand from deficiency of supply is placed in a still stronger light. After noticing the well-known fact that a small deficiency in the produce of corn, compared with the average rate of consumption, causes a rise in price very much beyond the ratio of the defect, he refers to some calculations of Gregory King, and confirms the principle on which they are founded, by a review of the state of the seasons and the state of prices from the year 1620.

In the next section (V. Part III.) he applies the principle of the ' *effect of quantity on price*' to the state of agriculture from 1793 to 1812. ' The first great burst of prosperity (he says) clearly followed the deficient harvests of 1794 and 1795;' and he then calculates, with much appearance of probability, that the rise in the price of grain occasioned by the deficiency of these two years, which was supposed to be about one-eighth, must have thrown into the hands of the agricultural interest in 1795 and 1796, when the prices were the highest, a clear profit of from 12 to 14 millions each year, or from 24 to 28 millions for the two years.

Now unless it can be distinctly shown, that this enormous increase in the price and value of the grain of the country, was counterbalanced by a proportionate diminution in the price and value of other commodities, it follows incontestably, that there must have been a great positive increase of demand in reference to the actual mass of products, that is, such a demand as would have been effectual to the purchase of a larger mass of commodities than were consumed in 1793, on the supposition that they were sold at the same price. But Mr. Tooke does not attempt to show that there was any such counterbalancing fall of prices in the goods of the other producing classes. Indeed, such a fall would have been quite inconsistent with the language which he makes use of, when he refers to these two years as the period of a great burst of prosperity; and if we look to the tables at the end of his work which contain a list of the prices of goods, chiefly foreign, exclusive of duties, since 1782, and the quantities of some of the principal articles imported since the same period, we shall find no proofs whatever that the greater amount of currency expended on the corn diminished the amount of expenditure on foreign commodities. If we pursue the inquiry to the end of the war, it will appear that, partly from the frequent recurrence of unfavourable seasons, partly from the obstructions to the supply occasioned by the war, and partly from a rapidly increasing consumption, the market for corn was on an average rather understocked for nearly twenty years together. We in consequence imported largely for a considerable part of the time in spite of the obstructions of foreign decrees, and high freights and insurances. Comparing an average of the three years ending with 1792, and an average of three years ending with 1813, the currency price of corn, (according to the Eton table, and reckoning the paper price of gold for the latter three years at £5) appears to have risen from £2 : 12s. 9d. to £5 : 18s. 8d., and the bullion price from £2 : 12s. 9d. to £4 : 12s. Yet this very great increase in the bullion price of corn, so far from diminishing proportionably the prices of other commodities, was not only accompanied by increased prices but by a greatly increased amount of the quantity consumed.

It is extremely fallacious to estimate the increase of demand by the increase of consumption, if we refer only to short periods; because a considerable increase of consumption may take place for some years together, not from what can with propriety be called an increase of demand, but from an overabundant supply occasioned either by the seasons, or by unfounded hopes and expectations relating to the employment of capital. It is unquestionably true that nothing is produced, which some persons or other have not a fair right and title to consume. It may also safely be affirmed that all which is produced will be consumed in some way or other, sooner or later. But it is cold comfort to the manufacturer to tell him that, if he cannot sell his goods for a fair price, he is entitled to consume them himself. Nor can the farmer be much relieved by the assurance that, all the superabundant quantity of wheat which he has produced will certainly be

157

consumed in the course of the next two years, if in the meantime he is obliged to sell it at such a price, that, without other resources, he will not be able to employ above three-fourths of the labourers which he employed before. According to Mr. Tooke a succession of two or three very abundant seasons at home, accompanied by similar seasons abroad, would necessarily produce a state of general stagnation and despondency. Yet during this period there would certainly be a greater consumption of corn than usual. But surely he would not designate as a time of brisk and increased demand the very same period which he would call a period of stagnation and despondency, that is, a period when the greater part of the commodities of the country were selling below what Adam Smith calls their natural price.

We cannot then, it is obvious, measure the increase of demand by the increase of consumption for a few years. But if we take a period of considerable length, and attend particularly to the rate at which the annual consumption increases, some judgment may no doubt be formed of the annual increase of effectual demand. Tried by this criterion, we believe it will be found, by a reference to Mr. Tooke's and other documents, that the products of the land, the labour, and the capital of this country, never in any period of our history increased for twenty-two years together with the same rapidity as in the twenty-two years from 1793 to 1814 inclusive. If we look to the corn and provisions, and recollect the very great increase of population which took place in the interval in question, between one-third and one-fourth, and amounting in England and Wales alone to above two millions and a half of people, we shall be compelled to acknowledge, that if we had the means of comparing with accuracy the agricultural products of the three years ending with 1792, with the agricultural products of the three years ending with 1814, it would be seen that the increase of them was absolutely unexampled in reference to any other period of the same extent in our history.

If we look to the quantity of imported commodities noticed in the second of Mr. Tooke's tables at the end of his work, we shall find that, although the natural tendency of war is to diminish the returns for our exported commodities, in order to furnish the means of foreign expenditure, yet the returns so diminished, indicate a great increase of home consumption. Comparing the imports of the nine articles which he has selected, sugar, coffee, cotton-wool, sheep's-wool, silk raw and thrown, tallow, hemp undressed, and flax, during the three years ending with 1792 and the three years ending with 1812,* it appears that the quantity of sugar imported

---

* The average ending with 1812 is taken on account of the failure in the returns of 1813, owing to the fire at the Custom House.

has much more than doubled, the quantity of coffee increased more than ten times, the quantity of cotton-wool more than three times, and the quantity of sheep's wool more than twice, while the other articles have increased in various proportions short of doubling.

If we look to the British produce and manufactures exported during the war we shall find that they rose to above double their former amount, although, in previous wars, the general effect was a decided diminution of them, and although in the thirty years preceding, they had not increased so much as one half.

If, from the imports and exports, we turn our view to the quantity of domestic industry set in motion, we believe that in no former period of the same extent has there ever been any approach to the same increase of draining and inclosures, roads and bridges, canals and harbours, paving and other local improvements, machinery, shipping, and exciseable commodities. We are quite at a loss, therefore, to understand on what grounds the great increase of consumption during the war is denied by Mr. Tooke. The conversion of capital into revenue which was taking place during the whole of the period must have powerfully co-operated with the seasons and the obstructions to importation, in occasioning a brisk consumption of all the produce brought to market, so as, with few and slight exceptions, to leave little on hand; and as it appears from all the documents which can be referred to that the yearly additions to this produce were unusually large, it follows necessarily that the consumption during the war was unusually great.

It is true, however, that the consumption has been still greater since the peace. This was certainly to be expected: first, on account of the continuance of that rapid increase of population which was occasioned by the war demand for labour and the great and increasing power to pay for it; secondly, by the sudden abundance of capital and labour thrown out of employment by the peace which would change the former proportion between productive and unproductive consumption; and thirdly, by the natural consequence of the last cause combined with favourable seasons, namely, an excessive supply of all sorts of produce, and such a fall of prices and of profits as occasioned a greater degree of distress, and for a longer period, among the main body of producers than had ever before been experienced. These causes, while in full operation, could not fail to be accompanied by a very great consumption. But if, instead of looking merely at the quantity produced and consumed during the first eight years of the peace, we consider the rate at which the quantity and value of the produce seems to have been increasing, the result will be of a very different character. Taking an average of the total exports from Great Britain during the years 1814, 15 and 16, valued officially, and therefore representing quantity, and comparing them with the exports during the years 1819, 20 and 21, it appears that the quantity of exports had decidedly diminished, the former three years amounting to £56,275,000 and the latter only to £52,696,000; and even taking the specific articles contained in Mr. Tooke's table of quantities exported, it appears that, with the exception of cotton and sheep's wool, for which new and increasing markets have been opened, there is not, we believe, one of which the quantity exported has not decreased, and some of them considerably. His table of quantities of imported articles presents no doubt a more favourable aspect. The war expenditure abroad being over, our imports ought greatly to increase; yet, notwithstanding this, the imports of four out of the nine articles noticed seem to have diminished rather than increased, terminating the average of the latter three years with the year 1822, which Mr. Tooke has given.

If from the *quantities* of goods exported and imported we turn to their *prices* and *value*, the falling off will appear to be greater and more general. Such has been the depression of prices since the war, that whereas formerly it was the custom to add fifty per cent. to the official value in order to get the real value, it is now said that the real or declared value is actually lower on an average than the official; and, according to a statement before us, the declared value of the exports of Great Britain of home produce and manufacture was, in 1818, £48,904,000, and, in 1821, had fallen to £35,826,000.

But, whatever may have been the favourable or unfavourable changes which have taken place since the peace, the period, though very long for a crisis of distress and unnaturally low profits, is much too short to be compared with the period of the war; and it may still most safely be said that in no twenty-two years of our history of which we have authentic accounts has there ever been so rapid an increase of production and consumption, both in respect of quantity and value, as in the twenty-two years ending with 1814.

The specific and immediate cause of this great stimulus to continued production has, it appears to us, been very clearly explained by Mr. Tooke in the principle which he has laid down on the *Effect of Quantity on Price*, and the numerous instances which he brings to show that this principle is well founded. The principle is, that whenever there is a relative diminution of supply, from whatever cause it may arise, it is immediately followed by a briskness of demand for the remaining produce, accompanied by a rise of prices and of profits which never fails to occasion a great stimulus to subsequent production. This process we have always been in the habit of considering as the great remedial law of nature in regard to production and consumption; and it will be observed that it is a remedy of very great power. Whenever, within certain limits, a portion of the produce of a country has been diminished, by the seasons, by obstructions to importation, or by an increase in the proportion of unproductive consumption, not only does the power of setting fresh industry in motion remain unimpaired, but by the universal law of the effect of quantity upon price it is greatly increased. The farmer who, in consequence of a deficiency of his crops of one eighth, sells them for nearly a third more than the usual price before the money wages of labour have risen, is obviously able to set in motion a much greater quantity of industry than before. The specific funds destined for the maintenance of labour, though diminished in quantity, are by this happy provision of nature increased in their efficiency to recover the loss that has been sustained, and to increase the produce of the next year; while the labourers, although they unquestionably sustain some privation, are, in a considerable degree, recompensed by the great and general increase of employment. There is, in the language of Mr. Tooke, a burst of prosperity to the producing classes; and we should certainly add, without a *proportionate* diminution in the prosperity of the labouring classes.

This doctrine of Mr. Tooke on the effect of quantity on price, is, it must be allowed, directly opposed to the doctrine of M. Say, in his chapter *Des Debouchés*, which teaches that all increase of demand depends upon increase of supply, and diminution of demand on diminution of supply. If this were so; if it were true, that when the produce of a country had been in part destroyed, the will and power to increase what was left was immediately diminished, we do not see how the recovery of the loss would be practicable within any moderate compass of time; and such an increased difficulty thrown in the way of restoration to plenty would be so directly contrary to all the usual healing processes of nature, and is so directly opposite to all experience, which shows with what rapidity losses are recovered, that we can only feel astonishment that such opinions should be held by men of distinguished ability.

The specific source of M. Say's error and of those who have followed him is, the not being aware of, or the not allowing sufficient weight to the principle of the *Effect of quantity on price and value.* As long as the increase of quantity increases the value of the funds specifically destined for the maintenance of labour, so long of course it increases effective demand, and gives a stimulus to production; and in reference to any length of time, and the absolute necessity of a great and continued increase of produce to a great and continued increase of population, it is obvious that the increase in the power of setting industry in motion at the end of fifteen or twenty years must depend mainly upon the increase of production. But whenever this production so exceeds the actual state of the demand, whatever that may be, as to disable the producers from putting in motion the same quantity of industry as before, to that extent exactly is the effective demand for a further increase of produce diminished and the stimulus to the increase of wealth abated.

This limitation to the principle of the effect of quantity on price and value is so simple and intelligible; it so clearly shows that in all ordinary cases the increase in the wealth of other countries, or new employments at home, must give a great stimulus to our industry, (a result which M. Say erroneously thinks is peculiar to his own views relating to production,) while at the same time it explains so distinctly and specifically the causes of the few exceptions which are observed to occur, that the principle thus restricted, and its particular application to the power of setting industry in motion, may be safely laid down, as one of the most universal and constantly operating principles in political economy. We decidedly think indeed that, without allowing due weight to this principle, the phenomena of the last hundred years, but more especially the phenomena of the last thirty, are absolutely inexplicable. Certainly nothing but the union of a greatly increased activity of general demand, a greatly increased power of commanding labour, a great increase of encouragement to the use of machinery, and a great increase of profits, particularly in agriculture, all owing mainly to the peculiar state of the supply compared with the demand in a country of great resources and great ingenuity, could possibly have occasioned so rapid a recovery of the immense mass of capital consumed by the government during the war, and have given at the same time such a prodigious extension to almost every department of industry and improvement.

As we have always been of opinion, therefore, that the sole use of political economy is its application to practice, and that no theories are entitled to confidence in reference to the future, which will not give a satisfactory solution of past phenomena, we were disposed to hail Mr. Tooke's work as specifically calculated to set aside a theory which is directly contradicted by the most general experience, and as far as it has prevailed has wrested the science of political economy from its only just and safe foundation. What then was our disappointment to find that, although Mr. Tooke has written in such a way as, we trust, will convince

others, he does not seem to be convinced himself! In a note to
the last *Part* of his work (Part IV. p. 5.) he still declares his
adherence to the doctrine of M. Say on supply and demand as
explained by Mr. Mill in his *Elements of Political Economy.*[*]
This, we own, puts us in mind of the declaration of the learned
editors of the Jesuits' edition of Newton's works, (see the note
p. 163 of this Number,) who after having co-operated with the
illustrious author on whom they were commenting, in proving,
beyond the possibility of doubt, that, from the universal law of
gravity, the earth must necessarily revolve round the sun, still professed it to be their creed that the sun revolved round the earth.

To us it appears that Mr. Tooke has distinctly and luminously
proved both by a correct train of reasoning, and what is of much
more importance a constant appeal to a crowd of well-attested
facts, that a small diminution in the proportion of the usual supplies of such a country as this, invariably calls forth a larger
amount of currency and credit, and increases very decidedly the
general demand for produce, or the power of devoting such a
value to the purchase of the whole mass, as without the rise of
prices occasioned by the deficiency, would command a much
greater quantity; yet in the note above referred to he professes
to believe that the aggregate of demand must always be equal to
the aggregate supply, which if it means any thing beyond the
very futile proposition, that all which is produced will sooner or
later be consumed, must mean something directly opposed to the
whole spirit and bent of his work. We must however take leave
to consider Mr. Tooke's work as better authority than this inad-
vertent declaration; and to this work we can confidently refer
the reader as containing the most satisfactory proofs of the third
proposition stated, namely, That when the supply of commodities is in some degree deficient compared with the demand,
whether this arises from increase of demand, or diminution of
supply, the state of trade is brisk, profits are high, and mercantile speculations are greatly encouraged; and on the other hand,
when the supply is abundant compared with the demand, there is

[*] The fallacy of Mr. Mill's argument depends entirely upon the effect of quantity on price and value. Mr. Mill says that the supply and demand of every individual are of necessity equal. But as supply is always estimated by quantity, and
demand only by price and value; and as increase of quantity often diminishes price
and value, it follows, according to all just theory, that so far from being always equal,
they must of necessity be often very unequal, as we find by experience. If it be said
that reckoning both the demand and supply of commodities by value, they will then
be equal; this may be allowed; but it is obvious that they may then both greatly fall
in value compared with money and labour; and the will and power of capitalists to
set industry in motion, which is the most general and important of all kinds of demand,
may be decidedly diminished at the very time that the quantity of produce, however
well proportioned each part may be to the other, is decidedly increased.

a period of comparative stagnation, with low profits, and very little encouragement to mercantile speculation. We now proceed to consider the proofs which Mr. Tooke's work affords of the fourth proposition, namely, that when periods of abundant or deficient supply are of considerable duration, which is found by experience to be frequently the case, they are necessarily accompanied by a fall or rise of the value of the precious metals in the country where they take place, according to any mode of estimating their value which has ever been considered as approximating to the truth.

Mr. Tooke has clearly shown that the effects of the seasons in raising prices may last for twenty years together, so as very greatly to increase the average price of corn; and it has already been stated as a matter of fact, that taking an average of the three years ending with 1792, and the three years ending with 1813, the bullion price of wheat rose from £2 : 12s. 9d. to £4 : 12s. Now, though it is well known that a year of scarcity or even two years, may pass over without a rise in the price of labour, yet when the rise of provisions is very considerable in itself, and extends over a considerable period, a rise in the money price of labour must follow, or the population will be quite unable to support itself, and the prices of corn must fall again from the destruction of the consumers. In the case immediately under our consideration, we well know that this alternative did not take place. On the contrary, the population increased with extraordinary rapidity, which necessarily implies such a rise in the money price of labour as, combined with more general employment, and other advantages in the purchase of clothing and foreign commodities, would enable the labouring classes to bring up larger families than before.

We had then, it is allowed, a great and general rise in the bullion price of corn and all sorts of provisions, a great and general rise in the bullion price of labour; and, with few exceptions, a general, though more variable rise in the bullion price of other commodities. Now the question is, whether this state of things does not necessarily involve *a fall in the value of bullion*, according to any intelligible meaning which has ever been attached to the terms; or any mode of estimating the value of the precious metals which has ever been considered as an approximation to the truth.

Adam Smith in the fifth chapter of his first book, after explaining the distinction between the real and nominal price of commodities, has the following passage: ' Labour, therefore, it appears evidently, is the only universal as well as the only accurate measure of value, or the only standard by which we can compare the values of different commodities at all times and all places. We cannot estimate, it is allowed, the real value of different commodities from century to century by the quantities of silver given for them. We cannot estimate it from year to year by the quantities of corn. By the quantities of labour we can with the greatest accuracy estimate it, both from century to century and from year to year.' This is no doubt laying down labour as the measure of value in the most positive terms. But owing to some obscurity in the enunciation of this doctrine in other passages, and still more to his not adhering to it steadily and consistently in other parts of his work, it was not generally adopted. Mr. Malthus has lately revived it, with new proofs of its correctness, in a pamphlet entitled, ' *The Measure of Value stated and illustrated ;*' and as he does not seem likely to fall into the error of Adam Smith, in its application, it may be expected that it will receive a fair trial; and should it finally be established, it will, without doubt, give that distinctness and precision to all questions relating to value, of which it must be acknowledged they stand at present very greatly in need.

If, on these authorities, we should in the case before us take the labour which a commodity will command as the measure of its value, it will appear at once from the acknowledged rise in the bullion price of labour, that bullion had fallen just so much in value.

If we were to take corn,—the measure unfortunately adopted in practice by Adam Smith, instead of his professed standard, it would appear that the value of bullion had fallen still more ; and if we were to take a mean between the two, as was formerly suggested by Mr. Malthus, the fall would appear to be greater than if measured by labour, and smaller than if measured by corn.

If we were to take Mr. Ricardo's measure—the labour worked up in a commodity, the same conclusion of a fall in the value of bullion would unquestionably follow. Indeed, on Mr. Ricardo's principles, this fall must have been very considerable. According to him, while gold retains its value, a rise in the price of labour is invariably accompanied by a fall of profits. We witnessed, however, a very great rise in the bullion price of labour, not only without a fall of profits, but with a decided rise of them. And this, it is evident, could only have happened in consequence of the rise in the bullion price of labour being occasioned exclusively by a fall in the value of bullion.

If, rejecting any single criterion, or the combination of one or two, we proceed to compare an ounce of gold with all the commodities of the country in succession, though the measure would be a most clumsy one, and by no means well calculated to deter-

165

mine the degree of variation; yet we cannot for a moment doubt that the result would indicate a great fall in the value of bullion. As the great rise in the bullion price of labour is acknowledged, and as it must be allowed that profits had also risen compared with what they were in 1792, it is quite obvious that what Adam Smith calls the natural prices of all the domestic commodities of the country, in the production of which improvements had not been introduced, must have increased fully in the proportion of the increase in the price of labour. The only exceptions, therefore, to a general rise of this extent in the bullion prices of commodities would be imported commodities, and the commodities on which, on account of the improvements in machinery, a smaller quantity of labour had been employed. With regard to the first of these classes of commodities, though they would not probably rise so high as domestic commodities, yet they would necessarily rise considerably on account of freight, insurance, and taxes; and with regard to the second, as the extent to which improvements in the saving of labour may go is quite uncertain, and as such improvements might equally prevail under any value of the precious metals, it must be allowed that they are the last class of commodities which should be referred to, with a view to any estimate of value. Reckoning, however, the value of money as synonimous with the power of commanding the mass of commodities, including the effects of improved machinery, (which we do not think a just view of the subject,) still the value of bullion will appear to have fallen greatly.

Further, if we measure metallic money and other commodities by the relative conditions of their supply, the value of such money will appear still more strikingly to have diminished. The main conditions of the supply of commodities are allowed by political economists to be, the labour which it is necessary to employ both on the article, and on the portion of the capital used in producing it, together with the ordinary profits upon the advances. If either the necessary labour, or the ordinary profits of the time cannot be obtained, the supply will naturally fail.

Now let us try the variations and the relative values of commodities and of bullion by this general criterion. Taking the corn produced by the poorest land, in cultivation on which, the rent compared with the value of the produce, would be quite trifling, we shall find that the natural conditions of the supply of a quarter of corn from such land, during the three years ending with 1813, were not essentially different from what they were in the three years ending with 1792. Probably the quantity of labour employed was very nearly the same, but the profits of stock being higher, the quarter of corn, though it had cost in its production no more labour than in 1792, would necessarily command rather more, when brought to market. This was confirmed by the acknowledged fact, that the corn wages of labour, notwithstanding the great demand for men, and the great advance of money price, were rather lower than before the war.

If we proceed to the examination of cloth, leather, houses, ships, tin, &c.; or any commodities in the production of which no decided saving of labour had been introduced, it is obvious, that the natural conditions of their supply, must have been nearly the same as in 1792, with the exception of the rise of profits, which would cause all these commodities to exchange for rather more labour than before. But when we come to examine the conditions of the supply of bullion, the case is quite different. They will appear to have experienced such a change, as must necessarily lower its value, just as if a great saving of labour had been introduced into its mode of production. When countries which have no mines possess the precious metals, they must have been purchased by some exportable commodities; and we conceive that no man in his senses would knowingly send goods abroad, which he could sell for an ounce of gold at home, unless he could obtain for them, after exportation, the same value estimated in the same medium, with the addition of the necessary expenses of carriage. But at home the ounce of gold bullion, owing to the rise in the bullion price of labour, will command a much smaller quantity of labour than before, and it follows that the cotton goods which will exchange for an ounce of gold at home, and are destined to purchase more than an ounce of gold abroad, will also command a much smaller quantity of labour than before. But the quantity of labour which a commodity will command, is obviously the same as the quantity of labour worked up in it with the addition of profits, and therefore represents the natural and necessary conditions of the supply. Consequently the natural conditions of the supply of the muslins which were to purchase the ounce of gold were lowered. To use the language of M. Say, the productive services required to obtain gold in England were diminished, and the value of gold naturally fell.

It appears then, that, according to any mode which has ever been adopted for estimating the value of commodities, whether we take one object, a few objects, all objects, the labour worked up in commodities, or the quantity of labour and profits, which is the necessary condition of their supply, the value of bullion must, on an average,* have fallen considerably from 1792 to 1813,

---

* We say on an average, because there were unquestionably certain periods between 1809 and 1815, when the great demands of the government for its foreign expenditure,

and by the same criterions it will appear that the value of bullion must have risen considerably since 1813.

We are quite at a loss, therefore, to understand the grounds on which Mr. Tooke confines this fall and rise in the value of the whole currency, during the last thirty years, to the difference between paper and gold. He distinctly acknowledges the rise in the bullion price of corn in the great mass of labour, and in numerous other articles, both domestic and foreign, during the war. He acknowledges also a state of prices directly opposite, since the termination of it. But he strangely supposes that the natural inference from these prices, in respect to the value of bullion, will be destroyed by his showing the specific causes of scarcity, freights, insurance, taxes, or, generally speaking, the obstructions to supply which occasioned these high prices, upon the principles of supply and demand. Now we are quite willing to agree with Mr. Tooke in all the causes of the high and low prices of the last thirty years, which he has summed up at the conclusion of his *Third Part* (pp. 83, 84). But we must strongly protest against his conclusion, that the statement of these causes ' leaves no ground for imputing to the alterations in our currency any effect beyond the difference between paper and gold.' Because the causes which he states are specifically those which, according to the principle of the *effect* of *quantity on price,* are calculated to raise bullion prices generally, or, in other words, to alter the value of bullion. Mr. Tooke, we repeat, has very happily explained how this is effected, by showing that a deficiency of supply calls forth at once an increased quantity of private paper and credit, without any necessary separation of the paper from the gold, thus making the gold conform itself in value to an increased quantity of currency divided among a diminished quantity of commodities. To this cause of the high prices of commodities occasioned by the sudden extension of private paper and credit, we should be strongly disposed to add a more rapid circulation of the currency, which, we believe, is the almost constant concomitant of what is called a brisk demand. And we cannot help considering these two causes combined as of very great power, and as affording the true explanation of events which would be otherwise unintelligible.

To what extent bullion prices might rise from the causes just stated, called into action by a diminished proportion of the supply to

did really raise the price of gold in reference to its low preceding value. This is clearly shown by Mr. Blake in his late publication, and it is much to be regretted, that he should have mixed up with so many interesting and important observations, a proposition so entirely untenable, as that the average value of gold should rise amidst the acknowledged average rise of the gold price of labour, and of all other commodities.

the demand, it is not easy to say. The specific limit to them seems to be the turn of the exchange, and the impossibility of a country's maintaining its exports under an advance in the bullion price of labour, beyond what was balanced by peculiar skill and machinery, or the peculiar raw products which might be sold abroad at advanced bullion prices with little diminution of quantity. It is justly observed by Mr. Mill, in his *Elements of Political Economy*, (p. 129) that ' The increase of the quantity of the precious metals which diminishes the value of them, gradually diminishes and tends to destroy the power of exporting other commodities : the diminution of the quantity of the precious metals which increases their value, increases, by a similar process, the motive to the exportation of other commodities.' But an increase or decrease in the quantity of currency and credit, while paper exchanges at par with gold, or an increase or decrease in the rapidity with which the currency circulates, must, while it lasts, have precisely the same effects on the value of bullion and the state of the exports, as an increase or decrease of bullion. Mr. Mill, however, goes much too far, and probably much farther than he really intended, when he says, that ' a country will export commodities other than the precious metals only when the value of the precious metals is high,' 'and import only when the value of the precious metals is low.' Experience informs us that the two greatest exporting nations of the world, England and America, are the two nations where the value of the precious metals is the lowest. But still the tendency, though counterbalanced in the way above stated, is exactly such as is described by Mr. Mill; and, accordingly, it was the turn of the exchange in 1800 which first separated the paper from the bullion.

Whether it is desirable that a deficiency in the supply compared with the demand, occasioned either by the seasons, or an increased proportion of unproductive consumption, should take place in order to call into action the stimulus of an increased currency and an increased power among capitalists of commanding labour, is quite another question. To wish for such a state of things seems to be something like wishing for a wound in order to see the energy and skill of nature in healing it. But however this may be, we cannot doubt that when such a state of things does occur, it is attended with the effects which have been stated; and we can safely refer to what we have said, and to the facts and general reasonings of Mr. Tooke's work, for the proofs of the fourth proposition, which we consider him as having established, namely, ' That when periods of deficient or abundant supply compared with the demand are of considerable duration, which is found by experience to be frequently the case, they are necessarily accompanied by a fall or rise in the value of the precious metals in the country where they take place, according to any mode of estimating their value which has ever been considered as approximating to the truth.

The four propositions, which we have separately examined, appear to us to be of vital importance to the science of political economy, as affording the only just explanation of the events of the last thirty years; and we consider Mr. Tooke as justly entitled to the thanks of the public for the indisputable proofs which his work affords of their truth.

For the reasons which have compelled us to think that some of the conclusions which Mr. Tooke intended to establish are not borne out by the facts brought forwards, we refer the reader to the different parts of our examination in which these points are treated of; but it is important to add, with a view to one of the main questions which he has proposed to discuss, that though we are most decidedly of opinion that the facts and general reasonings of his work distinctly prove that the alterations in the value of the whole currency were considerably greater than the difference between paper and gold, yet we are equally convinced they do not prove that these alterations, beyond such difference, were occasioned by the Bank restriction and Mr. Peel's bill. The direct effects of these measures were obviously confined to the difference between paper and gold; and it would be exceedingly difficult to form any sort of estimate of their indirect effects. The Bank restriction must no doubt have afforded some facilities to the economising of the currency; but the great rise of paper prices which it occasioned, by throwing a large proportion of the produce of the country into the hands of the productive classes would be likely so to increase the supply, as to prevent the rise of bullion prices from going so far as it otherwise would have done ; and, altogether, these indirect effects must have been very trifling : there is every reason to believe, from the well ascertained power of the currency to increase in quantity and efficiency without separating from the standard, that if our paper had always been exchangeable for gold, we should still have seen a great rise of bullion prices during the war, and a great fall of them since; and that if another war should occur some time hence, accompanied by an under supply of corn, high freights and insurance, a great increase of population, and greatly increasing exports, but without a Bank restriction act, and its necessary consequence, a bill like that of Mr. Peel, we must expect the same fluctuations in the value of bullion, and in bullion prices, as have distinguished the last thirty years.

THE

QUARTERLY REVIEW

JANUARY, 1824.

Art. I.—*Essay on Political Economy. Supplement to the En-cyclopædia Britannica.* Vol. VI. Part I. Edinburgh. 1823.

THE purpose of this Treatise, as stated by the author, is to de-fine the objects and limits of the science of political economy —to trace its progress—to exhibit and establish the fundamental principles on which it is founded—and to point out the relation and dependence subsisting between its different parts.

Much of what is here stated is ably accomplished, particularly a very useful sketch of the progress of the science ; and the whole is executed with so much talent and general knowledge of the subject, as to give considerable weight to the opinions ad-vanced. Yet, we think, that the author, in exhibiting the funda-mental principles on which he conceives the science of political economy to be founded, has fallen into some most important errors ; and as both his ability as a writer, and the depository in which his treatise is found, will necessarily give it a wide circula-tion, the interests of the science seem to require that these errors should be pointed out.

Of the work of Adam Smith, on the *Nature and Causes of the Wealth of Nations,* the author says, (p. 233.) that it ' has done for political economy, what the Principia of Newton did for physics.' The principles of a work which will admit of being so characterized, should not certainly be rejected or modified but on grounds which will stand the test of the strictest examination. We should be among the last to check free and continued inquiry in any science, particularly in one which is most justly described in the present treatise as a science, ' *not of speculation, but of fact and experiment.*' On such a subject, no writer, however great, can be expected to produce a work which may not subsequently require some modifications and corrections. We do not therefore object to the author of this treatise and the school which he repre-sents, that they differ from Adam Smith ; but that, in rejecting some of the fundamental principles of that great master, they pro-pose to substitute others, which not only do not so well account for the facts with which we are surrounded, but are in many cases absolutely inconsistent with them. They seem to have pro-

171

For Semmel's commentary on this review by Malthus of McCulloch's *Essay on Political Economy,* see especially pp. 24-27. (*Publisher*).

ceeded upon a principle just the very reverse of the position above laid down by the author, and to have altered the theories of Adam Smith upon pure speculation; and not because they do not accord with facts and experience.

The Treatise is divided into four parts—
I. The Definition and History of the Science.
II. The Production of Wealth.
III. The Distribution of Wealth.
IV. The Consumption of Wealth.

We shall make some remarks on the principles laid down in each of these parts.

The author begins with a definition of the science, to which we see no objection, although we do not think that it expresses so clearly and happily the precise object in view as the title of Adam Smith's work. He then notices the importance of making a proper distinction between value in exchange, and utility. In this we entirely agree with him, and have always thought that M. Say, whose opinions seem chiefly to be alluded to, by applying *utility* in a sense altogether inconsistent with the common meaning of the term, has obscured a part of the subject which was before sufficiently clear: we were not, however, aware that Mr. Malthus, whose name is coupled with that of M. Say, had fallen into a similar error. Our impression is, that he has adhered to the distinction stated by Adam Smith, which is plain and intelligible, and requires neither the rejection nor the alteration of common terms— changes which it is always desirable to avoid, unless really necessary.

The author next proceeds to the definition of the term wealth; and here he has made a useful addition to the definition of Mr. Malthus. He says, Mr. Malthus has defined wealth to consist of ' those material objects which are necessary, useful, or agreeable to man'—(p. 217.) but that this definition is too comprehensive, as it would include such material products as atmospheric air, and the heat of the sun, which are highly useful and agreeable, yet, by universal consent, are excluded from the investigations of political economy: he proposes, therefore, to limit the definition of wealth to those objects alone which have exchangeable value, and it will then stand thus, *those material products which have exchangeable value, and which are either necessary, useful, or agreeable to man;* and to this definition we see no objection.

The author is very decided as to the propriety of confining the definition of wealth to *material objects,* as the following passage will show. Having observed that some economists had considered wealth as synonimous with *all that man desires as useful and agreeable to him,* he goes on to say,—

'But if political economy were to embrace a discussion of the production and distribution of all that is useful and agreeable, it would include within itself every other science ; and the best Encyclopædia would really be the best treatise on political economy. Good health is useful and delightful ; and, therefore, on this hypothesis the science of wealth ought to comprehend the science of medicine. Civil and religious liberty are highly useful, and, therefore, the science of wealth must comprehend the science of politics. Good acting is agreeable, and therefore, to be complete, the science of wealth must embrace a discussion of the principles of the histrionic art, and so on. Such definitions are worse than useless. They can have no effect but to generate confused and perplexed notions respecting the objects and limits of the science, and to prevent the student ever acquiring a clear and distinct idea of the nature of the inquiries in which he is engaged.' —p. 217.

In all this we agree with the author, and the author agrees with Adam Smith : we were, therefore, greatly surprised to find him afterwards totally differing on a point so very closely connected with the definition of wealth, as the definition of productive labour. To us, indeed, it appears that the term productive labour, when used in an *Inquiry into the Nature and Causes of the Wealth of Nations,* is absolutely unmeaning and useless, unless it be applied, according to the intention of Adam Smith, to signify the labour which is directly productive of wealth ; and if the term wealth be confined to material products, this must be the labour which is so fixed and realized on these products as to be estimated in their value when they become the subjects of exchange. But, according to our author, this distinction is ill-founded: let him, however, speak for himself. Having quoted the passage of Adam Smith, in which he clearly explains the difference between what he has denominated productive, and what unproductive labour, he thus proceeds :—

'Such are the opinions of Dr. Smith, and it will not we think be very difficult to show the fallacy of the distinctions he has endeavoured to establish between the labour, and consequently, also the consumption of the different classes of society. To begin with the case of the menial servant :—Dr. Smith says that his labour is unproductive, because it is not realized in a vendible commodity, while the labour of the manufacturer is productive, because it is so realized. But of what, may we ask, is the labour of the manufacturer really productive ? does it not consist exclusively of comforts and conveniences required for the use and accommodation of society ? The manufacturer is not a producer of matter, but of utility only ; and is it not obvious that the labour of the menial servant is also productive of utility ? If, for example, the labour expended in converting the wool of the sheep into a coat be, as it unquestionably is, productive; then surely the labour expended in brushing and cleaning the coat, and rendering it fit to be worn, must be so too. It is universally allowed that the labour of the husbandman in raising corn, beef, and other articles of provision is productive; but, if so, why is the labour of the menial servant, who performs the *necessary* and indispensable task of preparing and dressing these articles, and fitting them to be used, to be stigmatized as unproductive? It is clear to demonstration, that there is no difference whatever between the two species of industry, that they are both productive or both unproductive. To produce a fire, is it not just as necessary that coals should be carried from the cellar to the grate, as that they should be carried from the bottom of the mine to the surface of the earth? and if it be said that the miner is a productive labourer, must we not also say the same of the servant who is employed to make and mend the fire? The whole of Dr. Smith's reasoning proceeds on a false hypothesis. He has made a distinction where there is none, and where *there can be none.* The end of all human exertion is the same—that is, to increase the sum of necessaries, comforts, and enjoyments; and it must be left to the judgment of every man to determine what proportion of these comforts he will have in the shape of menial services, and what in the shape of material products. It is an error to suppose that a man is impoverished by maintaining menial servants, any more than by indulging in any other species of expense. It is true he will be ruined if he keeps more servants than he has occasion for, or than he can afford to pay; but his ruin would be equally certain were he to purchase an excess of food or clothes, or to employ more workmen in any branch of manufacture than are required to carry it on, or than his capital can employ. To keep two ploughmen when one might suffice, is just as improvident and wasteful expenditure as to keep two footmen to do the business of one. It is in the extravagant quantity of the commodities we consume, or of the labour we employ, and not in the particular species of commodities or labour that we must seek for the causes of impoverishment.'—p. 274.

'This passage appears to us to be totally inconsistent with that which we before quoted respecting wealth, and to merit all the severity of remark which was applied by the writer to those political economists who do not confine wealth to *material objects.* If the production of utility and enjoyment, as here stated, be the point in question, then, beyond all doubt, not only the labour of the menial servant is productive, as well as that of the manufacturer, but the exertion necessary to learn to dance, to get to a pleasant party, to read the public papers, or to acquire any useful or agreeable kind of accomplishment or information, must come under the same denomination.

But when Adam Smith gave his definition of productive labour, be obviously did not mean to refer simply to utility and enjoyment, but to *wealth*; that is, to the utility and enjoyment resulting from *material products.* He most expressly, indeed, notices the high utility and importance of many other kinds of labour besides those which he has denominated productive, and had not the slightest idea of *stigmatizing* them, as the use of this expression by the author would imply. Could he, indeed, for a moment doubt that the labours of a just magistrate, a skilful physician, or an able legislator, were, beyond comparison, more *useful* than the labour of the lace-maker? We have not the least objection to agree with the author in saying that ' the end of all human exertions is the same; that is, to increase the sum of necessaries, comforts and enjoyments:' but if political economy be, as he states, ' the science of the laws which regulate the *production,* distribution and consumption of those *material products* which have exchangeable value, and are either necessary, useful, or agreeable to man,' then it is certain that the term production, or productive labour, as it ought to be used in the science of political economy, can only apply to the labour which increases the quantity or value of material products.

That in this classification there may be a few anomalous cases we are perfectly ready to admit, but we hardly know what classification is without them. It is true that the labours of some menial servants sometimes increase the value of material products; but the amount of this value, as it affects the wealth of the society, never comes to be estimated, like the labours of the agriculturist, the manufacturer, the carrier, and the shopman; and even if it could be estimated, it would be found so trifling compared with *the material products consumed by them,* that as a class their labour may most fairly be denominated unproductive. In fact, menial service, when most like productive labour, may be characterized as assisting in the convenient and agreeable *consumption* of wealth, and not essentially in its production. But what puts the matter beyond doubt, and makes a very marked and striking distinction between them is, that menial service is always employed by revenue with a view to consumption and enjoyment, and never by capital with a view to production and profit; and as this is the only intelligible and useful distinction between unproductive and productive consumption, it is clear that menial servants, even when they most resemble productive labourers, must come under the head of unproductive consumers. It may be true, as stated by the author, that ' to keep two ploughmen where one only might suffice, is just as improvident and wasteful expenditure as it is to keep two footmen to do the work of one.' But the agriculturists who raise corn with a view to profit are in no danger of offending in this way; whereas

the rich landlord, who keeps menial servants with a view to gratification and sumptuous expenditure, almost always maintains
much greater numbers than are necessary to keep in order and
prepare for immediate use his material products. Dr. Clarke, in
his Travels in Russia, says, if we recollect right, that some of the
Russian noblemen of Petersburgh and Moscow keep one or two
hundred servants and attendants of various kinds. This would
be generally thought much more than sufficient. Yet we agree
with the author, that it must be left to the judgment of every man
to determine what proportion of comforts he will have in the
shape of menial services and what in the shape of material products. We agree with him also that it is an error to suppose that
a man is impoverished by maintaining menial servants any more
than by indulging in any other species of expense. Though he
is no doubt likely to be ruined if he employs more servants than
he can pay, yet a rich landlord may employ forty servants to do
the work of four, and still live decidedly within his income. To
the income of the individual it matters not whether the same sum
be laid out in the maintenance of menial servants and followers,
or in the material products of carpets, curtains, and carriages.
But Adam Smith was inquiring about the *causes* of the wealth of
nations; and if wealth consist, as our author allows, of material
products, then one of the most powerful causes of wealth must
be the general prevalence of such a taste for material products as
will occasion the employment of a great and increasing quantity
of that kind of labour which produces them. It is true that
there would be no use in employing a greater quantity of productive labour than is necessary to supply the demands of society for material products. We must wait the inclinations of the
owners of property : and as we cannot force them to prefer the
results of one kind of labour to those of another, the capitalists
would be very unwise to ruin themselves in the attempt. But
that the difference between the two kinds of labour consists in
quality and not in *quantity* is further manifest from this, that there
is scarcely any amount of demand for the results of productive
labour which would not tend very greatly to increase the wealth
of a nation, or the quantity and value of its produce; whereas a
great preference of the results of unproductive labour or a great
demand for menial servants and followers, would destroy more
than half of the capitals which are generally employed by a rich
and prosperous country in manufactures, and in domestic and
foreign commerce, and leave it merely with its landlords surrounded by poor dependants. And yet it is said that Adam
Smith has made a distinction where there is none, and can be
none !

With regard to the labour *indirectly* productive of material objects, which the author seems to consider in the same light as if it were *directly* productive, (p. 275.) we really believe that there is scarcely any exertion, and certainly not any regular consumption, which may not be shown to come under this head. If the exertions of the physician are to be considered as productive according to our author, because he has been instrumental in preserving the health or saving the life of an Arkwright or Watt, that is, of some of those who increase the value of material objects, we do not know how indirect productiveness can be denied to the walks, rides, and drives which are instrumental in preserving the health, strength, and lives of all the productive labourers of Adam Smith. And, with regard to consumption, it must be allowed to be so decidedly the *indirect* cause of all production, except that of the spontaneous fruits of the earth, that it cannot but have the most extensive and powerful operation, *indirectly*, in increasing the mass of material wealth. But if, because it is true, that the end of all human exertion is the same, that is, to gratify some want or wish of mankind, we are to make no distinction between exercise for health and the labours of the loom, or between the act of consumption and the act of production, in an inquiry into the *nature and causes of the wealth of nations*, we are totally at a loss to conceive how the student in political economy is to explain the effect of capital in increasing national wealth, the operation of saving as distinguished from spending, and the causes which make the balance of produce exceed that of consumption. Surely, to a description of productive labour which leads to such results, the observations, which, as we have seen, the author himself makes on some of the vague descriptions of wealth, may most justly be applied: ' Such definitions are obviously worse than useless: they have no effect but to generate confused and perplexed notions respecting the objects and limits of the science, and to prevent the student ever acquiring a clear and distinct idea of the nature of the inquiries in which he is engaged.'—(p. 217.)

On the other hand, the definition which Adam Smith gives of productive labour is not only quite consistent with the definition of wealth, which is of great importance, but it is at once as distinctly marked as such subjects will admit of, and in the highest degree useful. It amounts in substance to this. Having defined wealth to be the material products, possessing exchangeable value, which are necessary, useful, and agreeable to man, productive labour is that labour which is so directly productive of wealth as to be estimated in the value of the objects produced. This naturally includes the labours of carriers, shopmen, and of all those persons who are paid by capital, and give a definite increase of value to material products; while all those exertions the results of which are immaterial, indirect, or indefinite, are excluded. And having thus got a name for the labour which is directly productive of wealth, we may proceed with much more clearness in our inquiries into the quantity of unproductive labour or of unproductive consumption, which may be necessary in a flourishing society, either on account of its great intrinsic utility, or its tendency to increase the demand for material products.

We have to apologize to our readers for going at once from the beginning to the end of the treatise, in the discussion of this subject; but we consider the definition of wealth and of productive labour as so very closely connected, that they cannot with propriety be treated separately.

The author begins the second division of his Treatise with a definition of *production*, which he says is never ' the production of matter, for that is exclusively the attribute of Omnipotence, but the production of utility, and consequently of exchangeable value.'—(p. 234.) This may be strictly true; but, as Adam Smith had before called those modifications of matter which adapt it to the various tastes and wants of society, *production*, we see no advantage in the change of terms. On the contrary, it appears to us obviously calculated to mislead; because exchangeable value is never proportioned to utility, though it may be to the tastes and wants of society. The cobweb piece of muslin, produced by a great quantity of labour and skill, is not nearly so *useful*, according to the natural and common acceptation of the term, as a piece of cotton obtained by a third part of the exertion; yet the former would unquestionably be considered as the production of the greater amount of wealth. This is exactly the error into which M. Say has fallen, and which the author had before noticed with disapprobation.

The author next proceeds to insist very strongly on labour being the only source of *wealth*, and to assert that the earth, ' however paradoxical it may at first sight appear, is not a source of wealth.'—(p. 235.) He says that, ' independently of labour, matter is rarely of any use whatever, and is never of any value. Place us on the banks of a river, or in an orchard, and we shall infallibly perish either of thirst or hunger, if we do not, by an effort of industry, raise the water to our lips, or pluck the fruit from its parent tree.' This last position we are most ready to admit, but we cannot think it follows from it, that labour is the only source of wealth. If it were indeed the sole source of wealth, the legitimate conclusion would be, that wealth might be produced without the assistance of land; yet we strongly suspect that, if we were to make the same *effort of industry* in a place where the earth had not been the source of water or apples, such a degree of labour would do but little towards saving us from thirst or hunger. It is necessary to exert much more labour than the effort of industry here described to obtain the use of silver and gold; but to say that human labour is the sole source of these metals would surely be a most strange and useless perversion of terms. As well might we say, when two men were co-operating in carrying a log of wood, which was too heavy for either of them separately, that one was the sole carrier, because, without the effort of industry made by him, the log might have remained unmoved and useless. We totally disapprove of such futile and unnecessary attempts at simplification. We are disposed to consider labour as a most essential source of wealth; but knowing, with Adam Smith, the absolute necessity of the co-operation of land to give us food, clothing, lodging, &c. &c. we see no kind of reason why we should not acknowledge, with him, what is so obviously true, that both land and labour are sources of wealth.

It is not our intention to notice, among much that is good, in this and the other divisions of the treatise, all the passages in which we think the author has unnecessarily deviated from Adam Smith, or has otherwise advanced propositions which are unfounded. Our chief object is to call the attention of the reader to some of the main principles which characterize what may be called the new school of political economy, as contradistinguished from that of Adam Smith. But before we proceed more especially to this subject, we cannot refrain from adverting to a passage quoted in this division of the treatise, of which it is said, ' this is perhaps the most objectionable passage in the *Wealth of Nations,* and it is really astonishing how so acute and sagacious a reasoner as Dr. Smith could have maintained a doctrine so manifestly erroneous.'—(p. 249.) The passage is the following :—

' No equal quantity of productive labour or capital employed in manufactures can ever occasion so great a reproduction as if it were employed in agriculture. In manufactures nature does nothing, man does all, and the reproduction must always be in proportion to the strength of the agents that occasion it. The capital employed in agriculture, therefore, not only puts into motion a greater quantity of productive labour than any equal capital employed in manufactures, but in proportion too to the quantity of productive labour which it employs it adds a much greater value to the annual produce of the land and labour of the country, to the real wealth and revenue of the inhabitants. Of all the ways in which a capital can be employed it is by far the most advantageous to the society.'—(B. II. c. v.)

Now, admitting that Adam Smith has in one part of this passage underrated the operations of nature in manufactures, perhaps because he might think, with the author of this treatise, that political economy was the ' *science of values,*' (p. 216.)—and that, as the boundless gifts of nature confer no value, he was not called upon to consider them; yet we maintain that, in the principal part of the passage, he is fully justified in what he has said, and that it is strictly and most incontrovertibly true that ' the capital employed in agriculture, in proportion to the quantity of labour which it puts in motion, adds a *much greater value* to the annual produce of the land and labour of the country, to the real wealth and *revenue* of its inhabitants, than any equal capital employed in manufactures.'

A dam Smith evidently does not here refer, nor ought he in this case to refer, to the returns of the *last* capital employed on the land, but to *all* the capital employed on the land ; and unless we are prepared to affirm that wrought cotton, worth a hundred pounds, is of more value or confers greater wealth than raw produce worth a hundred pounds, we shall be compelled to acknowledge that the whole of the labour and capital employed to obtain the whole of our raw produce, bears a much less proportion to the value of that produce, than the whole of the labour and capital employed to obtain the whole of our manufactures does to the value of those manufactures; and consequently, that a given quantity of labour employed on the land, taking an average of the rich and poor land together, is actually productive of a *greater value and revenue* than the same quantity of labour employed in manufactures ; which is the statement of Adam Smith. Nor do we see that he has shewn a greater want of sagacity in attributing more importance to that species of industry which is the prime mover of the whole, and without which every thing would stop, than the man who might naturally enough be tempted to consider the main spring of a watch as of more importance to its movement than some of the subordinate wheels, or its ornaments. The sweeping generalizations which make no difference in the different parts of a work that co-operate to form a whole, appear to us, we confess, to be fatal to all clear explanation of the means by which the final result is attained. We feel certain, at least, that if the watchmaker, the anatomist, and the natural philosopher, were to proceed in this way, they would dreadfully confuse their pupils ; and we do not see why it should be different with the political economist. To establish the very great importance of manufactures it is not necessary to deny the superior importance of food and raw materials. Yet it does not at all follow, nor is it considered as a consequence by Adam Smith, that any forced

encouragement should be given to agriculture, which would probably defeat the very end in view.

The author further observes on this subject, that

' The rent of the landlord is not, as Dr. Smith conceives it to be, the
recompence of the work of nature remaining after all that part of the
produce is deducted which can be regarded as the work of man. But
it is, as we shall hereafter show, the excess of the produce obtained from
the best soils in cultivation over that which is obtained from the worst.'
—(p. 250.)

Now, even allowing this last position of the author, we do not
see how it essentially contradicts that of Adam Smith. Let us
suppose two nations with exactly the same rate of profits and
corn wages, but that one had previously cultivated a large quantity of very fertile land, while the whole of the land cultivated
by the other was little better than the poorest then in use.
Would not the prodigious difference which would exist in the
rents of the two countries in this case be clearly attributable to
the excess of the produce above what was necessary to pay the
labour of man? and would not this excess arise from the natural
fertility of the soil, or the work of nature? An approximation to
this state of things is indeed by no means uncommon. In countries
which have been long peopled, the returns of the last capital employed on the land are more nearly the same than the productiveness of the richest lands which have been cultivated. Independently of the great difference of natural fertility, it is certain that
with every increase of skill and saving of labour, the mass of rich
lands becomes more productive, compared with the labour employed upon it, while these improvements enable the farmer
gradually to cultivate poorer lands with the same returns, so that
the difference between the most productive and the least productive capitals employed on the land may be increasing for a century
together without any diminution in the quantity of produce
divided between the labourer and capitalist, or any essential rise in
the value of corn. In fact, this is what has really taken place in
our own country during the last hundred years. The severity of
remark, therefore, upon Adam Smith on account of the passage
above quoted, seems to be by no means warranted.

We now proceed to consider the main principles which more
especially characterize the new school of political economy.
These appear to be three.

1. That the quantity of labour worked up in commodities determines their exchangeable value.

2. That the demand and supply have no effect upon prices and
values, except in cases of monopoly or for short periods of time.

3. That the difficulty of production on the land is the regulator of profits, to the entire exclusion of the cause stated by Adam Smith, namely, the relative abundance and competition of capital.

The first of these principles is maintained partly in the second division of the treatise and partly in the third, and the inferences from it naturally run through the whole.

In page 237 of the second division, the author says, ' It is to labour therefore, and labour only, that man owes every thing possessed of exchangeable value.' And a little farther on he observes, ' having established this fundamental principle, having shown that it is labour only that gives exchangeable value to commodities, it is plain, &c. &c.'

In the beginning of the third division, he states repeatedly and strongly, that in the early periods of society when the whole produce of labour belonged to the labourer, the quantity of labour which had been expended in the procuring of different articles, would form the only standard by which their relative worth or exchangeable value could be estimated.—(p. 253.) He quotes Adam Smith, who says exactly the same thing; he then adds, ' thus far there is no room for doubt or difference of opinion:' and as, in this case, labour would be the sole condition of the supply of commodities, we are fully prepared to agree with him. Setting out from this point, he proceeds to investigate the laws which regulate the exchangeable value of commodities in an advanced period of society; and after an inquiry of considerable length concludes as follows, ' the analysis we have now completed shows that labour is not only essential to the existence of exchangeable value, but that it is, in every stage of society, from the rudest to the most improved, *the single and only principle which enters into its composition.*'—(p. 268.)

We are in no degree disposed to underrate the prodigious effect of the labour employed to produce a commodity in determining its exchangeable value even in the most improved stages of society. Of whatever other elements this value may be composed, the labour worked up in it must at all times be beyond comparison the most influential. It would indeed be most absurd to compare generally the difference of value occasioned by any other ingredient to the difference occasioned by the quantity of labour employed being that of one day, one hundred days, or one thousand days. This is so very obvious as scarcely to require stating. But though the labour worked up in a commodity is thus allowed to be beyond comparison the main ingredient of value ; yet if there really are other ingredients, and they are at the same time of such a nature as essentially to encourage or discourage production, and thus operate powerfully on the progress of wealth, it would be inexcusable in the political economist, from a desire of simplification, not to allow them their separate and due weight.

Adam Smith, in his chapter on the Component Parts of Price, (B. i. c. 5.) resolves the price of the great mass of commodities in every improved society into wages, profits, and rent. And in his next chapter, he considers natural price as made up of wages, profits, and rents, each at their ordinary and natural rates.* There is obviously in every society, as stated by Adam Smith, an ordinary or natural rate of wages and profits, ; but it is not the same with rents. On account of the very different fertility of different soils in the same country, the portion of the produce of land which is resolvable into rent, is extremely various. Sometimes it is a half, a third, or a fourth, and sometimes little or nothing. But if the price of a bushel of corn be the same, whether it be resolvable into more or less rent, rent cannot have much influence in determining its exchangeable value; and we think, on the whole, that satisfactory reasons have been given why, in tracing the causes of exchangeable value, in reference to the most important commodities, rent may be considered as having only a very inconsiderable effect.

But supposing this to be allowed, and the influence of rent on value excluded, as the author would wish, profits will still be left, besides wages or labour. And it remains to be considered whether profits do or do not influence, and if they do, to what extent they influence, the exchangeable value of commodities.

The author has distinctly allowed, that in the early periods of society, when labour alone is concerned in production and the returns are almost immediate, the value of commodities so obtained is determined by the quantity of labour employed to obtain them. But in every stage of society there are a few commodities which are obtained nearly in the same way; and if the value of these commodities, where no profits are concerned, may be correctly

---

* ' These three parts seem either immediately or ultimately to make up the price of corn. A fourth part, it may perhaps be thought, is necessary for replacing the stock of the farmer, or for compensating the wear and tear of his labouring cattle, and other instruments of husbandry. But it must be considered that the price of any instrument of husbandry, such as a labouring horse, is itself made up of the same three parts, the rent of the land upon which he is reared, the labour of tending and rearing him, and the profits of the farmer who advances both the rent of this land, and the wages of this labour. Though the price of the corn, therefore, may pay the price as well as the maintenance of the horse, the whole price still resolves itself either immediately or ultimately into the same three parts of rent, labour, and profit.' (*Wealth of Nations,* B. 1. c. vi.)—Consequently, if it appear that rent has little effect on price, the whole will be determined by labour and profits.

estimated by the quantity of labour employed to obtain them, we may make a fair calculation of the additional value given by profits, by comparing the value of such commodities with the value of those where profits have entered as a component part.

If, for instance, a useful stone inclosure, built from materials on the spot, were constructed in eight days by fifty common masons paid at half-a-crown a-day, the inclosure, when completed and fit for use, would, on account of the very small quantity of profits concerned, be worth but little more than the labour employed on upon it, that is, 400 days, or, in money, fifty pounds. Now, if we suppose a pipe of wine to be worth, when it is first put into the cask, exactly the same quantity of labour, and money, but that it is to be kept two years before it is used, and that the rate of profits is fifteen per cent., it is obvious that, at the expiration of that time, it must be sold at above £65, or its value must be above 520 days instead of 400 days labour, in order that the conditions of its supply may be fulfilled. We have here, then, two commodities which, by the hypothesis, have had the same quantity of labour employed upon them, and yet the exchangeable value of one of them exceeds that of the other above 30 per cent., on account of the very different quantity of profits worked up in each.

Now let us suppose that the rate of profits falls from 15 per cent. to 6 per cent., then the value of the article, in which profits had very little concern, would remain nearly the same, the conditions of its supply being nearly the same; while the conditions of the supply of the wine will have so essentially altered, without the slightest alteration in its quality, that, instead of being worth above 30 per cent. more than the walls, it would now only be worth a little above 12 per cent. more.

These cases are far from being merely imaginary. Wine is frequently kept much more than two years. Ships are often much above two years in building. The final returns for the commodities which purchase teas in China, reckoning from the period when the first advances required to produce them were made, can hardly be less than that period; and the same may be said of the wrought cottons sold in India after the raw material had been brought from that quarter of the globe and worked up in England. Of some other articles of exchange, particularly coppice-wood and timber, the proportion of the value resolvable into profits is very much larger; while it is universally allowed that the quantity of profits which enters into the composition of commodities, is greatly increased in all cases of an increase of fixed capital as compared with circulating. On the other hand, though, in an improved society, there are but few commodities in which labour is concerned exclusively, yet there are some; and there are unquestionably a great many where the tools are so cheap and the returns so little distant, that the profits on the advances necessary to such productions form but a small part of their exchangeable value. In short, the conditions of the supply of commodities at the same period in improved countries, with reference to the quantity of profits which must be repaid in their value when sold, are extremely various; and though it does not often happen that, in short periods, profits fall from 15 per cent. to 6 per cent., yet in the progress of nations greater changes must necessarily occur; and taking only what really happens, we are strongly disposed to believe that the variations of value arising from profits are in many commodities frequently more than 20 per cent., and that variations of 10 or 12 per cent. are common. How then can it be asserted that commodities exchange with each other according to the quantity of labour worked up in them? As far as we can trust our senses, the fact is notoriously otherwise.

The author, however, says, that ' the profits of stock are only another name for the wages of accumulated labour.'—(p. 263.) And it is no doubt true, that if the value of commodities be resolvable into wages and profits, and profits be only another name for wages, the whole is resolvable into wages. It is equally true, that if five be another name for four, two and two will equal five. But whether it will not tend to confuse matters either to consider five as another name for four, or profits as another name for wages, deserves our serious consideration.

We have always understood the wages of labour to mean the remuneration paid for some kind of human exertion; and it is certain that the accumulated labour worked up in machinery, raw materials, or any other species of capital, is just of the same nature as immediate labour, and paid for exactly in the same way: but the profits both upon the accumulated labour and the direct labour are totally a different kind of thing, and obey a different set of laws. This is justly and strongly stated by Adam Smith. He observes, ' the profits of stock, it may perhaps be thought, are only a different name for the wages of a particular sort of labour, the labour of inspection and direction. They are, however, altogether different, are regulated by quite different principles, and bear no proportion to the quantity, hardship and ingenuity of this supposed labour of inspection and direction.' He then proceeds to explain the nature of the fundamental distinction between profits and wages; and concludes as follows: ' in the price of commodities, therefore, the profits of stock constitute a component part altogether different from the

wages of labour, and regulated by quite different principles.'—
(B. II. c. vi.) In this view of the subject we entirely agree
with Adam Smith. But perhaps the author means to place it in
a different light. In replying to a case urged by Colonel Torrens, he seems to intimate that the effect of capital employed to
keep a cask of wine till it is fit for drinking, is to set in motion
the agency of nature, or the processes which she carries on in the
casks, instead of the agency, or the labour of men : and that the
only difference is in the agents employed.—(p. 268.) But the
assistance of nature to give this kind of improvement to wine is at
the command of every one who has capital, and certainly, therefore, requires no wages; and that in this case she gives her
labour gratis, is quite clear from this, that the increased value
which the wine acquires is in no degree proportioned to the efficiency of her workmanship, as is mainly the case in rents, but is
entirely regulated by the time during which the returns of the capital are delayed, and the ordinary rate of profits. We have already
seen, that an alteration in the rate of profits from 15 to 6 per
cent. would make the value of a cask of wine, after being kept
two years, compared with its value when first put into the cask,
fall from 30 per cent. to 12 per cent., while the processes of nature remained unchanged: and it is quite certain, that all wine
kept for two years must be paid for at the same price, whether it
improved by keeping or not, provided that the keeping of all
wines were enforced, and the returns of the capital employed on
them were delayed, for that period, by an arbitrary decree.

In no view of the subject, therefore, is there the slightest
ground for confounding the profits of stock with the wages of
labour : yet without this strange and most uncalled for misnomer,
how is it possible to say that commodities exchange with each
other according to the quantity of labour worked up in them, that
is, that fifty pounds worth of kept wine has had the same quantity
of labour worked up in it, as fifty pounds worth of stone walls
sold as soon as built? or that fifty pounds worth of young firs
planted thirty years ago on a barren heath had cost in their production the same quantity of labour as fifty pounds worth of
Scotch pebbles picked up on the sea shore, or fifty pounds worth
of straw plat?

Cases of this kind are, indeed, so numerous and palpable, that
they force themselves to be acknowledged. Very large concessions and modifications were, in consequence, repeatedly made
by Mr. Ricardo, which, though not sufficient to meet the real
truth, are quite sufficient to destroy the assumption that the products of the same quantity of labour in the same country, always
remain of the same value. And it is certainly most remarkable

that, in the last edition of his work, after having introduced modifications which he himself calls *considerable,* he should have the following passage, which we believe is a new one :—

'It is necessary for me to remark that I have not said, because one commodity has so much labour bestowed upon it as will cost £1,000, and another so much as will cost £2,000, that, therefore, one would be of the value of £1,000 and the other of the value of £2,000 ; but I have said that, their value will be to each other as two to one, and that in these proportions they will be exchanged. It is of no importance to the truth of this doctrine whether one of these commodities sells for £1,100 and the other for £2,200 ; or one for £1,500 and the other for £3,000 ; into that question I do not at present inquire. *I affirm only, that their relative values will be governed by the relative quantities of labour bestowed on their production.'*—(c. i. p. 46.)

And on this assumption, so contrary to our every-day experience, the whole of the calculations and reasonings throughout the remaining part of the work is founded ; although, in two sections of the first chapter expressly devoted to the subject, it is specifically allowed, that the principle that the quantity of labour bestowed on commodities regulates their relative value, is *considerably* modified both by the employment of machinery, and by the unequal rapidity of the returns of capital to its employer.

Similar concessions are made in the present treatise. It is stated that, when wages rise and profits fall, one large class of commodities will fall in exchangeable value, another will rise, and a third will remain the same (p. 265.); and it is rather oddly proposed to lump them all together, and to assume that, notwithstanding these changes, the products of the same quantity of labour always remain of the same value. If we want to know the general price of corn during a certain period, or even the general rate of profits, it may be well enough to take an average; but if our object be to ascertain the effects of the *seasons* on the price of corn, it would surely be passing strange to resort to the same proceeding: and it appears to us, we confess, equally strange to propose the taking of an average, when the specific object of our inquiry is to ascertain the effects of the varying quantity and varying rate of profits on the value of the products of the same quantity of human labour. Very considerable effects of this kind are most distinctly acknowledged by our author, varying according to the amount of profits worked up in different commodities, compared with the amount worked up in that commodity which is taken as their measure. They prove incontrovertibly that the cases of exception to the rule are, both in theory and in fact, beyond comparison more numerous than the cases in which the rule holds true. It is therefore absolutely inconceivable to us, on what ground, other than that of utterly confounding all distinction between wages and profits, the author could arrive at the conclusion before adverted to on the subject of *value*, namely, that labour ' *is, in every stage of society, from the rudest to the most improved, the single and only principle which enters into its composition.*' (p. 268.) We trust that we have shown that this doctrine, which peculiarly characterizes the new school of political economy, and from which all their peculiar tenets flow, is a most unwarranted deviation from Adam Smith, and rests on no solid foundation. But this truth will still more fully appear as we proceed to examine the two other most important principles which flow from it.

The second principle which we proposed to consider is, that demand and supply have no influence on prices and values, except in cases of monopoly, or for short periods of time.

On this subject the author is very decided in his opinion. Having referred to the admirable chapters of Adam Smith, in which, as it is justly observed, the general equality of wages and profits was first fully demonstrated; he goes on to say,—

' The principle of the equality of wages and profits once established, it is easy to show that variations in the demand and supply of commodities can exert no lasting influence on price. It is the *cost of production*, denominated by Smith and the Marquis Garnier *necessary or natural price*, which is the permanent and ultimate regulator of the exchangeable value or price of every commodity which is not subjected to a monopoly, and which may be indefinitely increased in quantity by the application of fresh capital and labour to its production.'—(p. 255.)

He then enters into the subject at considerable length; but as the passage we have quoted clearly expresses the substance of the doctrine, it will be sufficient for our purpose.

Though we cannot by any means accede to the statement that demand and supply exert no lasting influence on price; yet we are very willing to allow that the natural prices of commodities are determined by the natural costs of production, according to the meaning of the term, as used by Adam Smith, or even after we have excluded the effects of rents: but as profits will still remain a component part of price, it is absolutely necessary, before we can exclude demand and supply from a lasting influence on exchangeable value, to show that they can have no influence on the natural rate of profits. Adam Smith, in using the term natural rate of wages and profits, says, that he means by it ' the ordinary or average rate which is found in every society or neighbourhood, and which is regulated partly by the general circumstances of the society, their riches or poverty; their advancing, stationary, or declining conditions; and partly by the particular nature of each employment.' This reference to the varying circumstances of the society strongly savours of the effects of demand and supply ; and, by ordinary and average profits, cannot be meant an average for fifty or a hundred years, but an average of the varying profits of the time, as long as they are sufficient to encourage the employment of capital by the owners of stock. An average of ten or a dozen years, therefore, may fairly be considered as sufficient or more than sufficient to determine the ordinary rate of profits. But it is a matter of universal notoriety that, in the progress of a nation towards wealth, considerable fluctuations take place in the rate of profits for ten, twelve, or twenty years together out of one or two hundred: and the question is, to what cause or causes these fluctuations are mainly to be attributed.

Of all the truths which Mr. Ricardo has established, one of the most useful and important is, that profits are determined by the proportion of the whole produce which goes to labour. It is, indeed, a direct corollary from the proposition, that the value of commodities is resolvable into wages and profits ; but its simplicity and apparent obviousness do not detract from its utility. It is, however, only one important step in the theory of profits, which of course cannot be complete till we have ascertained the cause which, under all circumstances, regulates this proportion of the whole produce which goes to labour immediate and accumulated.

When the productiveness of labour employed on the land is continually diminishing, it is easy to see that the corn wages of labour cannot go on diminishing in the same degree without starving the labourer ; and that, therefore, of the produce of the same quantity of labour, a greater proportion must go to labour and less to profits. But we know, from experience, that the operation of this cause may be suspended by improvements in agriculture, for a hundred years together; and we are to inquire what it is which, independently of this cause, determines the proportion in which the produce of a given quantity of labour is divided between labour and profits. On this important point the present treatise is silent ;* but the prevailing opinion is, that it depends upon the greater or less demand for labour. If this opinion were correct, it would still show that the rate of profits must, so far, depend upon the principle of demand and supply. It appears, however, from experience, to depend rather upon the demand and supply of *produce*, than of labour. And it will be found that the specific reason which occasions a larger or smaller

---

* The author says, ' The limits to which this Article has already extended prevent our entering into an investigation of the various circumstances which determine the market rate of wages.' (p. 269.)

189

proportion of the produce of a given quantity of labour to go to labour, is the fall or rise in the value of the whole produce of such labour resulting from the temporary or ordinary state of the supply, compared with the demand. If we refer to the value of the whole produce of a given quantity of labour, this proposition is true, whatever may be the variations in the productiveness of labour; but if we are considering the value of a given quantity of produce as determining profits, we must refer to the state of the demand and supply, while the productiveness of labour remains the same.

Thus, to take one of the most familiar cases : if cottons fall in value from an abundant supply, not occasioned by improved machinery, will not a larger proportion of the produce of the same quantity of accumulated and immediate labour be necessary to repay that labour? and will not a smaller proportion be left for profits, although, instead of an increased demand for labour, the capitalist will neither have the power nor the will to employ so much as before? On the other hand, if cottons rise in value from a diminished supply, not occasioned by the diminished productiveness of labour, will not a smaller proportion of the produce of the same quantity of accumulated and immediate labour go to repay that labour? and will not a larger proportion of the produce be left for profits, although, instead of a diminished demand for labour, the capitalists will have both the power and the will to employ more labour? It appears, therefore, that in these cases of varying profits, it is specifically the varying state of the demand compared with the supply of produce while the productiveness of labour remains the same, which determines them. And does it not follow that the ordinary state of profits, or the ordinary *proportion* of the produce which goes to repay the advances of accumulated and immediate labour necessary to obtain it, is determined by the ordinary state of the demand compared with the supply of such produce?

But to make this important point more clear, let us consider what is meant by the amount of effectual demand, in the simplest form which it can assume so as to be correct. Adam Smith says, very justly, that labour was the original purchase-money of all commodities. If certain commodities were the objects of desire, but not attainable without a good deal of exertion, the person so desiring them would or would not have an effectual demand for them according as he was able and willing to purchase them with the necessary sacrifice of labour; and the quantity of labour which he was able and willing to give for them, might, with propriety, be considered as the amount of his demand; while the supply would depend upon the quantity of such commodities which the labour applied to obtain them could procure. In this case, it is obvious that the value of the articles would be as the demand directly and the supply inversely, or each article would be worth the quantity of labour which would arise from dividing the amount of labour employed by the amount of the articles obtained.

We have here supposed the returns to be rapid, and immediate labour only to be employed. But supposing the returns of some commodities to be necessarily very much slower than those of others, and further to require for their production expensive tools, or some form of accumulated labour; is it not quite certain that these commodities would be more scarce and valuable compared with the quantity of human labour worked up in them, than the commodities produced and brought to market rapidly? There would, in this case, be two causes influencing the supply of the commodities obtained by the same quantity of human labour : first, the productiveness of such labour; and, secondly, the plenty or scarcity of those accumulations called capital, and the time for which it was necessary to employ them; and the supply of such commodities compared with a given quantity of immediate labour would cease to be proportioned to the productiveness of that labour, and would only be proportioned to its productiveness after subtracting what was necessary to repay the profits of the capital employed.

To make an effectual demand for commodities of this description, we must transfer to the owners of them the means of obtaining a quantity of labour equal to the accumulated and immediate labour worked up in them, with such an additional quantity as will compensate for the use of the capital employed according as it is plentiful or scarce, compared with immediate labour, and according as it has been employed for a short or a long time.

In this case, the quantity of immediate labour necessary to make an effectual demand for the commodities will exceed, in various degrees, the quantity of accumulated and immediate labour worked up in them. But it will still be strictly true that the value of the commodities will be as the demand, directly, and the supply inversely. In the same manner, if the palms, yams and bananas belonging to a chief of Otaheite were in great request, the demand for them would be represented, not by other commodities similarly circumstanced, nor by the very small quantity of labour which they had cost in production, but by the great quantity of labour and service, that original purchase-money which the inhabitants were able and willing to give him in order to obtain them; and their value would be determined by the demand directly, and

191

the supply inversely ; or the quantity of service offered divided by the quantity of produce received. This last is a case of monopoly; but the value of all commodities is determined exactly in the same way, whether they are the subjects of any kind of monopoly, or of the freest competition ; whether they are produced by labour alone, or by labour and profits combined. In fact, all that is necessary to constitute value is, that a commodity should be wanted by more persons than can obtain it for nothing. When this is the case, some sacrifice must be made by the competitors. This sacrifice can seldom be measured with any approach towards precision by other commodities, the ever varying *products* of labour ; but it may be measured with tolerable exactness by labour itself; that is, by the quantity of their own or of other people's labour of a given description, which the competitors are willing to offer ; and the value of the commodities to those whose demands are effectual, will be just in proportion to the amount of their demand, compared with the supply which they obtain.*

This may be considered as the universal proposition applicable in all cases, temporary and permanent, and in whatever way the commodity is produced. The other proposition, namely, that the value of commodities is determined by the costs of their production, is limited in various ways. In the first place, it necessarily involves the supposition that profits form a part of *costs;* a supposition, the propriety of which has been controverted ; secondly, it refers always to the average and ordinary values of commodities, and not to the variations of their actual and market values; and, thirdly, it is confined to commodities which are produced by free competition, and excludes all those which are affected by monopolies either strict or partial, either natural or artificial, which are more numerous than people are aware of. With these limitations, however, the proposition is unquestionably true, and for this specific reason, that, under the circumstances supposed, the necessary condition of the continued supply of commodities is, that the demand or the amount of labour offered for them, should be such as to replace their costs, or the quantity of labour and profits required to bring them to market. Their value evidently cannot long be less than this, and when the competition is free, it is not necessary to the supply that it should be greater. It appears, therefore, that the value of all commodities, whether regulated by the costs of production or not, is determined by the supply compared with the demand, and that, as a

---

* In civilized societies, where the precious metals are in use, *a given demand* may be safely represented by the *variable* quantity of money which will command a *given quantity of labour* of the same description: but it cannot be represented by any given quantity of commodities,

given demand may be represented by a given quantity of labour, the supply of commodities compared with this demand which determines their value, must, while the productiveness of labour remains unaltered, determine, at the same time, the proportion of the whole produce which goes to labour, or, under similar circumstances, the rate of profits.

It is now generally allowed that, in almost every department of industry, the labourer who is employed at the present average rate of money wages, receives a larger proportion of what he produces than he did during the war. It is almost as generally allowed that this is mainly occasioned by the abundance of the supply compared with the demand; and the natural and necessary consequence is, that fall of profits which is the subject of universal remark.

In referring, therefore, to the costs of production, including profits, as the regulating principle of price and value, instead of demand and supply, we really refer to two elements, one of which is essentially determined in its value by the demand and supply. Independently of any question relating to the greater or less productiveness of labour, the costs of production, including profits, have diminished during the last eight or nine years, owing to a fall in the value of profits occasioned by the state of the demand and supply. Thus, the hardware, which in reference to the accumulated and immediate labour worked up in it, was produced both during the war and since, by the same advances, which we will call a hundred days' labour, was, in the former period, worth perhaps 114 days, and is probably now only worth 108 days, owing to the great supply of hardware compared with the demand. If the average term of the advances on which profits would be reckoned were a year in both cases, then, in the former case, profits would be 14 per cent., and in the latter, 8 per cent. The value of the produce of the same quantity of labour would have fallen in that degree; and it is certain that, if the producers were able and willing to continue the same proportionate supply, at the same rate, owing to the abundance of capital, this state of things might continue for twenty or thirty years together.

It is clear then, that in denying the influence of demand and supply on prices, except for short periods, the friends of the new school have totally mistaken the nature of the principle, and the mode and extent of its operation. This, indeed, is strikingly obvious from the following passage in the present treatise. Speaking of cottons, the author says, ' no one can deny that the demand for them has been prodigiously augmented within the last fifty or sixty years ; and yet their price, instead of increasing, as it ought to have done, had *the popular theory of demand and supply been well founded,* has been constantly and rapidly diminishing.' (p. 256.) Now, we should like to know, what ' popular theory' of demand and supply ever supposed that an increased consumption, specifically and exclusively caused by an increased supply, and increased cheapness, ought to occasion increased prices. That such increased consumption may prevent prices from falling so low as they otherwise would do, is natural enough ; but that it should raise prices is the grossest contradiction in terms ; and the statement only proves how totally the author has misapprehended the nature of that kind of demand and supply which affects prices and value. The specific reason why cottons have fallen during the last fifty or sixty years is, that they have been supplied in much greater abundance compared with a given demand, or a given quantity of labour. The main cause of this no doubt is, the greater productiveness of labour in this species of industry, or the power of producing the same quantity of cottons at a less cost of production in labour; but to show how exclusively the effect is owing to the principle of demand and supply, it would be universally acknowledged that, if a greater quantity of cottons had not been produced compared with the demand, or a given quantity of labour, no change whatever would have taken place in the value of cottons, however great might be the improvements in machinery:—but this, of course, could only have happened under a monopoly.

If, then, the nature of the principle of demand and supply be properly understood, it must be allowed that the rejection of this principle in the determination of value, except in cases of monopoly or for short periods, is totally unwarranted ; and that, in reality, the only difference between market prices and natural prices is, that the former are determined by the actual and temporary state, and the latter by the more permanent and ordinary state of the demand and supply.

The third important principle which we propose to consider, as peculiarly distinguishing the new school of political economy, is, that the difficulty of production on the land is the regulator of profits, to the entire exclusion of the cause stated by Adam Smith, namely, the relative abundance and competition of capital.

This principle, which is adverted to in various parts of the treatise, is broadly laid down in the last section of the third division, in the following passage :—p. 296.

' Dr. Smith was of opinion that the rate of profit varied inversely as the amount of capital, or in other words, that it was always greatest where capital was least abundant, and lowest where capital was the most abundant. He supposed that, according as capital increased, the principle of competition would stimulate capitalists to endeavour to encroach on the employment of each other, and that, in furtherance of this object, they would be tempted to offer their goods at a lower price, and to give higher wages to their workmen. This theory was long universally assented to. It has been espoused by MM. Say, Sismondi and Storch, by the Marquis de Garnier, and, with some slight modifications, by Mr. Malthus. But, notwithstanding the deference due to these authorities, it is easy to see that the principle of competition could never be productive of a general fall in the rate of profit. Competition will prevent any one individual from obtaining a higher rate of profit than his neighbours; but no one will say that competition diminishes the productiveness of industry, and it is on this that the rate of profit must always depend. The fall of profits, which invariably takes place as society advances, and population becomes denser, is not owing to competition, but to a very different cause—" *to a diminution of the power to employ capital with advantage, resulting either from a decrease in the fertility in the soil which must be taken into cultivation in the progress of society, or from an increase of taxation.*"

' Mr. Malthus has clearly demonstrated that population has a constant tendency not only to equal, but to exceed the means of subsistence. But if the supply of labourers be always increased in proportion to every increase in the demand for their labour, it is plain the mere accumulation of capital could never sink profits by raising wages, that is, by *increasing the labourer's share of the commodities produced by him.* It is true that a sudden increase of capital would, by causing an *unusually* great demand for labourers, raise wages and lower profits; but such a rise of wages could not be permanent; for the additional stimulus which it would give to the principle of population, would, as Mr. Malthus has shewn, by proportioning the supply of labour to the increased demand, infallibly reduce wages to their former level.'

On these observations it is first necessary to remark, that the opinion of Adam Smith on the subject of profits, is not properly understood. It is quite clear, from the context of the passage referred to, that he never meant to state generally, that the rate of profit varies inversely as the amount of capital, without any reference to the difficulty or facility of finding employment for it, which would be saying that England must have lower profits than Holland, on account of the greater quantity of capital employed in England, or that the rate of profits in any country whose capital was increasing, must go on falling regularly, and be always lower at every subsequent period, whether new channels of trade, and more productive means of employing capital, were opened to her or not. What Adam Smith says is this, (B. ii. c. iv.) ' As capitals increase in any country, the profits which can be made by employing them, necessarily diminish. It becomes gradually more and more difficult to find within the country a *profitable* method of employing any new capital. There arises in consequence a competition between different capitals, the owner of one endeavouring to get possession of that employment which is occupied by another.' This very distinctly implies, not merely *absolute amount of capital,* but relative difficulty of finding *profitable* employment for it. Abundance and competition, indeed, always have a relative signification; and by the abundance and competition of capital, Adam Smith obviously means an increase in the *share* of the ' annual produce which, as soon as it comes from the ground, or from the hands of the productive labourers, is destined for replacing a capital.' But it is quite certain, that whenever this share increases profits must fall.

With regard to the statement that competition cannot diminish the productiveness of industry, we most readily allow it ; but we utterly deny, that it is on this that the rate of profit must always depend. There is a very frequent, but certainly no *necessary* connection between the productiveness of industry and the rate of profits. The rate of profits depends upon the *proportion* of the whole produce which goes to replace the advances ; but this proportion may obviously be the same when the productiveness of industry is very different. And that practically, it very seldom increases or decreases according to the degree of productiveness, is manifest from this, that in the various countries of the commercial world so different in natural fertility, the rate of profits, allowing for difference of security, is much more nearly the same than the rate of corn wages. Nothing indeed can be more entirely unwarranted by facts, than the assumption of any thing like a constant rate of corn wages. In our own country great variations have taken place for twenty, thirty, and even sixty years together ; and in the United States the corn wages of labour have long been considerably more than double those of England. Yet, in order to be able to say with truth, that the rate of profit must always depend upon the productiveness of industry, we must assume, that the corn wages of labour are always the same,

On the subject of the difficulty of production on the land, we have to observe, that we are by no means disposed to overlook the effects resulting from the necessity of resorting to poorer land in the progress of cultivation and population. The principle founded on the gradations of soil not only shows clearly why rent, though generally considered as the consequence of monopoly, appears in an early period of society, while land is still in great plenty ; but it explains specifically the reason why the continued increase of capital, in a limited territory, must unavoidably terminate in a fall of profits. In both these views it is of the highest importance, and most decidedly confirmed by experience. But if it be considered as *regulating* profits, that is, if we assume, that while the productiveness of the last capital employed on the land remains the same, profits will continue the same, and that when it increases or diminishes, profits will necessarily increase or diminish, then it will be found to be almost universally contradicted by facts.

Is it possible, for instance, to attribute the fall of profits which has taken place during the last eight or nine years, to the difficulty of production on the land? Corn, it is well known, has been unusually cheap during the greatest part of the time; the capitals of many farmers have greatly suffered, and it is the universal impression, that they have been unable, on account of their losses, to keep their lands in the same high state of cultivation as before. Under these circumstances, and with a falling money price of labour, the doctrines of the new school teach us that profits ought to rise. The fact, however, has been exactly the reverse. Nor is there the least reason to say, that the effect is peculiar, or merely temporary. A similar fall of profits has taken place in almost every state at all similarly circumstanced, with which we are acquainted; and at a former period, in our own country, for nearly thirty years together, from the accession of George II. to the year 1757, the interest of money was at 3, 3½, and even, during an intermediate war, only at about 4 per cent., and profits must have been low nearly in proportion. In neither of these cases can we attribute the low profits to the difficulty of production on the land. Corn was plentiful and cheap; and nothing indicated that the labour employed on the last land taken into cultivation had become less productive.

What then was the cause of the fall of profits? It was obviously and unquestionably a fall in the value of produce owing to the abundance and competition of capital, which would necessarily occasion a different division of what was produced, and award a larger proportion of it to the labourer, and a smaller proportion of it to the capitalist. Accordingly, we find that, while the productiveness of labour on the land remained nearly the same, the labourer was paid greater corn wages than usual. It was during the thirty years of low profits just referred to, that he earned on an average about a full peck of wheat a day, which was more than he had earned, during any ten years together, for nearly a century and a half before, or could earn for above half a century afterwards. The same circumstance has attended the fall of profits since the war. It is well known, that the money price of wheat has fallen more than the money price of labour; and consequently, the labourer who has been employed, has earned a greater quantity of wheat than usual.

When the difficulty of production on the land really increases, the corn wages of labour almost uniformly fall, and the money price of corn almost uniformly rises. In these cases exactly the opposite effects were experienced, corn wages rose, and the money price of corn fell considerably; while, with these two symptoms so strongly negativing all idea of the diminished productiveness of the last capitals employed on the land, there was not a single symptom which could be brought forwards tending in the slightest degree to establish such diminished productiveness.

Here then we have two glaring instances in our own country of a fall of profits, one of thirty years continuance, and the other of eight or nine years, which cannot, with the slightest semblance of probability, be attributed to the difficulty of production on the land. Both instances, however, accord most perfectly with the more general proposition of Mr. Ricardo respecting profits, namely, that they are determined by the proportion of the whole produce which goes to labour. It is matter of incontrovertible fact, that in both these cases the labourer absorbed a larger proportion of what he produced: but it is of the highest importance to remark that, in neither case, could the increased corn wages be attributed to the increased demand for labour. In the former period, when the average corn wages of common day labour were a peck a day, if there had been the same demand for labour, and it had been equally easy for the wife and children of the labourer to find full employment, as it was from 1793 to 1815, it is quite impossible to suppose that we should not have had a nearly equal increase of population; while it is well known that the population from 1727 to 1756 increased very slowly, and from 1793 to 1815 very rapidly. In the period which has elapsed since the return of peace, the difficulty of finding employment, particularly on the land, has been too notorious to require proof; and if, owing to the extraordinary stimulus given to the population by the previous demand for it, it still continues to increase with rapidity, yet there is reason to think that the present demand would not nearly have kept pace with the rate of increase, and that great distress would have been the consequence, if the happy opening of new and large channels of foreign commerce, combined with the improved views of our government in commercial legislation, had not prepared the way for a renewed demand for labour. As it is, it is universally allowed that the money price of corn and commodities has fallen during the last nine years more than the money price of labour; and while the merchant sees that on this account the workmen which he employs are paid a larger proportion of the commodities which they produce, we believe that there is not a single unsophisticated person in business who would not at the same time acknowledge, that this was not owing to the scarcity and increased demand for labour, but to the abundance and cheapness of the commodities produced, occasioned by the abundance and competition of capital in every department of industry.

We fully agree with the author of the present treatise, that when it is said that profits depend on wages, they must not be understood to ' depend on wages estimated in money, in corn, or in any other commodity, but on proportional wages, that is, on the share of the commodities produced by the labourer, or of their value, which is given to him.' But innumerable facts concur to show, that this increased proportion awarded to the labourer continually takes place without being accompanied with any circumstances which indicate either an increased demand for labour, or an increase in the value of the same quantity of labour.

We are in the habit, and we believe justly, of considering the precious metals as a commodity less liable to sudden changes of value than any of the other products of human industry, and it is well known that the money price of the same kind of labour often remains the same for many years together. But during such periods there are frequently variations in the prices of commodities produced by a given quantity of labour, owing to the state of the demand and supply, without any alteration in the power of production, or the amount of produce obtained by the same quantity of labour and capital.

Now what is the consequence of these variations? If the *prices* of calicoes fall, it is quite obvious that while the workman continues to earn the same money wages, he will obtain a larger proportion of the calicoes produced by him. We have already shown that this does not imply an increased demand for labour, and it is equally certain that it does not imply an increased *value* of labour. Measured in money, the value of which for short periods is considered as being steady, labour remains of exactly the same value as before, and the additional quantity of calicoes earned by the workman is exclusively owing to the fall in their money price.

On the other hand, if, under the same circumstances, calicoes rise in money price, the workman must necessarily earn a smaller proportion of what he produces; but this, so far from implying a decrease in the demand for labour, implies, on the part of the capitalist, both the power and will to employ more than before. Nor does it imply a diminished *value* of labour. Measured in the steady article of metallic money, labour has continued exactly of the same value; and though the workman earns a smaller quantity of calicoes, yet this is exclusively owing to the rise in the price of calicoes, while the price of his labour has remained the same. Instances of this kind are occurring all around us every day of our lives; and we believe that there is no political economist who would venture to say, that, in these individual cases, the variations of profits, arising from wages absorbing a greater or smaller proportion of the produce, were occasioned by the rise or fall in the value of the labour, instead of a rise or fall in the value of the produce.

But, in reality, the principle is as applicable generally as it is individually, and will be found to be true for periods of considerable length, as well as for those short periods, during which we are in the habit of considering metallic money as practically of the same value. If the competition of capital in any particular department of industry may so lower the value of the produce as to occasion a larger proportion of the produce to be paid to the labourer, there seems to be no reason why the competition of increasing capital in all departments should not so lower the value of the mass of commodities, compared with labour, as to award generally a larger proportion of what is divided between the labourers and the capitalists to the labourers, and thus occasion a general fall on profits.

The only argument against this natural and obvious conclusion is taken from the principle of population stated by Mr. Malthus, and referred to in the passage before quoted. His doctrine is considered as proving, that ' the supply of labourers will always be increased in proportion to every increase in the *demand* for their labour;' and in this statement we are disposed to agree with the author. But the great question, and a most important one it must be acknowledged to be, is, whether an accumulation of capital coming upon a slack demand for produce, which will certainly award a larger share of this produce to the labourer, will always be accompanied by that increase in the demand for labour which is so necessary to occasion a rapid increase of population? It is well known, that the effect of increase of quantity on price and value is frequently to lower the exchangeable value of commodities in a much greater degree than in proportion to the increase. But when this is the case the mass of such commodities, after their increase, must command a smaller quantity of any object which had not altered its value, than before. Now, supposing this increase to have taken place, under the circumstances stated, in the funds specifically destined for the maintenance of labour, the necessary consequence would be, that, instead of an *unusually great demand* for labourers, there would be a *diminished demand*,

and the mass of these funds would not be adequate to set so many people to work as before. Either a part of the labourers must be thrown entirely out of work, or the whole must be only partially employed—a state of things exactly calculated to generate those indolent habits, which, while they occasion a larger proportion of the produce to go to labour, owing to the greater number employed, tend to reduce to but a scanty allowance the annual remuneration of each labourer. Under these circumstances it is evident, that, notwithstanding the increased produce awarded at first to the labourers actually employed, the progress of population is likely to be but slow. The theory on the subject is very simple and clear, and it only remains to be considered whether it is confirmed by experience.

In the first place it is obvious, that whenever the money price of the funds for the maintenance of labour so falls as to lower the value of the whole mass, while the money price of labour remains nearly the same, the labourer must earn a larger proportion of the produce, and profits must fall; and it must be allowed that this event is practically frequent. It is continually happening for short periods, owing to a fall in the price of corn, occasioned by the state of the seasons; and for longer periods, owing to more permanent causes. It occurred in the latter part of the fifteenth century and the beginning of the sixteenth, in this country, for sixty years together; it occurred in the early part of the last century for above thirty years together, and has been taking place for the last nine years, since 1814; and whatever may have been the increase of population during the latter period, occasioned by the *impetus* previously received, and the fortunate opening of new channels of trade, it is certain that in the two former periods of very considerable duration, the high corn wages earned by the labourer were not accompanied by anything like so rapid an increase of population as at periods when the corn wages were lower, and the demand for labour greater. But, if it appear both from theory and experience, that an increased rate of corn wages is not always accompanied by an increased demand for labour, and on that account does not necessarily occasion a more rapid increase of population, it is perfectly clear that a distribution of the produce which awards a larger share to the labourer, may occasion a fall of profits for a very considerable time together, without any increase in the difficulty of production on the land.

But if this be so, it is equally certain that it is specifically the competition of capital, or the increase of capital compared with the value of the produce to be derived from it, which can alone occasion such a distribution. The relative difficulty of production on the land accounts for none of those considerable variations in the rate of profits which are practically found to occur during those long periods when the improvements in agriculture, and the saving of labour, have compensated the disadvantage of resorting to naturally poorer soils, and when, in consequence, the productiveness of labour on the land has remained nearly the same; while the principle of the competition of capital not only gives the true explanation of all these variations, but equally applies to those variations which arise from the diminished productiveness of labour on the land. In both cases the immediate cause of the fall of profits is the increase or abundance of capital greater than the demand for the produce; in both cases the effect depends *solely* on the altered distribution of what is produced. And the only difference is, that, in the latter case, this altered distribution is absolutely necessary and unavoidable, in the actual state of the land, and of the skill with which it is cultivated; while in the former, it depends upon the tastes and habits of the effectual demanders, and is susceptible of change, without any alteration in the state of the land, by a better proportion of the supply to the demand.

In denying, therefore, the effects of the relative competition of capital on profits, and referring exclusively to the relative productiveness of labour, the friends of the new school have rejected a principle which will account for almost every variation of profits which can possibly occur, and have endeavoured to substitute another, which will only account for one class of cases, and those of such a nature that they may not occur in the course of one or two centuries.

It appears, then, that their theory of profits does not account for things, as they have been, and as they are, in any degree so well as the theory of Adam Smith which they have rejected.

We have already anticipated most of the remarks which we wished to make on the fourth division of the present treatise, in what we said of productive and unproductive labour, and productive and unproductive consumption as necessarily connected with the definition of wealth given in the first division. But we cannot quit this last division, without referring to a passage in it which strikes us as peculiarly illustrative of the impracticability and inapplicability of some of the opinions maintained by the new school. The author fully adopts the doctrine of M. Say, laid down in his chapter *Des Debouchés*, that is, *that effective demand depends upon production:* and to show that a general glut is impossible, he has the following argument.

‘ In exerting his productive powers every man's object is either directly to consume the produce of his labour himself, or to exchange it for such commodities as he wishes to obtain from others. If he does

202

the first—if he directly consumes the produce of his industry, there is an end of the matter, and it is evident that the multiplication of such produce to infinity could never occasion a glut: if he does the second—if he brings the produce of his industry to market, and offers it in exchange for other commodities, then and then only there may be a glut; but why? Not certainly because there has been any excess of production, but because the producers have not properly adapted their means to their ends. They wanted, for example, silks, and they offered cottons in exchange for them; the proprietors of silks were however already sufficiently supplied with cottons, and they wanted broad cloths. The cause of the glut is therefore obvious. It consists not in over-production, but in the production of cottons which were not wanted, instead of broad cloths, which were wanted. Let this error be rectified, and the glut will disappear.

' Even supposing the proprietors of silks to be not only supplied with cottons, but with cloth and every other commodity that the demanders can produce, it would not invalidate the principle for which we are contending. If those who want silks cannot obtain them from those who have them by means of an exchange, they have an obvious resource at hand—let them cease to produce the commodities which they do not want, and *directly produce the silks which they do want, or substitutes for them.* It is plain, therefore, that the utmost facility of production can never be the means of overloading the market. Too much of one commodity may occasionally be produced ; but it is quite impossible that there can be too great a supply of every species of commodities. For every excess there must be a corresponding deficiency. The fault is not in producing too much, but in producing commodities which do not suit the tastes of those with whom we wish to exchange them, or which we cannot ourselves consume.'

It is here stated, that for every excess there must be a corresponding deficiency. If this means any thing, it must mean, that if, in some departments of industry, the fall in the value of the produce from excess of quantity destroys nearly all the profits of the producer, this must necessarily be accompanied by such a rise in the value of produce in other departments of industry, as to yield to the capitalists engaged in them an unusually high rate of profits. Now we would appeal to the experience of every person who, without being biassed by some previous prejudice, had turned the smallest attention to the subject, whether, at the time when a general glut was talked of, there was the least ground for the assertion, that, although the state of the trade in cottons was ruinous, the capitalist engaged in making broad cloths or silks, or some other article which would absorb a large capital, was in the most prosperous and flourishing state, and inviting additional stock by high prices and high profits. This assertion of corresponding deficiency, as applied to what is known to have taken place since the peace, appears to us as strange as if it were gravely asserted that every man in the streets of London who was observed to have his head covered, would be found upon examination to have his feet bare. All people have not been in London, and could not therefore personally contradict such an affirmation ; but on account of its extreme improbability none would believe it, and in justification of this disbelief they would naturally say that, if it were true, they must have heard more of it. Now we will venture to say, as a matter of fact from competent authority, that, for some years together since the peace, there was a marked deficiency of produce in any one considerable department of industry.

If, however, in spite of the general principles of political economy, which inculcate an equality of profits; in spite of the intelligence and skill of our merchants and manufacturers, who are not apt to be obstinately inattentive to their interests, and in spite of an abundant quantity of floating capital ready to go any where for the chance of a tolerable profit, some capitalists are absolutely unable to obtain the commodities they want by means of an exchange; what is their resource? Our author says it is obvious, and at hand.—' Let them cease to produce the commodities which they do not want, and *directly produce the silks which they do want, or substitutes for them.*'

Let us for a moment consider the nature of this remedy. In the first place no capitalist ever wants a large quantity of any one commodity with a view to his own consumption. If he could most readily exchange his cottons for silks, or any other commodity which he might prefer, and were to consume such commodity, he would at once be ruined, as he would have consumed his capital. What, then, does he really want? Besides the raw materials to be worked up, which he can seldom obtain but by means of an exchange, his main want is the means of supporting his workmen. Is he to set about producing these means? If he does, he will proceed but slowly in his new manufacture; and in the interim must produce all the various articles required for the consumption of his family, and thus give up the benefits derived from the division of labour. We feel quite certain that if the reason why a general glut cannot happen is, that the producers have this remedy at hand, gluts might take place over and over in civilized countries, without its ever occurring to a single producer that he might relieve himself by resorting to so impracticable and barbarous a resource.

The doctrine of the equality of profits teaches us that partial gluts cannot be of long duration. The interest of individual producers to move their capitals to more profitable employments is so obvious and pressing, that it cannot long be unattended to, though the change may occasion temporary loss. But when the warehouses are generally full, and there is a sudden and unusual fall of profits in *all* employments, which is what is meant by a general glut, the producer cannot relieve himself. It is of little consequence in this case, that all the articles are produced in their proper proportions to each other, and that cottons, broad cloths, silks, hardware, &c. &c. exchange among themselves exactly at the same rate as they did before. If without improvements in machinery, they have all fallen compared with labour,* which they may very easily do from the competition of capital acting on a slack demand, foreign and domestic, there must necessarily be a general fall of profits accompanied with all the appearances of a general glut. How long this might last, it would not be very easy to say: it would depend entirely upon the tastes and habits of the effectual demanders, and the perseverance and competition of the producers. Such a state of things, however, would at once be put an end to by the opening of new and large channels of trade, which would absorb a great mass of capital, and raise the price of produce, by altering the state of the demand compared with the supply. But during the time of its continuance, it is manifest, from what has been said, that the large proportion of the produce awarded to the labourer would not necessarily occasion an increased demand for labour; and it is equally manifest that a greater quantity of cheaper commodities being given to the labourer would not imply an increased *value* of labour. It would be, as Adam Smith has most justly stated, the goods which had fallen, not the labour which had risen.

It has been our object in this Article to point out to the reader the main characteristic differences which distinguish the new school of Political Economy from that of Adam Smith and Mr. Malthus. For this purpose, we have laid our chief stress on three very fundamental points;—1. The new principle which has been laid down on the subject of value; 2. The new principle

* Upon a former occasion the author had fallen into a similar error. Speaking of a rise in the price of wages and of commodities, he observes, (p. 264.) ' If wages rise 50 per cent., a producer, a farmer for example, would be precisely in the same condition whether he sold his corn for 50 per cent. advance, and gave an additional 50 per cent., as he would be obliged to do, for his hats, shoes, clothes, &c. &c., or sold his corn at its former price, and bought all the commodities which he consumed at the prices he had formerly given for them.' Now we consider it as quite certain, that if the price of labour were to rise 50 per cent., and the price of the produce of such labour were to continue the same, the producer would infallibly be ruined, and would be utterly unable to carry on his business, at whatever price he might buy his shoes and clothes; whereas, if the price of his produce rose proportionally, it would be merely a fall in the value of money, and he might go on as before. It is of the utmost importance to remember that every commodity is mainly exchanged against labour, and that a moderate alteration in the value of labour, compared with produce, would at once destroy all profits, if they were not before very high.

which has been laid down on the subject of demand and supply; and 3. The new principle which has been laid down on the subject of profits, and the competition of capital.

We are inclined, however, to think that these differences may be still further concentrated; and that it will not be incorrect to state, that all the peculiar doctrines of the new system directly and necessarily flow from the first of these new principles; namely, that *the exchangeable value of commodities is determined by the quantity of labour worked up in them.* It follows, directly and necessarily from this principle, that neither the demand compared with the supply, nor the relative abundance and competition of capital, can have more than a mere temporary effect on values and profits.

This draws a strongly marked line of distinction between the two systems in reference to the main object of inquiry in the science of Political Economy, namely, the causes which encourage or discourage the increase of wealth. In both systems it is allowed that these depend mainly on the state of profits. And the grand distinction between the two may be stated shortly to be this :— The new school suppose that the mass of commodities obtained by the same quantity of labour remains always substantially of the same value, and that the variations of profits are determined by the variations in the value of this same quantity of labour : while Adam Smith and Mr. Malthus suppose that the value of the same quantity of labour remains substantially the same, and that the variations of profits are determined by the variations in the value of the commodities produced by this same quantity of labour. In the one case, the varying value of labour is considered as the great moving principle in the progress of wealth ; in the other, the varying value of the *produce* of labour. The difference is most distinct and important. And as political economy, according to the first description of it in the present Treatise, ' is not a science of speculation, but of fact and experiment,' the specific question is, which of the two views here stated best explains the broad and established facts of which we have had experience.

For our own parts we have no hesitation in saying that the events of the last thirty years, in this country, appear to us to be absolutely inexplicable on the supposition that the mass of commodities produced by the same quantity of labour, remained during that time of the same value;* while they are explained in

---

* It would imply, that, during the war, the value of labour was low, on account of the food of the labourer being obtained with great facility ; and that since the war the value of labour has been high, on account of the food of the labourer being obtained with great difficulty ;—positions which it is impossible to maintain.

the clearest and most obvious manner, by allowing, in conformity with all appearances, that the value of the produce of the same quantity of labour rose during the war, and has fallen since, owing to the state of the demand and supply, and of the relative abundance and competition of capital in the two periods. * And we believe it will be found, that no instance of a rise or fall of profits has ever occurred which may not justly be attributed to a rise or fall in the value of the produce of the same quantity of labour occasioned by these causes.

The reader will be aware that this proposition in no respect impeaches the very great advantages derived from that fall of price which arises from the saving of labour, the use of improved machinery, and the diminution of taxes, or any other outgoings. Such improvements, while they lower the value of any specific quantity of the article produced, have the strongest tendency to raise the value of the produce of the same quantity of labour; and this tendency can only fail to be effectual for short periods, or under particular circumstances.

The frequent fall of price arising from the saving of labour and other outgoings, is almost always beneficial. The frequent fall of price not arising from this cause, but from the state of the demand and supply, and the competition of capital, is often prejudicial. The rapid progress of wealth for a continuance, depends upon the produce of labour being of such a *value* as to occasion its division between the capitalist and labourer in the proportions which are at once the most advantageous to both,† and will increase most rapidly and steadily the quantity and *value* of the capital, and the number of the people.

The system of the new school of political economy has always struck us as bearing a very remarkable resemblance to the system of the French Economists. Their founders were equally men of the most unquestionable genius; of the highest honour and integrity, and of the most simple, modest and amiable manners.

---

* If the money price of labour had remained the same during the whole period, this rise in the value of corn and commodities in the first twenty years, and fall subsequently, would have been exactly expressed and measured by the rise and fall in the money prices of commodities. But under great changes in the state of the demand and supply of commodities, money rarely retains the same value. Still, it is of some use as a measure. And as the money prices of corn and commodities rose more during the first part of the period, and fell more during the second part than the money price of labour, this fact, which is absolutely incontrovertible, shows at once that the great change of value was in corn and commodities, while labour remained comparatively constant.

† It has been said that the manner in which the produce of labour is divided cannot alter the value. If it do not actually alter its value, it clearly shows that its value *is altered*. Properly speaking, indeed, it is the value of the produce, determined by the demand and supply, which regulates the division, not the division which regulates the value.

Political Economy.

Their systems were equally distinguished for their discordance with common notions, the apparent closeness of their reasonings, and the mathematical precision of their calculations and conclusions founded on their assumed data. These qualities in the systems and their founders, together with the desire so often felt by readers of moderate abilities of being thought to understand what is considered by competent judges as difficult, increased the number of their devoted followers in such a degree, that in France it included almost all the able men who were inclined to attend to such subjects, and in England a very large proportion of them.

The specific error of the French Economists was the having taken so confined a view of wealth and its sources as not to include the results of manufacturing and mercantile industry.

The specific error of the new school in England is the having taken so confined a view of *value* as not to include the results of demand and supply, and of the relative abundance and competition of capital.*

Facts and experience have, in the course of some years, gradually converted the economists of France from the erroneous and inapplicable theory of Quesnay to the juster and more practical theory of Adam Smith; and as we are fully convinced that an error equally fundamental and important is involved in the system of the new school in England as in that of the French economists, we cannot but hope and expect that similar causes will, in time, produce in our own country similar effects in the correction of error and the establishment of truth.

PART IV

Articles about
MALTHUS
and his views

From The *Westminster Review,*

January 1825

This is John Stuart Mill's riposte to Malthus' Review of McCulloch's article "Political Economy." See Semmel's article: pp. 27-28 *supra.* (*Publisher*).

[John Stuart Mill]

ART. IX. *The Quarterly Review*, No. LX. Art. 1. *On the Essay on Political Economy, in the Supplement to the Encyclopædia Britannica.*

HAD this article been particularly good, we might have left it to work its way by itself. Had it been bad, after the usual manner of the Quarterly Review, begging every question on the side of power, we should not have thought it necessary to add any thing to the exposure which we have already given of this branch of the aristocratic logic. It happens, however, that while the article is as bad as might naturally be expected, considering the quarter from which it comes, there are peculiarities in its badness, which take it out of the ordinary run of Quarterly Review articles.

The object of the writer, as described by himself, is, to upset what he terms the "new school of political economy;" of which school he is pleased to consider the very able essay * which he has taken for his text, as the manual. His predictions, with respect to the future fate of this school, are sufficiently appalling. He threatens them with a downfal similar to that of the French Economists, between whose system and theirs, he has discovered that there is a remarkable similarity; a piece of information which is as new to us as his menaces are alarming. We learn that they, to their unspeakable confusion, have set at nought the wisdom of their ancestors, and " altered the theories of Adam Smith upon pure speculation " (it would, indeed, have been somewhat surprising if they had altered them on any other ground). It was fitting that such unparalleled temerity should not escape unchastised. Happily, the old and orthodox faith was not left altogether destitute, for our author remained. It was reserved for him to carry back the science to its fountain-head—to restore the legitimate rule of Adam Smith, or, as he afterwards expresses it, of " Adam Smith and Mr. Malthus."

A writer who praises what is old and condemns what is new, is exactly suited to the Quarterly Review; and, considering him merely in the capacity of a Quarterly Reviewer, we are

---

* We cannot omit an opportunity of recording our feeble testimony to the merits of this essay, which deservedly ranks among the ablest productions of one of the first political economists of the age; and which, from the soundness of its principles, the aptness of its illustrations, and the perspicuity of its style, is one of the best elementary treatises of which the science has yet to boast.

only surprised that he should have pitched upon Adam Smith as the object of his idolatry; a writer who, whatever may be his other merits, cannot lay claim to that of being two centuries old ; and who not only did his utmost to promote an object so alien to the conceptions and wishes of a Quarterly-Reviewer, as the improvement of the great mass of mankind, but pursued that object by means which he cannot but regard as abominable; by pointing out the defects of existing institutions, and suggesting remedies.   If it was absolutely necessary to have a system, to set up in opposition to the new-fangled doctrines of later times, a purer source might have been found from whence to derive it; and the writings of St. Athanasius, St. Jerome, and St. Augustin, if read with faith, would, doubtless, have afforded thirty-nine articles of political economy, untainted with the poison of modern sedition and impiety.   Unfortunately, however, man is presumptuous, and will use his reason, unconscious that he is playing with edge-tools, and unmoved by the dangers with which he is threatened by his masters in this world and by his pastors in the next.   In vain does the anxious tenderness of the Quarterly Review represent to him, that the reason, on which he so arrogantly prides himself, was given by a benevolent Providence on purpose to delude and mislead him; that the only safe standard of belief is the faith of his fathers; and that, although the insufficient records of early times do not permit us to mount up to the creation of the world, and ascertain what were the opinions of Adam on the subject of political economy, it is our duty to approach as near to that summit of orthodoxy as we can.   Instead of listening to these pious exhortations with the reverence and submission which they deserve, the reader breaks out into a blasphemous laugh, and shuts the book ; for we live in an incredulous age, and we are even informed that there are some (we say it with horror) who doubt the whole Athanasian creed, and dispute the divine authority of tithes.   Being unable, therefore, to do what they would, the Reviewers wisely content themselves with doing what they can.   Being unable to drag back the public mind five thousand years, they are fain to try whether they can drag it fifty.

To do them justice, they resisted Adam Smith, as long as they could do so without falling into utter contempt.   When the reputation of the " Wealth of Nations" was not so well established as it now is, they called it " a tedious and hardhearted book, greatly over-valued, even on the score of ability;" it considered man (they said) in the light of a " manufacturing animal," and estimated his importance by the gain which can be extracted from him; nay, we almost shudder at the treatment which it inflicted upon him, since it actually " plucked the wings of his intellect," and " stripped him of the down and plumage of his virtues." Mr. Malthus, too, at that period surpassed, if possible, even Adam Smith in criminality; and it was with difficulty that they could find language adequate to express guilt of so black a dye. They described his reputation as disgraceful to the age; they made a collection of the most approved epithets, expressive of all the varieties of wickedness or folly, and heaped them on his devoted head.* Unfortunately, however, both Adam Smith and Mr. Malthus proved too strong for the Quarterly Review; and now that the public mind has got beyond them, the Quarterly Review courts an alliance even with such monsters of depravity, rather than tolerate that unholy spirit of progression which is so unhappily conspicuous in the human species.

This, we say, is quite in character, and can surprise no one; and if the present article had contained nothing more extraordinary, we should not have thought it worthy of a lengthened notice in our pages. But this is far from being the case; and the article is altogether so great a curiosity, that we could not refrain from drawing to it the attention of our readers.

When we commenced the perusal, we were considerably startled at the remarkable similarity of the style to that of Mr. Malthus himself; nor was our surprise lessened when we found the Reviewer to be a professed advocate of several opinions, which we had hitherto imagined to be held by Mr. Malthus exclusively. Whatever suspicions, however, we might have formed at the beginning of the article, they were effectually dispelled before we arrived at the close; nor was it long before we discovered that this writer, under the mask of a devoted adherent of Mr. Malthus, is, in reality, his concealed enemy, and affects to defend his doctrines, merely to have an opportunity of exhibiting them and him in a ridiculous and contemptible attitude. In this attempt, candour constrains us to own that he has completely succeeded : for the article is precisely such as the bitterest enemy of Mr. Malthus would have wished him to write; and the imitation is so close, that even we, who believe ourselves to be tolerably well versed in Mr. Malthus's writings, were, for a time, deceived by it. Not having heard, however, that Mr. Malthus has yet publicly disavowed the opinions which are here put forward as his, or disclaimed con-

---

* See a review of Colquhoun on the Poor, in the sixteenth number of the Quarterly Review.

nexion with the Reviewer, whom he probably deems altogether unworthy of his notice, we are apprehensive lest some incautious reader, misled by the confident tone of the Reviewer, and by the air of sincerity which finely characterises his irony, should unguardedly conclude that he is in earnest, and should mistake this grave piece of raillery for a serious *exposé* of Mr. Malthus's opinions.   Few persons are inclined to allow a larger scope to wit and ridicule than ourselves ; but when wit and ridicule assume so malignant a form, we should be wanting in our duty, if we did not come forward to unmask the cheat and put the public on their guard.

Among not a few other difficulties, however, with which we shall have to contend in the execution of our design, one, and that one not the least considerable, is the impossibility of making the malicious accuracy of the imitation perceptible to those who are but imperfectly acquainted with the original ; a description of persons including, we are greatly apprehensive, a very considerable proportion of the public.   Few, we fear, of our readers can boast, like ourselves, of having effected the reading of Mr. Malthus's " Measure of Value," and of his " Principles of Political Economy."   It is indeed a task by no means lightly to be engaged in, and upon which we cannot advise any person to enter without being aware what it is which he undertakes.   For if Mr. Malthus excels in any thing, it is not certainly in smoothing the road to knowledge ; and if any truths are contained in the works to which we have alluded, they must be of the number of those truths which lie hidden in the bottom of a well.

On reflection, however, it occurred to us, that if few have read Mr. Malthus, it is only the more necessary that some person who has read him should step forward to vindicate his reputation from the calumnious insinuations of this pretended disciple; who not only puts forward Mr. Malthus's peculiar doctrines in such a manner as actually to direct the assailant to all the points most open to attack ; but affects to consider as the opinions of Mr. Malthus, opinions utterly inconsistent with, and even contrary to, those which that gentleman has always professed to hold : nor does he stop here, but while he copies implicitly all the mistiness of Mr. Malthus's style, he never lets slip an opportunity of throwing in, by a side wind, some concealed joke at Mr. Malthus's expense.

Thus, because certain Political Economists differ somewhat from Mr. Malthus, he dubs them the " new school," thereby intimating, that Mr. Malthus's doctrines are exploded and out of date ; and he takes a malicious pleasure in coupling Mr.

Malthus with Adam Smith ; a compliment for which Mr.
Malthus cannot be too grateful, as it implies that all the discoveries of modern Political Economists are thrown away
upon him, and that he has not yet advanced beyond the
founder of the science. It may appear presumptuous to suppose, that so great a master of ridicule as this writer can
stand in need of any suggestions that we can give, for the
better amusement of his readers ; but, we think, that in
attempting to twist the systems of Mr. Malthus and of Adam
Smith into concordance, to be serious would have been by far
the best joke which he could have devised. The difficulty of
serving God and Mammon is proverbial, but it is a mere trifle
in comparison with that of reconciling Mr. Malthus and Adam
Smith : the former difficulty, whatever it may once have been,
the experience of modern times has proved to be by no means
insuperable.

The Reviewer proceeds, with well-feigned gravity, to criticise
the doctrines of the " new school." To say that he attempts
to criticise them without knowing any thing about them, would
be to say very little : since it would, on the contrary, be much
more surprising, were a Quarterly-Reviewer to be found, who
did know any thing about any subject which requires any intellect, or is of any importance to mankind. It is not, therefore, the blunders of this writer, which we wish especially to be
remarked, but the sang-froid with which he lays all of them to
the charge of Mr. Malthus, by pretending to fight on his side,
and to be the enemy of his enemies.

‘ The main principles,’ says he, ‘ which more especially characterize
the new school of political economy, appear to be three.

‘ 1. That the quantity of labour worked up in commodities determines their exchangeable value.

‘ 2. That the demand and supply have no effect upon prices and
values, except in cases of monopoly, or for short periods of time.

‘ 3. That the difficulty of production on the land is the regulator of
profits, to the entire exclusion of the cause stated by Adam Smith;
namely, the relative abundance and competition of capital ’—p. 307.

He afterwards [p. 332] continues :

‘ We are inclined, however, to think, that these differences may be
still further concentrated ; and that it will not be incorrect to state, that
all the peculiar doctrines of the new system directly and necessarily
flow from the first of these new principles ; namely, that *the exchangeable value of commodities is determined by the quantity of labour
worked up in them.* It follows directly and necessarily from this principle, that neither the demand, compared with the supply, nor the relative abundance and competition of capital, can have more than a mere
temporary effect on values and profits.’

We have been accustomed to believe that political economy, which was left, even by Adam Smith, in a state of great vagueness and uncertainty, had been raised to the rank of a science chiefly by three discoveries : the principle of *population*, the theory of *rent*, and Mr. Ricardo's theory of *foreign commerce*. If these discoveries be thought to constitute a *school*, Mr. Malthus must certainly be considered a leading member of that school : of the first, and most important of the three principles which we have named, he is generally believed to have been the discoverer ; of the second he has furnished one of the earliest expositions. Doctrines which make such havoc with the faith of our fathers, might naturally have excited the wrath of the Quarterly Review : and the duller geniuses among the orthodox, who cannot understand a joke, will wonder that in a professed attack upon the " new school," it should have passed over the most essential doctrines of that " school ;" but it is easy to see, that to refute their opinions, or any opinions, was the last thing which this writer had any thought of : all he sought was to ridicule Mr. Malthus, whom he wished to represent as actually not knowing what their essential doctrines are.

As for the three propositions which the Reviewer has hit upon, to distinguish the " new school" from that of Adam Smith and Mr. Malthus, the two last, as here stated, never were maintained by them at all : while the first, into which he resolves both the others, and which he holds up as the *most* important of all their doctrines, happens to be the *least* important ; and so far is it from being true, as he asserts, " that all the peculiar doctrines of the new system directly and necessarily flow" from this proposition, that not one of their doctrines, nor, so far as we know, of any other doctrines, flows from it at all ; it being, in truth, more a question of nomenclature and classification than one from which any important consequences are deduced. Granting, therefore, that the Reviewer has completely demolished these three propositions—two of which, indeed, we freely concede to him—all the fundamental principles of the " new school" remain untouched.

It must be owned, indeed, that Mr. Malthus is peculiarly sensitive on every thing which regards his measure of value ; a discovery, indeed, which he appears to cherish the more fondly, as no one, except himself, seems to be capable of appreciating it : but it is too much to attempt to persuade the public that Mr. Malthus is so wrapt up in the importance of his supposed discovery, as actually to believe that these insignificant disputes about value are the most important questions in political economy, questions upon which every thing depends—

questions of more consequence than the theories of rent, profits, and foreign trade!

We will now go a little deeper into the subject, and see what this pseudo-Malthusian has to say on each of the topics aforesaid. For this purpose we will follow his example, and begin with the first of the three principles; " That the quantity of labour worked up in commodities determines their exchangeable value."

The doctrine which our Reviewer comes out with, in opposition to this principle, proves how accurately he has imitated his great original : for it is no less than Mr. Malthus's favourite doctrine, with which all who have read his " Measure of Value" are familiar—that value depends upon labour and profits : a proposition which he supports in the following terms : —

' If, for instance, a useful stone inclosure, built from materials on the spot, were constructed in eight days by fifty common masons paid at half-a-crown a day, the inclosure, when completed and fit for use, would, on account of the very small quantity of profits concerned, be worth but little more than the labour employed upon it, that is, 400 days, or, in money, fifty pounds. Now, if we suppose a pipe of wine to be worth, when it is first ·put into the cask, exactly the same quantity of labour and money, but that it is to be kept two years before it is used, and that the rate of profits is fifteen per cent, it is obvious, that, at the expiration of that time, it must be sold at about £.65, or its value must be above 520 days instead of 400 days labour, in order that the conditions of its supply may be fulfilled. We have here, then, two commodities, which, by the hypothesis, have had the same quantity of labour employed upon them, and yet the exchangeable value of one of them exceeds that of the other above 30 per cent, on account of the very different quantity of profits worked up in each.

' Now let us suppose, that the rate of profits falls from 15 per cent to 6 per cent, then the value of the article, in which profits had very little concern, would remain nearly the same, the conditions of its supply being nearly the same ; while the conditions of the supply of the wine will have so essentially altered, without the slightest alteration in its quality, that, instead of being worth about 30 per cent more than the walls, it would now only be worth a little above 12 per cent more '— p. 310.

Now this is all very true, but " we think we have heard all this before :" it is, in truth, the old doctrine, about the influence of *time* on value ; and we think our readers will admit that it is at least as clearly and as forcibly stated in the following passage, as it is by the Reviewer : —

" It is hardly necessary to say, that commodities which have the same quantity of labour bestowed on their production, will differ in exchangeable value, if they cannot be brought to market in the same time.

" Suppose I employ twenty men at an expense of £1000 for a year in the production of a commodity, and at the end of the year I employ twenty men again for another year, at a further expense of £1000, in finishing or perfecting the same commodity, and that I bring it to market at the end of two years, if profits be 10 per cent, my commodity must sell for £2,310 ; for I have employed £1000 capital for one year, and £2,100 capital for one year more. Another man employs precisely the same quantity of labour, but he employs it all in the first year ; he employs forty men at an expense of £2,000, and at the end of the first year he sells it with 10 per cent profit, or for £2,200. Here then are two commodities having precisely the same quantity of labour bestowed on them, one of which sells for £2,310, the other for £2,200."

Now, to what author does the reader suppose we are indebted for this passage ?   To Mr. Malthus, or to Adam Smith ? No : to *Mr. Ricardo !**

So much for the novelty and importance of the Reviewer's first objection to Mr. Ricardo's doctrine of value. His second objection is, that " the quantity of profits which enters into the composition of commodities is greatly increased in all cases of an increase of fixed capital as compared with circulating :" this also, he himself admits to be " universally acknowledged :" indeed, Mr. Ricardo says, " This difference in the degree of durability of fixed capital, and this variety in the proportions in which the two sorts of capital may be combined, introduce another cause, besides the greater or less quantity of labour necessary to produce commodities, for the variations in their relative value : this cause is the rise or fall in the value of labour." Principles of Political Economy, p. 25.

So far, then, it seems, all parties are agreed ; and further objection, under this head, our Reviewer has none.

What then is this great question upon which we are to believe that the whole science depends? simply, as we have already observed, a question of nomenclature: the question, whether these facts, about which all are agreed, shall be contained in one expression or another ; whether this effect of *time,* and this effect of *fixed capital,* are ultimately resolvable into labour, and are included in the simple expression that value depends upon quantity of labour, or not : a question of pure curiosity, and of no practical use whatever. Yet this is the question upon

---

* Principles of Political Economy, 3rd edition, p. 34.

which our pseudo-Malthusian pretends to believe, that the whole of the peculiar doctrines of the "new school" depend '*

It is very well, if a Reviewer chuses to make a great noise about nothing. It is no novel practice, certainly, with Reviewers ; and as little so with Quarterly, as with any other Reviewers; but it is hard that Mr. Malthus should be held responsible for all the ignorance and confusion of ideas which the Reviewer chuses to impute to him, and should be deemed incapable of distinguishing between a question about words and a question about things, merely to afford a good joke to a Quarterly-Reviewer.

We have already remarked, that the second of the three propositions which the Reviewer puts into the mouth of the new school, " that demand and supply have no influence on prices and values except in cases of monopoly, or for short periods of time", never was maintained by them at all. They not only allow that demand and supply have *some* influence on value, but they assert that nothing else has any influence whatever, except in as far as it may be calculated to affect either the demand or the supply. When they say that cost of production regulates value, it is only because cost of production is that which regulates supply. If there be two commodities, produced by equal cost, what is the reason that they exchange for one another? The reason is, because if one of the two bore a higher value than the other, when the cost of production is the same, the profits of the two producers would be unequal, and it would be the interest of one of them to withdraw a portion of his capital from his own business and transfer it to that of the other; thus *increasing the supply* of the dearer commodity, diminishing that of the cheaper, until the equality of values is restored : and restored, as the reader will observe, not in contradiction to the principle of demand and supply, but in consequence of it. "It thus appears," says Mr. Mill [Elements of Political Economy, 2nd Ed. p. 88] "that the relative value of commodities, or, in other words, the quantity of one which exchanges for a given

---

* It is remarkable, that on this question of nomenclature, Mr. Ricardo actually *agreed with Mr. Malthus :* he did not indeed adopt the "measure of value," but he believed that those modifications of the principle that value depends upon quantity of labour, on which Mr. Malthus lays so much stress, were not included in the proposition, but required to be annexed to it by a qualifying clause. Some other political economists, indeed, particularly Mr. Mac Culloch and Mr. Mill, think differently; and in their opinion we ourselves concur : not, however, to weary our readers by discussing a question of no practical use, we shall content ourselves with referring them to the latter part of the chapter on exchangeable value, in the second edition of Mr. Mill's Elements.

quantity of another, depends upon *demand and supply*, in the first instance, but upon cost of production ultimately, and hence; in accurate language, upon cost of production entirely."

It is true that a variation in productive cost frequently takes place, and produces a corresponding variation in value, without any actual alteration of supply ; that an increase, for instance, of the productive cost of an article, raises its value without necessarily diminishing the supply, because all the parties concerned, whether as sellers or as purchasers, know that if the rise of value does not take place *without* a limitation of supply, it must take place *by* such a limitation. If, for example, a duty of a shilling per yard were imposed upon cloth, the dealers, in all probability, would quietly lay an additional shilling upon every yard of cloth which they might sell; and it would not necessarily follow that any capital would be withdrawn from the manufacture of cloth ; unless indeed the higher price had the effect of narrowing the demand, which is not improbable, but is altogether extrinsic to the question. Although, however, there would be no *actual,* there would even here be a *potential* limitation of supply ; upon which potential limitation, not only something would depend, but every thing would depend ; since cost of production itself would have no influence on value without it.

It is usual, indeed, to say that a fluctuation in demand and supply cannot have more than a temporary effect upon value: but this is merely because the fluctuation in the demand and supply must itself be temporary, unless accompanied by a change in cost of production. Could we suppose a permanent change in the proportion of the demand and supply to one another, independently of productive cost, value also would permanently vary, and cost of production would cease to have any influence over it. This, however, is to suppose the absence of free competition: an element which, in political economy, is always taken for granted unless otherwise expressed. There is not the smallest foundation, then, for the assertion, that the "new school" deny that values depend upon supply and demand.

But the malicious ingenuity of this Reviewer will not suffer Mr. Malthus to talk common sense, even when he is on the right side of the question : and though he is fighting shadows, yet even shadows baffle him, and drive him completely out of the field.

He begins by saying, that demand and supply, though they have no influence on labour, which is one of the ingredients of value, have an influence on profits, which is the other ingredient. To this proposition we shall not say whether we assent or not ; for this reason, that previously to committing ourselves for or against a proposition, we usually endeavour to attach some meaning to it, which, in this case, we confess our inability to do. We think we know what is meant by the influence of demand and supply : the demand and supply of cloth have an influence on the value of cloth ; the demand and supply of corn have an influence on the value of corn : but what is meant by " demand and supply" in the abstract, or what demand and supply it can be, which has an influence on *profits,* is a mystery which we cannot fathom.

When it has been our fate to peruse any of Mr. Malthus's lucubrations on the more intricate subjects of political economy, we have remarked, that although they are in general sufficiently obscure, yet if there is one part of them which is more obscure than another, it is where he attempts anything like explanation or illustration. This peculiarity of Mr. Malthus our satirist has very happily seized ; and so invariably has he adhered to the rule, that so soon as he begins to speak of throwing light upon a subject, from that moment we lose all hope of ever understanding it. Thus, under pretence of explaining the above proposition, which we thought had been of itself sufficiently incomprehensible, he has contrived to throw as thick a mist round it as would have sufficed to obscure the clearest demonstration in Euclid.

He begins by saying, that Mr. Ricardo has proved, that profits are determined by the proportion of the whole produce which *goes to labour;* this we at first thought we had understood ; for we have read Mr. Ricardo's work, and we know that he has proved that profits are determined by the proportion of the produce, which *goes to the payment of wages* : but we soon found what an egregious mistake we had committed, and how little we were capable of comprehending the fineness of our author's satire. This, he goes on to state, is " only one important step in the theory of profits, which, of course, cannot be complete till we have ascertained the cause which, under all circumstances, regulates this *proportion of the whole produce which goes to labour, immediate and accumulated.*" Now, as he himself has expressly excluded [p. 309] all consideration of rents, we were not a little puzzled by this last proposition; since, in our humble conception, the *whole* of the produce, with the exception of rent, goes to the payment either of immediate or accumulated labour—either of the labourer or of the capitalist : it is evident, therefore, that in using the expression, " the proportion of the whole produce which *goes to labour,*" he cannot have meant, the proportion which goes to the *payment of wages,* but that in this mysterious phrase there lurks some recondite meaning, to which the Reviewer, oracle-like, withholds from us the key.

To ascertain, then, what it is which regulates the proportion of the whole produce which "goes to labour," is his next object. The prevailing opinion he declares to be, that it depends upon the "greater or less demand for labour," compared, as we suppose, with the supply: in short, that wages depend upon the ratio between population and capital. This, however, we learn to be a vulgar error: the proportion of the produce which "goes to labour," really depending not upon the demand and supply of labour, but upon the demand and supply of *produce*. "The specific reason which occasions a larger or smaller proportion of the produce of a given quantity of labour to go to labour, is the fall or rise in the value of the whole produce of such labour, resulting from the temporary or ordinary state of the supply, compared with the demand"—p. 316.

We had been accustomed to believe, as we thought on pretty good grounds, and certainly in conformity with the doctrines of Mr. Malthus, in his Essay on Population, that the *ratio between population and capital* had been the regulator of wages: but we now learn it to be *the value of the whole produce*. Our satisfaction at the receipt of this new and unexpected information is greatly alloyed by the difficulty of comprehending it. We can understand what is meant by the *value of cottons*; namely, the quantity of other commodities for which a given quantity of cottons will exchange: we can understand in what manner cottons may rise or fall in value; namely, when a given quantity of cottons comes to exchange for a greater or less quantity of other commodities than before: but what is meant by the value of the *whole* produce, or how the whole produce of the land or labour of a country, or of the world, can be said to rise or fall in value, is a problem, of which we must leave it to wiser heads than our own to discover the solution. Value is a relative term. if it is not this, it is nothing: if any one talks about absolute value, or any other kind of value than exchangeable value, we know not what he means. One commodity may rise or fall in value, with respect to another; all commodities cannot rise or fall in value, with respect to themselves.

The Reviewer, however, thinks it incumbent upon him to know better, and the reader, we are sure, will join with us in admiring the originality and relevancy of the fact upon which his theory is founded. If cottons, says he, fall in value from abundant supply; of the cottons produced by the same quantity of labour, a greater proportion will be required to pay for that labour, and a smaller proportion will therefore remain for the capitalist; and, on the other hand, if cottons rise in value, from a diminished supply, a smaller proportion will suffice to pay the labourer, and a larger proportion will remain as profits to the capitalist. This is not only in itself altogether novel and of the highest importance, but seems to prove that (strange to relate!) the producer is benefitted by a high price of his goods—injured by a low one. The Reviewer next proceeds to generalize upon this grand discovery. The proportion, says he, of the *whole produce* which goes to labour, depends upon the *value of produce.* We at first regretted that he had not condescended to unfold to us the hidden process by which such a conclusion is drawn from such premises; but we speedily consoled ourselves with the reflection, that we have not lost much, since if he had, it is probable that we should not have understood him; nor, indeed, is there any just cause for wonder, that we should be unable to understand how a proposition is proved, when we cannot even comprehend the proposition itself.

In this chain of words, for we will not call them arguments, the experienced reader will not fail to recognize an exaggerated likeness of Mr. Malthus. Our anxiety, however, to convince him that we do not purposely conceal from him the connexion of ideas, but that we really give him the benefit of whatever meaning we can extract from those outward and visible signs of inward ideas, which, like other signs, frequently show themselves, when the reality which they are supposed to indicate does not exist, has induced us to withhold from him the best part of the joke; namely, a disquisition, of and concerning the " measure of value," which the Reviewer has contrived to intermix with the above *exposé,* as a remedy apparently for its unnecessary clearness. The disquisition itself certainly leaves no reason for complaint on the score of too great perspicuity; nor indeed on that of logic; from the rules of which, this writer holds himself completely exempt. He begins by laying down as a principle the proposition which he has undertaken to prove; and though this one assumption ought in all conscience to have been sufficient, he does not stop here, but bravely reiterates it in a variety of shapes in every succeeding sentence to the close. The proposition, and the logic by which it is proved, are worthy of one another; and there could not be a more bitter piece of satire, both upon the principle itself and upon its author.

We now approach the third of the propositions which " more especially characterize the new school of political economy." This is, as our readers have already been informed, " that the difficulty of production on the land is the regulator of profits, to the entire exclusion of the cause stated by Adam Smith, namely, the relative abundance and competition of capital." That the " new school" do not believe the " relative abundance and competition of capital" to be the regulator of profits, is no doubt true; nor do they even comprehend how there can be such a thing as competition of capital, unless it be competition for labour. Adam Smith supposed, that, when capital increased, the competition of capitalists induced them to lower their prices, and, by a necessary consequence, their profits. The " new school" dissent from this doctrine; first, because prices depend not upon the competition of capital, but upon the quantity of money in the country, compared with the quantity of commodities to be circulated, and the rapidity of circulation; and secondly, because, even granting that, as Adam Smith supposes, all prices would be lowered, profits would not be affected; for this very reason, because *all* prices would have fallen; in consequence of which every capitalist would be able to command, less money, it is true, but precisely the same quantity of all commodities which he desired to purchase, as before. The competition of capital, therefore, can, in no conceivable manner, operate to lower profits by lowering prices: and here Mr. Malthus is just as far from agreeing with Adam Smith as Mr. Ricardo himself. That there may be, and always is, a competition of capital for labour, is most true: this is the only competition of capital which Mr. Malthus acknowledges; and this competition has undoubtedly a tendency to raise wages, and, therefore, to lower profits; the limit to the rise of wages being the ratio between capital and population; wages, therefore, depend upon the ratio between population and capital, and profits depend upon wages: and this is the real doctrine of the " new school." Where the Reviewer found the doctrine, that " the difficulty of production on the land is the regulator of profits," he himself best knows.

The satire is here less refined than usual; for even had Mr. Malthus been capable of so grossly misunderstanding the doctrines of his opponents, he would scarcely, in that case, have been so simple as to expose his ignorance by *quoting*. Yet this the Reviewer has done [p. 320]. " This principle" (that the difficulty of production on the land is the regulator of profits), " which is adverted to in various parts of the treatise" (meaning Mr. M'Culloch's Essay on Political Economy), " is broadly laid down in the last section of the third division, in the following passage." A quotation follows; in which, after an attentive perusal, the passage most like the above proposition, which we can find, is the following :—

" The fall of profits, which invariably takes place as society advances and population becomes denser, is not owing to competition, but to a very different cause ; to a diminution of the power to employ capital with advantage, resulting either from a decrease in the fertility of the soil which must be taken into cultivation in the progress of society, or from an increase of taxation."

Here is a manifest insinuation, that Mr. Malthus is not only ignorant of the most elementary principles of the science, but that he is unable to understand a plain statement, conveyed in plain language. It is evident enough that Mr. M'Culloch, in the above passage, not only did not assert that the difficulty of production on the land is the sole regulator of profits (if he had he would have been the first man who ever maintained so preposterous a doctrine), but never intended even to speak of any fluctuation in profits, excepting that fall " which invariably takes place as society advances, and population becomes denser ;" that his meaning, in short, was, that whatever other causes might affect profits by affecting wages, there is one cause, namely, the increasing difficulty of producing the necessaries of the labourer, which must always ensure a rise of wages, and a consequent fall of profits, as population increases and cultivation is extended. Does the Reviewer deny this ? Mr. Malthus surely does not.

We pass over all that the Reviewer says, to prove that corn wages are not the same at all times and in all places ; never having heard of any body who asserted that they were, we think that he might have spared this portion of his labours. It is just as little to the purpose, that he triumphantly asks, how the fall of profits, which has taken place during the last eight or nine years, can be ascribed to the difficulty of production on the land ; as if it had ever been asserted, that profits could never fall from any other cause. But mark how the Reviewer himself accounts for the fall of profits. " What, then," says he, [p. 323] " was the cause of the fall of profits ? It was obviously a fall in the *value of produce !*" and not only this, but " a fall in the value of produce, owing to the abundance and competition of capital !"

The reader probably thinks that we have said enough on the subject of the " value of produce ;" but it is here that, for the first time, we get an incidental glimpse of what the phrase is intended to mean. This inveterate wag, who will never have done jeering Mr. Malthus, contrives once more to bring in our old acquaintance, the " measure of value." By a fall, it seems, in the *value of produce*, he all along meant a fall in the exchangeable value of commodities, *relatively to labour ;* in short, what any one else would have called a rise of wages : which is precisely the cause to which the " new school" ascribes the fall of profits. It is not to be supposed, however, that Mr. Malthus and the " new school" can be permitted to agree, on any one point. The sallies of our author's wit here become particularly lively. Only mark the figure which Mr. Malthus is made to cut, by this pretended disciple. This abundance and competition of capital, says he [p. 322], lowers profits by *occasioning a different division of what was produced, and awarding a larger proportion of it to the labourer, and a smaller to the capitalist.* Yet, though the labourer obtains both a greater *quantity* of commodities, and a greater *proportion,* he does not obtain *higher wages.*

' Innumerable facts concur to show, that this increased proportion awarded to the labourer continually takes place without being accompanied with any circumstances which indicate either an increased demand for labour, or an increase in the value of the same quantity of labour '—p. 325.

' It is universally allowed, that the money price of corn and commodities has fallen during the last nine years more than the money price of labour ; and while the merchant sees, that on this account the workmen whom he employs are paid a larger proportion of the commodities which they produce, we believe that there is not a single unsophisticated person in business who would not at the same time acknowledge, that this was not owing to the scarcity and increased demand for labour, but to the abundance and cheapness of the commodities produced, occasioned by the abundance and competition of capital in every department of industry '—pp. 324-5.

Nothing can be droller than the whole of this passage ; nor any thing more sarcastically humourous than the appeal to " unsophisticated persons in business." It only remains to intrust some competent person with the privilege of determining what " persons in business" are unsophisticated, and what the reverse ; a privilege which he seems to think can be confided to no one, with so great propriety as to himself.

But this inveterate enemy of Mr. Malthus is not even yet satisfied ; and having already made him, for the sake of his " measure of value," explain away almost all the fundamental principles of the science, he next proceeds to make him explain away the principle of population itself. Mr. M'Culloch had said, that an increase of capital, if unaccompanied by an increased difficulty of producing the necessaries of the labourer, is not likely to occasion a permanent fall of profits ; because, by raising the wages of labour, it stimulates the increase of population, so as, in all probability, to lower wages, and raise profits to the same rate as before. This opinion the Reviewer now finds to be erroneous : an increase of capital, provided it comes upon a *slack demand for produce* (that is, an eagerness on the part of the labourers to toil, none to enjoy), does not stimulate population. True it is, that it gives more and better food, clothing, and lodging, more necessaries, comforts, and enjoyments, to every labourer ; which we had hitherto believed to be the only way in which a rise of wages could possibly stimulate population ; but the labourers, to whatever degree better fed, clothed, and lodged, will not multiply. For why? because there is a slack demand for produce, and because they have not got a greater *value* than before.

It would have been satisfactory had the Reviewer informed us in what manner, upon this principle, a rise of wages can by possibility take place at all. If wages cannot rise, unless the labourer gets a greater value for his labour, and if commodities can never have a greater value unless they can command more labour, the supposition of a rise of wages involves a contradiction ; since, whatever quantity of food, clothing, and lodging a day's labour may command, it can never command more than the value of a day's labour. Although, however, it is not possible for wages to rise, it is possible for them to fall ; and (what is somewhat remarkable), it is when the labourer obtains the greatest quantity of necessaries, comforts, and enjoyments, and the greatest proportion of the produce, that his wages are lowest. The supposed increase of capital, instead of increasing, as we should have expected, the demand for labour, actually diminishes it, " and the mass of these funds would not be adequate to set so many people to work as before" [p. 327]. Now we have shewn that whatever is true of an increase of capital under the circumstances supposed, must necessarily be true of an increase of capital under any circumstances. If, therefore, capital continues to increase, and wages to rise, the demand for labour will continually diminish, and we may in time expect to see capital so plentiful and wages so high, that there will be no demand for labour at all ! At the close of this lucid exposition, the Reviewer cracks a bitter joke upon Mr. Malthus. " The theory on the subject," says he, " is very simple and clear." The reader, perhaps, thinks that the Reviewer himself has afforded as striking a proof as could be desired of the clearness and simplicity of the subject ; since, in spite of all his attempts to explain it, he has not succeeded in rendering it altogether unintelligible.

Although the three great fortresses of the " new school " are now utterly demolished, there remain, it would appear, certain outworks, from which it is still deemed necessary to dislodge them.   One of these is the doctrine of the impossibility of a general glut.   Having gone into this question at some length, in the article on War Expenditure in our third number, we shall not at present repeat the arguments which we then urged ; but the contrary side of the question is here supported by an argument which, for its strictness and relevancy, is worthy of notice. Mr. M'Culloch having said that for every excess in one commodity there must be a deficiency in another, the Reviewer observes, that this strikes him as peculiarly illustrative of the impracticability and inapplicability of some of the doctrines of the new school. " For," says he, " we would appeal to the experience of every person who, without being biassed by some previous prejudice, had turned the smallest attention to the subject, whether at the time when a general glut was talked of, there was the least ground for the assertion, that, although the state of the trade in cottons was ruinous, the capitalist engaged in making broad cloths or silks, or some other article which would absorb a large capital, was in the most prosperous and flourishing state, and inviting additional stock by high prices and high profits.   This assertion of corresponding deficiency, as applied to what is known to have taken place since the peace, appears to us," he facetiously observes, " as strange as if it were gravely asserted, that every man in the streets of London who was observed to have his head covered, would be found upon examination to have his feet bare. . . . We will venture to say, no one ever heard, as a matter of fact, from competent authority, that for some years together since the peace there was a marked deficiency of produce in any one considerable department of industry "—p. 330.

The *naïveté* with which he thus proposes to rebut demonstration by testimony, is truly amusing.   There is nothing, says Cicero, so absurd as not to have been maintained by some philosophers; and it may be said with equal truth, that in political economy there is no opinion, however absurd, whether on a question of fact or of principle, which may not easily be proved from " competent authority."   We are bold enough, however, in spite of " competent authority," to think that every one desires to consume to the extent to which he produces.   If he did not wish to consume either that which he produces or an equivalent, he would cease to produce.   But the demand of the community is made up of the demands of individuals : and if every individual have a demand exactly equal to his supply, so also must the demand of the whole community be equal to its supply. To say that there can never be a greater sum total of commo-

dities produced than the community wishes to consume, is merely
to say in other words, that people will not consent to labour
without a motive. The commodities, therefore,which are produced,
cannot, collectively considered, be in excessive quantity, though
they may be of the wrong kind. Too much may be produced
of one commodity; because, though all want some commodity,
all may not want *that* commodity. But as there cannot be an
excess on the whole, if there be too much of one commodity,
there must be too little of another. This reasoning is so clear
and convincing, that the idea of disproving it by a reference to
" competent authority " could have occurred to no one but a
Reviewer, who wishes to aim a side blow at the cause which he
professes to defend, and in behalf of which he insinuates (in
this instance justly) that there was nothing better to be said.

There is an attempt to prove, in opposition to Mr. M'Culloch,
that labour, employed in agriculture, is more productive than
labour employed in any other branch of industry ; which, if it
be meant as a joke, is so very dull a one, that if we could reconcile ourselves to a supposition which speaks so little for his
intellect, we should be half inclined to suspect that the writer
is in earnest. By wealth, we can understand nothing but necessaries, comforts, and enjoyments. How is it possible to say
whether agriculture, or manufactures, be most productive of
wealth? unless it is pretended to determine whether food or
clothing be most essential to the happiness of man. But manufacturing capital, it seems, yields no more than the ordinary
profits of stock ; while agricultural capital yields not only
profits but rent. True ; but rent (if Mr. Malthus's explanation
of it be correct) is the effect, not of the *greater* fertility of the
soil, but of the *unequal* fertility of different soils ; not of the
superior productiveness of agricultural, over every other capital,
but of the *unequal* productiveness of one agricultural capital and
another. So far is rent from being a proof of the superior productiveness of agriculture, that rent is highest when the productiveness of agricultural capital is the least; and when that
productiveness is greatest, that is, when none but the best land
is in cultivation, and when the return to capital from that land
is at its highest, there is no rent at all. At that time, according
to the Reviewer, the productiveness of agricultural and manufacturing capitals should be equal, and it is afterwards that
they become unequal : but in what manner? Does agricultural industry become more productive, or manufacturing industry less productive? Quite the contrary. As cultivation advances, the capital first applied to the land does not
become more productive than at first, while all capital subse-

quently applied is less so; nor is the productiveness of manufacturing capital diminished, but, on the contrary, it is probably increased by the invention of machinery and other expedients for abridging labour. If, then, at a time when there is no rent, agricultural capital, even that portion of it which yields the greatest return, is not more productive than capital employed in manufactures, it is difficult to see how the case should be altered by a mere change in the distribution; when the whole produce is no longer retained by the capitalist, but a part of it is given to the landlord.

We are aware, that, by arriving at this conclusion, we have laid ourselves open to the charge of " sweeping generalizations," which our author deems " fatal to all clear explanation" [p. 306]. However well-founded this censure may be, we think our remarks may bear, to say the least, a favourable comparison with his, in this respect; for, whatever may be our propensity to " sweeping generalizations," we doubt whether we have produced any thing so " fatal to all clear explanation" as some of his paragraphs. We have already had occasion to remark on the peculiar taste which this gentleman seems to entertain for the incomprehensible ; we might easily have adduced a greater number of specimens, but we have not room to transcribe the whole article into our pages. If, indeed, it be a merit to puzzle what is plain, to render intricate that which is simple, obscure that which is clear, and difficult that which is easy, it would be hard to find, in the whole circle of Political Economists, one with whose merits he might not vie.

But our readers have probably had enough of this merry writer ; and so have we. We cannot, however, conclude, without expressing (together with our sincere gratitude for the amusement which he has afforded to us) our anxiety (which, we hope, he will not consider unpardonable) to know whether he excels as highly in the serious as he does in the jocular mood. We hope that his genius will not prove to be of that kind, which can shine only in a single department of the field of human attainments. Having shown, when he unbends himself, and condescends to be facetious at the expense of a brother economist, what a pitch of perfection he can attain ; perhaps, when he next takes up the pen, to indite an article for the Quarterly Review, he may agreeably surprise us by writing common sense.

230

From *Edinburgh Review,*
January 1837

This is Empson's defense of Malthus which appeared in the 2nd ed., of
Principles. See Semmel's article, especially pp. 28-29 *supra.* *(Publisher)*.

[William Empson]

ART. IX.—*Principles of Political Economy considered with a
view to their Practical Application.* By the Rev. T. R. MAL-
THUS, F.R.S. Second Edition. To which is prefixed a Memoir of the Author's Life. 8vo. London : 1836.

MR MALTHUS first published his ' *Principles of Political Eco-
' nomy'* in the year 1820. The book was soon out of print :
and, although he continued to occupy himself more or less with its
revision, the present volume was left a posthumous, and, in some
degree, an unfinished work. On comparing the two editions together, the difference in their contents does not appear considerable enough to account for the number of years interposed between them. The two first chapters indeed are entirely rewritten ;
and a great variety of fresh matter is every where introduced.
But there is no change in the principles, except in the assumption that labour is a constant measure of value, and of this he
had given the public notice as far back as 1823. The arguments,
on which this new proposition was grounded, are, we think, the
least satisfactory part of all Mr Malthus's writings. This is to
be attributed mostly to the subject itself, and partly to his mode
of viewing it. It certainly arose by no means from want of attach-
ing sufficient importance to it, or of taking sufficient pains about
it, as all his friends, learned and unlearned, can bear witness.
Until some permanent measure of value had been agreed upon,
Mr Malthus considered that the very corner stone of a great portion of the science of political economy must be necessarily loose.
The last letters which he received from Mr Ricardo contain a

masterly criticism on his pamphlet of 1823. The objections stated in them appear to us to be conclusive. Mr Malthus himself frequently observed, that in political economy we must be content for the most part with approximations. And we should refer to the case in question, as an example of the truth of the general observation. There are but few things in life of which we have a perfect measure. Where we have not, we shall only aggravate our disadvantages by acting or reasoning as if we had.

Mr Ricardo and Mr Malthus lived together on the most friendly terms. Although, whenever they met or wrote, they appeared to meet and write only to discuss their differences, yet their friendship never suffered the slightest diminution on that account. On the contrary, like emulous alchymists, working by different processes, they found equal pleasure and profit in throwing their materials into each other's crucible; while their hearts were gradually and firmly knit by the discovery of those moral excellencies, which professed searchers after controverted truths are unfortunately seen to have more frequent opportunity than disposition to display. We have no intention of reviving, on this occasion, the discussion of the questions on which these eminent writers were at issue. But it may be of use to coarser natures to see a specimen or two of the manner in which great minds can differ and communicate their differences. On the original publication of the ' Principles of Political Economy,' Mr Ricardo wrote as follows :—

' I have read your book with great attention. I need not say that there are many parts of it in which I quite agree with you. I am particularly pleased with your observations on the state of the poor—it cannot be too often stated to them, that the most effectual remedy for the inadequacy of their wages is in their own hands. I wish you could succeed in ridding us of all the obstacles to the better system which might be established. I am sure I do not undervalue the importance of improvements in agriculture to landlords, though I may not have stated it so strongly as I ought to have done. You appear to me to overvalue them. I differ as much as I ever have done with you, in your chapter on the effects of the accumulation of capital.'—(*Letter, May* 4). ' I have been reading your book a second time with great attention, but my difference with you remains as firmly rooted as ever. Some of the objections you make to me are merely verbal ; no principle is involved in them. The great and leading point in which I think you fundamentally wrong is, that which Say has attacked in his Letters. On this I feel no sort of doubt.'—(*Sept.* 4.) ' I am quite sure that you are the last man who would mistate an adversary knowingly ; yet I find in your book some allusions to opinions which you represent as mine, and which I do not really hold. In one or two cases you, I think, furnish the proof that you have misapprehended me ; for you represent my doctrine one way in one place, and another way in another. After all, the difference between us does not depend on these points, and they are very secondary considerations. I have made notes on every passage in your book which I dispute, and have supposed myself about publishing a new edition of your work, and at liberty to mark the passage, with a reference to a note at the bottom of the page. I have in fact quoted three or four words of a sentence, noting the page, and then added my comment. The part of your book to which I most object is the last. I can see no soundness in the reasons you give for the usefulness of demand on the part of unproductive consumers. How their consuming without reproducing can be beneficial to a country, in any possible state of it, I confess I cannot discover.'—(*November* 24*th*, 1820).

Mr Malthus possessed in their utmost perfection the two great philosophical qualities of single-mindedness and patience. He could not contemplate any subject in the spirit of a partisan ; and his opinions were usually formed with a deliberation, and expressed with a reserve which left him next to nothing afterwards to undo. But in political economy he took more than his ordinary security against error. The boundaries of a new and extensive science were not likely to be extended, and its controversial chaos reduced to order by the partial incursions of amateurs. From the time that he first entered upon the study of it, he therefore made it the business of his life ; the one object on which the powers of his mind were steadily and systematically put forth. And he had his reward. The two great discoveries which have been made in it since the days of Adam Smith—those relating to population and rent—are identified with his name. During the whole interval between the two editions of his Political Economy, Mr Malthus was going over its principles and details, week after week, in his lecture-room and his study. If his opinions, meanwhile, underwent but little change, this was not owing to any unbecoming confidence in himself. No man's reason was ever less swayed by vanity or passion ; and the candid and equitable consideration for the understanding of others, which was general in him, was heightened with regard to Mr Ricardo, into sincere admiration and affection. The feelings under which the preparations for the second edition proceeded so slowly, were (we have no doubt) in great measure the same which had previously delayed the publication of the first. The following passage from one of Mr Ricardo's letters will probably explain their nature. ' By what you ' tell me in your letter, you have respected my authority much ' too highly ; and I do not consent that you should attribute to ' that respect the little activity you have displayed in getting ' your work finished.'—(Sept. 21, 1819.)—This friendly correspondence was closed only by death. Apparently it left both parties equally unconvinced. Mr Malthus had appreciated, however, so fully the philosophical talents of Mr Ricardo and the advantages which he had enjoyed from the interchange of criticisms with so kind and uncompromising an opponent, that the influence of his former deference in part remained with him, after the contest had passed into less favourable hands.   The periodical press, in the meantime, showed that he had all along active adversaries in the field, who would expect from him, on his reappearance, additional matter of greater novelty than he had it in his power honestly or usefully to produce.   On being reproached for his procrastination a little before his death, he replied, ' My views are before the ' public.   If I am to alter any thing, I can do little more than ' alter the language : and I don't know that I should alter it for ' the better.'   We have, therefore, this satisfaction.   The present edition is to be considered as unfinished only in point of composition.   In substance and in doctrine it contains the principles of Political Economy taught by Mr Malthus—the most original and successful of all its cultivators during a period when many have been distinguished ; and whom the importance of his discoveries has placed in the rank of its benefactors, next to Adam Smith.

A most interesting addition to the present volume is a Memoir of the Author, by the Bishop of Chichester.   The office of a biographer requires, above all others, a friendly and congenial nature.   Whether its duties are principally those of a testimony or a tribute they can seldom indeed have been so appropriately performed as in the present instance—by a Christian philosopher, the friend of the author for half a century, and worthy of his friendship.

This is a suitable opportunity for saying a few words on the nature of the services and character of Mr Malthus. Justice to his memory imperatively demands it.   While intemperate opponents rashly misrepresented him, and extravagant admirers as rashly misunderstood or caricatured him ; while he was abused by the vulgar, who knew not what they did, and neglected by the powerful, who had no such excuse, he himself was calm and silent.   But now that he is gone, what was highmindedness in him, would be baseness in the friends who survive him.   Injuries of this kind are among the things which are rightly held *contemnenda in nobis, non negligenda in nostris.*   But in doing justice to Mr Malthus more is concerned than the feelings of friendship, the sacredness of truth, or the grateful office of transmitting to posterity the light of a great and good example.   Disgraceful personalities have been prolonged for the purposes of public mischief.   Political economy—the science of civilisation—is sought to be discredited by the help* of private

---

* What do Mr Coleridge's literary executors expect that they are earning for themselves or for their author, by circulating posthumous

slander and the name of one of the best of men is made an igno-
minious by-word for inflaming the passions of the poor, against,
by far, the most sensible measure the English legislature ever
passed for the independence and relief of the classes that live by
labour. It is true, questions of this order ought to be discussed
on their own merits, independent of the merits of individuals.
But human nature it seems does not admit of so much reason.
Political economy is charged with hardness of heart. The science
can appear and call witnesses to character only in the persons of its
professors. We remember Sir James Mackintosh saying, that
he had known Adam Smith slightly, Ricardo well, Malthus intimately. He added, ' Is it not something to say for a science,
' that its three great masters were about the three best men I
' ever knew ?' The Poor Law Amendment bill is denounced as
a conspiracy on the part of the wealthier orders of society against
their poorer brethren. For the principles upon which this bill
has been constructed, the character of Mr Malthus, their veteran
advocate, is undoubtedly responsible. Now of this we are confident. First: that there were no limits to the personal humanity
of Mr Malthus, but what were imposed by his judgment, in order
that mere feeling might not do that which unenlightened feelings,

---

poisoned slaver against the name of Mr Malthus ? Against a man, remarkable with all who knew him for the faithful discharge of every duty
of private life : Of whom it is saying little to say that he was at least a
good husband and a good father. And under what authority is this
book-making outrage perpetrated ? The authority of one of those unlucky slaves to imagination and indulgence who dread the sight of a
duty, and whose lives and habits, even without the contrast of a comparison thus shamelessly provoked, push Christian forbearance to its
utmost limits. ' *Malthusianism.* Is it not lamentable—is it not even
marvellous—that the monstrous practical sophism of Malthus should
now have gotten complete possession of the leading men of the kingdom ! Such an essential lie in morals—such a practical lie in fact, as it
is too ! I solemnly declare that I do not believe that all the heresies
and sects, and factions, which the ignorance, and the weakness, and the
wickedness of man have ever given birth to, were altogether so disgraceful to man as a Christian, a philosopher, a statesman, or citizen, as
this abominable tenet.'—(P. 88.) ' The entire tendency of the modern
or Malthusian political economy is to denationalize.' (P. 327. Table-
Talk). ' Finally, behold this mighty nation, its rulers and its wise men
listening—to Paley and—to Malthus ! It is mournful, mournful.'—
(Literary Remains of S. T. Coleridge, p. 328). The representatives of
Mr Coleridge seem to be bent on doing their best towards destroying
the value of his opinion on any subject. Admiring much of his literary
criticism and all of his idolatry of Shakspeare, we are sorry for it.

as well as unenlightened consciences, are so often doing to defeat its own object. Next: that from the year 1798, when he first appeared before the public as an author, to the day of his death, there never fell a word relating to poor laws from his pen or from his lips, which, fairly construed, do not entitle him to be considered the advocate of the poor.

In his letter to Mr Whitbread, published in 1807, Mr Malthus expressly admits (p. 6, 13) that he did not wish, had he the power, to press his general poor law principles into practice in England, to the abolition, but only to the improvement, of our particular system. He declares, moreover, that, abstractedly, he would be an advocate for poor laws on principle (p. 11, 27, 30), the moment a poor law was proposed, which should not have the effect of lowering the rate of independent wages below the maintenance of an average family, and by increasing the proportion of dependent poor, leave them ultimately in a worse state than that from which it took them. ' To those who know me personally, ' I feel that I have no occasion to˙defend my character from the ' imputation of hardness of heart; and to those who do not, I can ' only express my confidence, that when they have attended to ' the subject as much as I have, they will be convinced that I ' have not admitted a single proposition which appears to detract ' from the present comforts and gratifications of the poor, without ' very strong grounds for believing that it would be more than ' compensated to them by the general and permanent improve- ' ment of their condition. The moral obligation of private, ac- ' tive, and discriminate charity, I have endeavoured to enforce in ' the strongest language of which I was capable ; and if I have ' denied the *natural right* of the poor to support, it is solely, to ' use the language of Sir F. M. Eden, after his able and labori- ' ous Inquiry into the State of the Poor, because it may be ' doubted whether any right, the gratification of which seems to ' be impracticable, can be said to exist.'—' I should indeed think ' that the whole, or a much greater sum, was well applied, if it ' merely relieved the comparatively few that would be in want, ' if there were no public provision for them, without the fatal ' and unavoidable consequence of continually increasing their ' number, and depressing the condition of those who were strug- ' gling to maintain themselves in independence. Were it possi- ' ble to fix the number of the poor, and to avoid the further de- ' pression of the independent labourer, I should be the first to ' propose that those who were actually in want should be most ' liberally relieved, and that they should receive it as a right and ' not as a bounty.' Yet there are hundreds of declaimers, like Mr Poulett Scrope, who seem either not to know or not to care for a word of this, but who tread and talk irreverently over a wise man's grave.

Mr Malthus was born in 1776. He enjoyed the inestimable blessing of having a clever and affectionate father. But he was still more fortunate. For, he was born with one of those temperate and discriminating natures, the possessor of which can profit not only by the excellencies but also by the defects and mistakes of those he loves. The father, Mr Daniel Malthus, was so intimate a friend of Rousseau's, that he was one of his executors. Their friendship is said to have been cemented by a similarity of tastes. There are symptoms in their characters of a more painful resemblance—something of that perilous union of strength and weakness, good sense and paradox, for which Rousseau was so remarkable. The following passage, in a letter from the father, gives us a glimpse of what the son must in the main have owed him. The author of the most sensible chapters in the Emilie could not have taken a wiser view of life, or have addressed his pupil in language more affectionately judicious :—

' You must make your way to us over bricks and tiles, and meet with five in a bed, and some of us under hedges; but every body says, they will make room for Robert. Every thing I have heard of you has given me the most heartfelt satisfaction. I have always wished, my dear boy, that you should have a love of letters ; that you should be made independent of mean and trifling amusements, and feel a better support than that of the next man who is idle enough to offer you his company. I have no doubt that you will be able to procure any distinction from them you please. I am far from repressing your ambition ; but I shall content myself with their adding to your happiness. Every kind of knowledge, every acquaintance with nature and art, will amuse and strengthen your mind, and I am perfectly pleased that cricket should do the same by your legs and arms. I love to see you excel in exercises of the body, and I think myself that the better half, and much the most agreeable one, of the pleasures of the mind, is best enjoyed while one is upon one's legs. This is pretty well for me to say, who have little else but my bed and my arm-chair. May you long enjoy all the delights of youth and youthful spirits, of an improving mind, and of a healthful body—but ever and above all, my dear boy, with virtue and its best affections in your heart.'

On the other hand, it is clear that the parental interposition was not always as reasonable in itself, nor the manner equally well calculated to win confidence and respect. The following letter represents their family relationship in rather a reversed position. It appears to have been written when Mr Malthus obtained his college fellowship. By the touching retrospect which it opens, it proves how early and insensibly in their intercourse the father had felt the superiority of the mild intelligence of his son :—

' I heartily congratulate you upon your success; it gives me a sort of pleasure which arises from my own regrets. The things which I have missed in life, I should the more sensibly wish for you. Alas! my dear Bob, I have no right to talk to you of idleness; but when I wrote that letter to you with which you were displeased, I was deeply impressed with my own broken purposes and imperfect pursuits. I thought I foresaw in you, from the memory of my own youth, the same tendency to lose the steps you had gained, with the same disposition to self-reproach, and I wished to make my unfortunate experience of some use to you. It was, indeed, but little that you wanted it, which made me the more eager to give it you, and I wrote to you with more tenderness of heart than I would in general pretend to, and committed myself in a certain manner which made your answer a rough disappointment to me, and it drove me back into myself. You have, as you say, worn out that impression, and you have a good right to have done it; for I have seen in you the most unexceptionable character, the sweetest manners, the most sensible and the kindest conduct, always above *throwing little stones into my garden*, which you know I don't easily forgive, and uniformly making everybody easy and amused about you. Nothing can have been wanting to what, if I were the most fretful and fastidious, I could have required in a companion; and nothing even to my wishes for your happiness, but where they were either whimsical, or unreasonable, or most likely mistaken. I have often been on the point of taking hold of your hand and bursting into tears at the time that I was refusing you my affections; my approbation I was precipitate to give you.'

The admirers of Rousseau will doubt whether he was manly enough to have written such a letter even to such a son. But yet how humiliating was the necessity! What a lesson to characters that give undue precedence in the heraldry of our nature to impulse and imagination—that suppose a passionate susceptibility can come in any form but what is poor and apologetic before the presence of majestic reason! In a case of this kind, unless they are well regulated, the greater the powers the greater the disorder. But all regulation proceeds upon proportion. It is probable that the irregularities which Mr Malthus cannot have observed without much uneasiness in his father's ill-adjusted mind, early directed his attention to this fundamental truth. It was a truth he was constantly repeating in different ways. The dependence of wealth upon proportion is the main doctrine of the latter part of his Principles of Political Economy. He believed in the universal prevalence of a law resembling the law *de maximis et minimis* in fluxions. And he has added a note (Principles, p. 376), for the express purpose of reminding the reader that it is not in political economy alone that so much depends upon proportions, but throughout the whole range of nature and art. The lesson which he sought to impress on others, he faithfully applied to himself; and so successfully, that few characters have ever existed of more perfect symmetry and order.

Some of the peculiarities of Mr Daniel Malthus were likely to reappear in the persons of those whom he took into partnership with him in the education of his son. It is difficult to guess what was the principle of selection which carried the young pupil, from between the age of nine or ten and his entrance at Cambridge, under the successive roofs of Richard Graves, the Warrington Academy, and Gilbert Wakefield. The influence, however, of these instructors was evidently confined to the general encouragement and mechanical direction of his studies. The real formation of his moral and intellectual nature was in wiser hands. In this higher department, he appears throughout to have been so much his own great schoolmaster, that neither upon the surface of his mind nor in its depths was there any thing to be perceived that could be traced to the schools in which he had been brought up—nothing either of the wayward father or the eccentric novelist, of the scrupulous nonconformist or the presumptuous polemic. Difficulties which would be ruinous to an ordinary disposition, may accordingly have been serviceable in the strengthening and perfecting of his. The early habit of having to think and decide for himself, would force on him a steadiness beyond his years. While the necessity, in which he was often placed, of differing from those whom he otherwise regarded with affection and esteem, doubtless contributed essentially to that combination of universal kindliness towards others, with strict personal self-respect, which met so happily in his character. For this purpose his temperament had indeed been excellently well commingled from the first, qualifying him to enter into and come out of all encounters with goodwill and honour. The account sent home by Mr Graves of his juvenile prowess is a picture of the spirit with which he was ready to the last to carry on the literary battles in which his after life involved him. ' Don ' Roberto, though most peaceably inclined, and seeming even to ' give up his just rights rather than to dispute with any man, yet, ' paradox as it may seem, loves fighting for fighting's sake, and ' delights in bruising; he has but barely recovered his eyesight, ' and yet I have much ado to keep him from trying again the ' chance of war; and yet he and his antagonist are the best friends ' in the world, learn together, assist each other, and, I believe, ' love each other better than any two boys in the school.' This reads like an apt prelusion to the correspondence with Mr Ricardo—all contention and all affection. Should there be any among his later adversaries with whom the analogy does not answer in all its parts, they may be assured that they have had only themselves to blame.

At the University, the principle *esse magis quam videri*, which Mr Malthus made the motto of his life, led him to distribute his attention generally among the different studies of the place —a mode of proceeding he entirely reversed as soon as his general education might be considered to be completed. We have already remarked that he embraced political economy as his intellectual profession. From that time he gave up other subjects, except occasionally. In his views of life and in his management of himself, he was a utilitarian of the right sort. Under this conviction, he had set about learning to make himself useful from an early age. His quarrel with the followers of Bentham was only in their narrow conception of utility, and in their apparent ignorance of human nature. Otherwise, he was as stout a utilitarian in faith and practice, as ever mounted that cockade. While at the University, he observes of himself, in answer to an injudicious interference which his father had sought to make with the course of his reading :—
‘ I am by no means inclined to get forward without wishing to
‘ see the use and application of what I read. On the contrary, I
‘ am rather remarked in college for talking of what actually exists
‘ in nature, or may be put to real practical use.’ From the turn of mind which he thus mentions as a characteristic of his academical habits, he never departed. He had no notion of theory being any thing but science grounded upon and amenable to experience. Mr Ricardo and Mr Malthus had both minds eminently philosophical. But they differed chiefly in this, that, in looking at their subjects philosophically, the man of business delighted to dwell among and follow out abstract principles, while the professor was constantly enquiring after practical results. Mr Malthus entitled his work, ‘ Principles of Political Economy, *considered*
‘ *with a view to their practical application.*’ Mr Ricardo, observing upon the criticisms on himself which his friend had introduced, notices this distinction in their points of view :—‘ After the frequent
‘ debates between us, you will not be surprised at my saying that I
‘ am not convinced by your arguments on those subjects on which
‘ we have long differed. Our differences may, in some respects,
‘ I think, be ascribed to your considering my book as more prac-
‘ tical than I intended it to be. My object was to elucidate prin-
‘ ciples, and to do this I imagined strong cases that I might show
‘ the operation of those principles.’ This latter mode of writing gives a much more masterly air to its speculations ; and a species of inventive logic may be applied in it of a higher order. But there is a previous point for consideration. It should be first

settled whether political economy approaches most nearly to the conditions of mathematical or moral science.   For upon this must depend the choice of the mode of proceeding and of reasoning which may be most successfully employed in the developement of its truths.   In all things appertaining to politics and morals, extreme cases alter the whole question. Whatever depends upon proportion must necessarily be always matter of degree.

At the age of thirty, Mr Malthus felt prepared to enter the lists. He began with politics—the politics of 1796. The pamphlet still exists in MS., but was never printed. It was to have been called ' The Crisis, a View of the Present Interesting ' State of Great Britain, by a Friend to the Constitution.'   His first object was, as a friend of freedom, to protest against Mr Pitt's administration. His second, as the friend of order and moderation, to arbitrate between extreme parties. The allies whom he looked to in this patriotic cause, were to come from the camp of penitent country gentlemen ; the means which he recommended were the redress of grievances.   On the one hand, he says— ' The corresponding society is, I fear, little calculated to answer ' any useful purposes of reform.'   On the other, ' In the country ' gentleman of 1796, it is impossible to recognise that old and ' noble character, the jealous guardian of British freedom.'   He goes on therefore to state—

' It appears to me that nothing can save the Constitution but the revival of the true Whig principles in a body of the community sufficiently numerous and powerful to snatch the object of contention from the opposing factions.   In the Portland party, it is in vain to look for a revival, fettered with blue ribbands, secretaryships and military commands : freedom of action may be as soon expected from prisoners in chains. Where then are we to look for the principles that may save us ? The only hope that Great Britain has, is in the returning sense and reason of the country gentleman, and middle classes of society, which may influence the legislature to adopt the safe and enlightened policy, of removing the weight of the objections to our constitution by diminishing the truth of them.'

If Mr Malthus had any predilections which it may be thought that he was disposed to extend further than reason would strictly justify, they would seem to be his views, whether in politics or in political economy, concerning what is called the landed interest. We see here what he expected from the squires in 1796. Unknown to himself, these partialities may have helped to bias a little the balancing powers of his mind, when, after the peace, he attempted to weigh in a scale of the greatest nicety the advantages and disadvantages of corn laws. At a later period, in his investigation of the question, whether the nation would be richer if the law of primogeniture were abolished, he could not help adding—

‘ In all cases of this kind there are higher considerations to be attended to than those which relate to mere wealth. It is an historical truth whick cannot for a moment be disputed, that the first formation, and subsequent preservation and improvement of our present constitution, and of the liberties and privileges which have so long distinguished Englishmen, are mainly due to a landed aristocracy. And we are certainly not yet warranted by any experience to conclude that without an aristocracy, which cannot certainly be supported in an effective state but by the law of primogeniture, the constitution so established can be in future maintained. If then we set a value upon the British Constitution, if we think that, whatever may be its theoretical imperfections, it has practically given a better government, and more liberty to a greater mass of people for a longer time than any which history records, it would be most unwise to venture upon any such change as would risk the whole structure, and throw us upon a wide sea of experiment, when the chances are so dreadfully against our attaining the object of our search.’

Mr Malthus was a reformer long before reform became the fashion. But, always moderate and always consistent, it seems that it was not without an effort that he admitted the necessity of the Reform Bill of Lord Grey. The course of his conversion on this question coincided with that of Sir James Mackintosh, and of most other thinking men who were really at heart reformers. The following note to the above passage shows the mixed feelings of hope and fear with which his cautious judgment accepted the Reform Bill in the first instance. We think that we may now congratulate our countrymen that the conditions, upon which the philosopher suspended his unqualified approbation, have been substantially fulfilled.

‘ This was written in 182). Imperious circumstances have since brought on a reform of a more sudden and extensive nature than prudence would have perhaps suggested, if the time and the circumstances could have been commanded. Yet it must be allowed, that all which has been done, is to bring the practical working of the constitution nearer to its theory. And there is every reason to believe, that a great majority of the middle classes of society, among whom the elective franchise has been principally extended, must soon see that their own interests, and the interests and happiness of those who are dependent upon them, will be most essentially injured by any proceedings which tend to encourage turbulence, and shake the security of property. If they become adequately sensible of this most unquestionable truth, and act accordingly, there is no doubt that the removal of those unsightly blots, of those handles, which, with a fair show of reason, might at any time be laid hold of to excite discontents and to stir up the people, will place the British Constitution upon a much broader and more solid base than ever.’

Particular trades have particular diseases. So different professions are exposed to different moral dangers. Mr Malthus was a clergyman—a most conscientious one, pure and pious. We never knew one of this description so entirely free from the vices of his caste. Among the remedies which the youthful politician proposed in the *Crisis*, there was one the wisdom of which his personal acquaintance with the nonconformists authorized him to enforce. He lived to witness at last the partial application of his mild prescription, and to rejoice in its success. When will the principle of Paley's chapter on Religious Establishments be allowed to bring peace to Ireland? If men of the spirit of Malthus and Paley had represented the class of churchmen from which, during the last fifty years, English bishops had been recruited, dissenters would by this time be quietly studying at the English universities, and their church itself would be comparatively at rest. In church reform, a more equal distribution of its revenues is by no means an advantage of as much unmixed good as would follow from an extensive infusion of a more liberal spirit among its members. A generation or two of real Whig bishops would make the general temper of the Church of England quite a different thing. Mr Malthus is writing in 1796 on the policy of religious exclusions :

' An instance of the evil effects of this kind of policy occurs in the present state of the Dissenters in England. As a body, though there are certainly many individual exceptions, they may now almost be considered as professed enemies to the State as well as the Church ; yet at the revolution of 88, when the constitution was fixed in its present state, the nation was greatly indebted to them for their assistance ; and since that time, till of late, they have been among the firmest friends of the constitution. If during this period, the tests that related to them had been removed, and they had been admitted to equal privileges with the rest of the community ; we should never have seen the present violent opposition from them to the established government. And perhaps if the mother church prompted by an universal charity, had extended her pale to admit a set of men, separated by such slight shades of difference in their religious tenets, such a conduct, so far from endangering the holy building, I must ever think would have added strength and safety both to the Church and the State. Admitted to equal advantages, and separated by no distinct interests, they could have no motives peculiar to themselves for dislike to the government. And as neither religious nor political principles are born with men, the next generation, educated at the same seminaries, and mixing indiscriminately in other society, would quickly be lost and undistinguished in the great mass of the community. An observation on this subject which is given to Mr Courteney, though it has at first the air of one of his usual witticisms, is founded on the justest reasoning, and a knowledge of mankind. " For my part, I hate the Dissenters, and I vote for a repeal of the tests that I may hear of them no more." '

But as for hating, Mr Malthus could hate nobody—which, considering the strength of his feelings, public and private, and the provocations which for forty years he was perpetually receiving, was almost as wonderful a circumstance, as that any body could be found capable of hating him.

The object of our present notice is not so much to make a statement or offer proof in behalf of Mr Malthus's talents, as to bring before the public, in a connected form, the means of judging of his character. It is with this view that we have extracted the above political passages from his unpublished pamphlet. His later writings were almost purely scientific, and his nature was utterly averse from all display, political as well as otherwise. It is probable, therefore, that the public may not generally have been aware of the largeness of his popular sympathies, and the sterling liberality of his political opinions.

The part of the *Crisis*, which, with reference to Mr Malthus's literary history is the most curious—that is, its political economy—remains to be mentioned. In the course of his argument, he enters at large into the distresses and the dissatisfactions of the labouring classes of 1796, and discusses the nature of the relief which he conceives poor laws might and should supply. Many persons have been desirous of tracing the source and current of Mr Malthus's doctrines. A passage in this essay contains the earliest intimation which exists, of his having already begun to think upon the principle of population. But, from all the observations, by which the passage is surrounded, concerning the condition of the poor and the means by which poverty may be most effectually alleviated, it is evident that as yet he was only at the threshold. At this time he was as little aware, as any other writer who had stumbled upon the principle before him, of the immense importance of the practical applications which it involved. 'On ' the subject of population,' he observes, ' I cannot agree with ' Archdeacon Paley, who says, that the quantity of happiness in ' any country is best measured by the number of people. In- ' creasing population is the most certain possible sign of the hap- ' piness and prosperity of a state ; but the actual population may ' be only a sign of the happiness that is past.'

Mr Malthus owed the discovery, which will immortalize his name, mainly to his benevolence. Instead of his speculations on population having hardened his heart against the interests of the poor, it was the eartnestness and the perseverance with which he set himself to work in behalf of those very interests, that first fixed

his attention upon these particular speculations. In the same manner, his progressive conviction of the extent to which the interests
of the lower orders were comprised in them, alone gave them, in
his sight, the value which he so justly set upon them.   The consideration of the several schemes for reducing the hardships of the
poor within the smallest compass, was the task which he originally
undertook. He brought to it a resolute purpose and a philosophical
mind; and he never quitted it, until, by degrees, the whole subject
of population in all its relations and consequences had spread
itself out before him. The consequence was, that his views as to
the means by which the pains of poverty might be most effectually relieved were completely reversed. It was not that his humanity became narrowed, but that his knowledge became enlarged.
If popular declaimers ever put themselves in the way of learning
humility and charity, it might do something towards teaching
them these virtues, to be informed, that when Mr Malthus first
entered upon the enquiries, among which he passed the remainder of a retired and thoughtful life, he entertained most of
the erroneous opinions in which they are immersed at present.
He had to do what they refuse to do—to unlearn false knowledge,
and to master the prejudices of his age and country. This made
him frequently remark that there was no science in which first
impressions were so generally wrong as in political economy. We
have repeatedly heard him say that the two converts of whom he
was most proud, were Dr Paley and Mr Pitt. It will be seen,
however, that he had had to begin with himself—the great victory
of all.
    No contemporary volume produced so powerful an effect upon
the age in which it was written as the Essay on Population. It
has this distinction too. Popular fictions drop like May flies into
the stream. Even many truths, now thought much of, will lose
their value with posterity. But the importance of the truths announced in the Essay on Population must last for ever. Any one
who has taken the trouble to enquire into this subject, will learn
what was the state in which Mr Malthus found it. A swarm of
inconsistencies—light and darkness mixed together, even in
minds like those of Montesquieu and Süssmilch. The real ignorance, in which the little knowledge that was possessed upon the
matter was held suspended, and was in consequence rendered
worse than useless, cannot be better shown than by Mr Malthus's notice of the writer, from whose publications more than
from those of any other person he picked up the hints which
directed him to the truth.
    'I own that I felt myself obliged to draw a very opposite conclusion
from the facts advanced in Dr Price's two volumes. *I had for some*

time been aware, that population and food increased in different ratios ; and a vague opinion had been floating in my mind, that they could only be kept equal by some species of misery or vice ; but the perusal of Dr Price's two volumes of Observations, after that opinion had been conceived, raised it at once to conviction. With so many facts in his view, to prove the extraordinary rapidity with which population increases when unchecked; and with such a body of evidence before him, to elucidate even the manner by which the general laws of nature repress a redundant population; it is perfectly inconceivable to me how he could write* the passage that I have quoted. He was a strenuous advocate for early marriages, as the best preservative against vicious manners. He had no fanciful conceptions about the extinction of the passion between the sexes, like Mr Godwin, nor did he even think of eluding the difficulty in the ways hinted at by M. Condorcet. He frequently talks of giving the prolific powers of nature room to exert themselves. Yet with these ideas, that his understanding could escape from the obvious and necessary inference, that an unchecked population would increase, beyond comparison, faster than the earth, by the best directed exertions of man, could produce food for its support, appears to me as astonishing, as if he had resisted the conclusion of one of the plainest propositions of Euclid.'—(Edition of 1798.)

It is always interesting to trace the degrees by which great truths have ripened, and the circumstances under which they are safely harvested at last. In this instance Mr Malthus has enabled us to do so. In 1796 he had seen so little of his way, that he was a warm advocate of Mr Pitt's Poor Law Bill, and of the *jus trium liberorum.* Between 1796 and 1798, the truth was forced upon him (as he has mentioned in the last extract) by the evidence which Dr Price had brought forward in the controversy with Mr Howlett, concerning the increase or decrease of the population of England since the Revolution. About that time he happened to have an eventful conversation with his father upon the prospects opened to society by a paper in Godwin's Enquirer. The father, as might be expected, took flight, and floated along with the visions of human perfectibility. The son opposed the law of population as a fatal obstacle in the way. The zeal of this family discussion, and the temporary excitement of the rhapsodists to whose serious refutation it was addressed, made an author

---

* The passage alluded to expresses an opinion that if we would only live in the country, and lead natural lives, diseases would disappear, and death come upon us as a sleep, by imperceptible decay. Dr Price believed that the intrinsic prolific powers of the human species decreased with civilisation. Mr Godwin could not say whether the human race began with a pair, but he thought from appearances that, it was very likely, it would end with one.

1837.   *Life, Writings, and Character of Mr Malthus.*

of Mr Malthus on this occasion rather before his time. The Essay of 1798 establishes that he had then got at the principle, but little more. By 1803 he had collected his evidence, arranged his argument, and verified its permanent connexion with the happiness of mankind. Whether he saw originally the extent to which moral restraint may operate as a check on population, is comparatively indifferent. It is probable that he did not. It was incidentally and strikingly alluded to,* but not formally enumerated among the checks in his first Essay. Operate as extensively as it may, it can never operate so universally as to prevent the pressure of population from lowering the standard of human happiness below the expectations of Condorcet and Godwin. Therefore it can never affect the substance of that limited argument. But the Essay of 1803 was a new, matured, and comprehensive work. This, therefore, is the year in which Mr Malthus may be said to have taken out the patent for his discovery. He now for the first time claimed his own. In doing so, he notices the previous authors who had treated on the subject; and points out what they had done already—what they had left for him to do—and what he should leave to be done by others. After naming them—

‘ Much, however, (he states) remained yet to be done. Independently of the comparison between the increase of population and food, which had not perhaps been stated with sufficient force and precision, some of the most curious and interesting parts of the subject had been either wholly omitted or treated very slightly. Though it had been stated distinctly, that population must always be kept down to the level of the means of subsistence; yet *few inquiries had been made into the various modes by which this level is effected ; and the principle had never been sufficiently pursued to its consequences, and those practical inferences drawn from it, which a strict examination of* its effects on society appears to suggest.”

This is what Mr Malthus has done hImself. He adds, in 1806—

‘ The chief object of my work was to enquire what effects these laws, which I considered established in the first six pages, had produced, and were likely to produce on society ; a subject not very readily exhausted. The principal fault of my details is, that they are not sufficiently particular ; but this was a fault which it was not in my power to remedy. It would be *a most curious, and to every philosophical mind a most interesting piece of information, to know the exact share of the full power of increase which each existing check prevents ;* but at present I see no mode of obtaining such information.’

---

* As there is no index to the volume, that class of readers is referred to the passages, p. 217–276.

247

This is Mr Malthus's legacy for his successors. So completely had Mr Malthus at this time proved his case, that, on this part of his argument, he neither added nor altered any thing of much importance during the course of thirty years. Yet he was not only open to conviction but grateful for criticism. For example, he weeded out, from time to time, a few obnoxious metaphorical expressions which had given offence to certain readers; and he always spoke in the highest terms of the ability with which Dr Sumner had fought the religious part of the battle in the *Records of the Creation.* Mr Malthus might have been forgiven for not having anticipated this necessity. So capricious and contradictory are mankind, that, among the religious sects of the earlier ages, there was one which had taken up as their peculiar symbol, the probation comprised in the principle of population. The Shakers have since adopted the doctrine. ' Times and seasons ' —fixed for generation in animals—left to man as a trial—abused ' by him, typified by eating the apple.' From his narrative of the consequences of the forbidden fruit on our first parents, Milton might have studied ' the summary view of the Millennial *Church* ' *or United Society of Believers.*' Mr Malthus all along conceived that the particular case of physical and moral evil connected with the proportion between population and food, was only distinguished from other cases belonging to the general and unfathomable question of the existence of evil, by our being enabled to see a little more of our way towards an explanation of its object in this case than in many others. The extensive nature of the trials which the difficulty raises is very evident; while in every particular instance, the degree in which the difficulty exists is a circumstance eminently under the control of the particular individual.

It would not be surprising if, in his analysis of the causes of poverty, Mr Malthus should have discovered the peculiar nature of the evil to which the lower atmosphere of society is exposed, before he discovered the principle of the safety lamp by which the danger may be, to a considerable degree, evaded. In point of fact, however, the discoveries were, as far as we have the means of judging, nearly contemporary. In the title-page of the edition of 1803, the Essay on Population is announced to be ' a view of ' its past and present effects on human happiness; with an en- ' quiry into our prospects respecting the future removal or miti- ' gation of the evils which it occasions.' The subject thus branches off into three periods, the past, the present, and the future. The checks on population in them are divided into the positive and preventive. Misery and vice, in some shape or another, constitute the former, moral restraint the latter. With regard to the degree that these checks have respectively operated, both formerly and at present, Mr Malthus has expressed the decisive opinion which experience and observation warrant. For the future, it would have been very unlike him to have spoken with equal assurance, or to have done much more than offer up encouraging hopes and earnest prayers. As far as past times are concerned, Mr Malthus uniformly retained his original classification, by which the checks then actually in force are confined to misery and vice, and the words, vice and misery, are left to be understood in their coarser meaning. ' I believe Mr Godwin would ' find it difficult to name any check, which in past ages has ' contributed to keep down the population to the level of the ' means of subsistence, that does not fairly come under some ' form of vice or misery ; except, indeed, the check of moral ' restraint, which I have mentioned in the course of this work ; ' and which, to say the truth, whatever hopes we may en- ' tertain of its prevalence in future, has undoubtedly, in past ' ages, operated with inconsiderable force.' In what proportion the different checks are taking hold of society in its present state, every body who will be at the pains of making the requisite observations has the same means of judging for himself as the author of the Essay on Population. It is a question of fact, where within a certain circle we have all of us the facts before us. Mr Malthus, in 1803, on apportioning the apparent improvement which has taken place in modern times, carefully distinguished the moral restraint, which is satisfied only by entire sensual forbearance, from the prudential restraint, by which a party is prevented from marrying, and nothing more. A moralist and a clergyman, he necessarily considered that simple abstinence from marriage might be only a mitigated species of vice. In the prudential restraint thus explained, he thought that he saw the principal cause, by means of which modern Europe has superseded, to a considerable extent, the more violently penal forms by which vice and misery were formerly represented. ' An infrequency of the marriage union, from the fear of a ' family, is the most powerful of the checks which in modern ' Europe keep down the population to the level of the means of ' subsistence.' Mr Malthus had nothing of Mandeville in his composition. It was not likely, therefore, that he should be morally content with the modification of vice, which he has here described. A considerable difference of opinion may probably prevail with respect to the average point which a pure moral restraint has hitherto reached in a large portion of any community. This difference will of course be greatly increased, as soon as we come to prognosticate for after times. On this subject, as on all others, the future presents a tempting field for speculation. It is a field on which every one may and will take his own line : and where it will be much more easy to assert and contradict, than to offer either proof or probabilities of any very imposing order, upon either side. On introducing the principle of moral restraint into his classification in 1803, Mr Malthus stated, that, in doing so, he hoped that he had ' not violated the principles of ' just reasoning, nor expressed any opinion respecting the proba- ' ble improvement of society, in which he was not borne out by ' the experience of the past.' Mr Malthus gladly recognised the possibility that, as civilisation practically descended into the mass of the people, the influence of moral restraint upon the course of population might become more and more perceptible. But he was too cautious a philosopher to venture far into the unknown regions of wild analogy or mere conjecture. The day-dreams of Condorcet and Godwin had showed him the lengths we may be carried, if we once abandon experience for more enchanting guides. Human nature remaining the same as at present, his expectations on this point were by no means sanguine. Having satisfied, however, his conscience argumentatively by noticing the limits, indefinite as they were, within which he had felt compelled to circumscribe his hopes, he committed his work to the judgment of the public with the following forcible and affectionate appeal :—

' From a review of the state of society in former periods, compared with the present, I should certainly say, that the evils resulting from the principle of population have rather diminished than increased, even under the disadvantage of an almost total ignorance of their real cause. And if we can indulge the hope that this ignorance will be gradually dissipated, it does not seem unreasonable to expect that they will be still further diminished. The increase of absolute population which will, of course, take place, will evidently tend but little to weaken this expectation, as every thing depends upon the relative proportions between population and food, and not on the absolute number of people. In the former part of this work it appeared, that the countries which possessed the fewest people, often suffered the most from the effects of the principle of population; and it can scarcely be doubted, that, taking Europe throughout, fewer famines and fewer diseases arising from want have prevailed in the last century, than those which preceded it. On the whole, therefore, though our future prospects respecting the mitigation of the evils arising from the principle of population, may not be so bright as we could wish, yet they are far from being entirely disheartening, and by no means preclude that gradual and progressive improvement in human society, which before the late wild speculations on the subject, was the object of rational expectation. To the laws of property and marriage, and to the apparently narrow principle of self-love, which prompts each individual to exert himself in bettering his condition, we are indebted for all the noblest exertions of human genius, for every thing that distinguishes the civilized from the savage state. A strict enquiry into the principle of population obliges us to conclude, that we shall never be able to throw down the ladder by which we have risen to this eminence; but it by no means proves that we may not rise higher by the same means. The structure of society, in its great features, will probably always remain unchanged. We have every reason to believe, that it will always consist of a class of proprietors and a class of labourers ; but the condition of each, and the proportion which they bear to each other, may be so altered as greatly to improve the harmony and beauty of the whole. It would indeed be a melancholy reflection, that while the views of physical science are daily enlarging, so as scarcely to be bounded by the most distant horizon, the science of moral and political philosophy should be confined within such narrow limits, or at best be so feeble in its influence, as to be unable to counteract the obstacles to human happiness arising from a single cause.'

In a question of proportion between food and population, Mr Malthus was not likely to overlook so plain a proposition as that every successive addition to the food must have a favourable effect towards improving that side of the proportion. But, in order to avoid doing more harm than good, by raising our expectations in that quarter too highly, he thought it expedient to point out so much the more strongly how little, in comparison, any increase of food, taken by itself, could contribute towards a permanent improvement of the condition of the poor.

' In an endeavour to raise the proportion of the quantity of provisions to the number of consumers in any country, our attention would naturally be first directed to the increasing of the absolute quantity of provisions ; but finding that as fast as we did this, the number of consumers more than kept pace with it, and that with all our exertions we were still as far as ever behind, we should be convinced that our efforts directed only in this way would never succeed. It would appear to be setting the tortoise to catch the hare. Finding, therefore, that from the laws of nature, we could not proportion the food to the population, our next attempt should naturally be to proportion the population to the food. If we can persuade the hare to go to sleep, the tortoise may have some chance of overtaking her. We are not however to relax our efforts in increasing the quantity of provisions ; but to combine another effort with it, that of keeping the population, when once it has been overtaken, at such a distance behind, as to effect the relative proportion which we desire ; and thus unite the two grand desiderata, a great actual population and a state of society in which squalid poverty and dependence are comparatively but little known ; two objects which are far from being incompatible.'

Such was the language of Mr Malthus in 1803, upon the mode in which this proportion would be best considered for practical purposes. The following passage from the new edition of his

251

Political Economy, will prove what little occasion he had found to vary it:—

'It is of the utmost importance always to bear in mind that a great command over the necessaries and conveniences of life may be effected in two ways, either by a rapid increase in the quantity and value of the funds destined for the maintenance of labour, or by the prudential habits of the labouring classes; and that as the former mode of improving their condition, is neither in the power of the poor to carry into effect themselves, nor can in the nature of things be permanent, the great resource of the labouring classes for their happiness must be in those prudential habits, which, if properly exercised, are capable of securing to them a fair proportion of the necessaries and conveniences of life, from the earliest stage of society to the latest.'—(P. 260.)

The mind of Mr Malthus was not so positively set upon permanent measures as to think lightly of temporary ones; he only wished that we should know that they were but temporary, and that when we had made the most of them, we could make them nothing more. He has himself objected to the habit in theoretical writers of overlooking intervals of brightness and depression. Eight or ten years not unfrequently recurring, are, he observes, serious spaces in human life. Nobody, therefore, contended more strenuously in behalf of occasional relief for occasional distresses. At the same time, it is by a wise or fortunate co-operation with general principles, not only that measures of relief, but that the various chances which at its several stages civilisation may present, will be enabled to accomplish in this respect any lasting good. The greatest openings during the progressive advancement of society—the breaking up of feudal properties—a vast augmentation in the funds for the maintenance of labour—the discovery of remedies for mitigating diseases and saving the waste of human life, are all advantages which may be easily thrown away. Every thing depends upon the turn which the people happen to take under these new circumstances. Emigration may drain off the excess in the supply of labour on one hand, the abolition of restraints on commerce may extend the labour market on the other. But unless the lower orders avail themselves of the opportunity to raise their standard of comfort and to preserve it, when it has been once raised, by a prudent regulation of their numbers, the gleam will vanish with a single generation. There are many measures which are desirable as measures of occasional assistance; some, which may be indispensable as the means of giving prudential habits a space to form and act in. It is nevertheless equally true, that in prudential and moral habits, and in these alone, is lodged the specific remedy for the ever impending danger, with which the principles of population, at the same time that it excites, also menaces society.

Truth travels slowly even when she has left her well.ꞏ .Perhaps, of all books much talked about—certainly, of all books that ever exercised any thing like its influence, none has been so little read, or so frequently misunderstood, as Mr Malthus's celebrated essay. The problem to be solved, was, the means by which the existing proportion between food and population is regulated in different countries. Mr Malthus has tendered an explanation satisfactory to political economists. But there are numerous and clamorous objectors still. Some cannot comprehend it out of mere stupidity: among these Mr Grahame entitled himself to a distinguished place. Others will not give it a hearing from a sentimental or religious horror. For instance, Dr Southey, Mr Coleridge, and Bishop Huntingford. The last was wont, when we were schoolboys, to stop audacious argument with one word from the Scriptures, 'increase and multiply.' Others deny the testimony of all experience. Such was Mr Weyland. Others, rather than submit to a natural solution of the phenomena, call in a special interposition of Providence at every step. Of this class, were Mr Godwin and Mr Sadler; who followed the romantic precedent of Dr Price and M. Muret, and imagined arbitrary laws of fecundity in the human species —varying according to the occasion. Under the same standard, although flocking in from another quarter, are philosophers, of the calibre of Mr Anderson, Mr Owen, and Mr Poulett Scrope. These cause-mongers go also to the storehouse of their fancy for visionary laws. The only difference is, that the new laws which they are in search of do not regard the prolific powers of mankind, but the conditions which determine the augmentation of human food. According to their statistical information, it is, has been, and for ages will be, the food which is kept down to the level of population, and not the population which is kept back within the limits of the food. No wonder that among adversaries of this description there are found persons who still persist that Mr Malthus must be a friend to the small-pox, the plague, the slave-trade, and to every species of misery and vice. He is charged with having lost sight of the interests of the poor, while looking only to wealth; he who has declared, ' if a coun- ' try can only be rich by running a successful race for low wages, ' I should be disposed to say at once, perish such riches !' He is accused of underrating moral causes; although he has expressly stated, ' how very dangerous it is in political economy to ' draw conclusions from the physical qualities of the materials ' which are acted upon, without reference to the moral as well as

' the physicial qualities of the agents.' It is imputed to him that
he held slighting and dishonourable views concerning marriage.
Yet, in truth, no body ever put its desirableness higher. This
reproach was the more unjust: since in reality it was founded
solely on the anxiety which he had manifested to preserve the
marriage state in its purity and dignity, by holding it out to be
the reward of virtue, and by seeking to secure it in comfort
and independence. ' It should always' (he observed), ' be
' represented as, what it really is, a state peculiarly suited to
' the nature of man, and calculated greatly to advance his hap-
' piness, and to remove the temptation to vice; but like pro-
' perty, or any other desirable object, its advantages should be
' shown to be unattainable, except under certain conditions.'
A man has no more right to set up a wife unless he can afford it,
than to set up a carriage. The blameless life of Mr Malthus
served him as a shield which arrows could not pierce, and on
which dirt could not stay. He never paused or turned aside, or
seemed even for a moment to take notice of abuse. To have
made it of so much importance would have been an offence to
the imperturbable rectitude and tranquillity of his nature. When
he was obliged to speak of himself, he knew, however, that he had
a moral as well as an intellectual right to tell Mr Weyland, and
through him, the host of his abusers:—' I trust that I am dis-
' posed to attach as much importance to the effects of morality
' and religion on the happiness of society even as Mr Weyland;
' but among the moral duties, I certainly include a restraint upon
' the inclination to an early marriage, when there is no reason-
' able prospect of maintenance for a family; and unless this
' species of virtuous self-denial be included in morality, I am
' quite at issue with Mr Weyland: and so distinctly deny his
' proposition as to say that no degree of religion or morality, no
' degree of rational liberty and security of person and property
' can, under the existing laws of nature, place the lower classes
' of society in a state of comfort and plenty.'

We have said that the Essay on Population has been much
more talked about than read. This seems to have been almost
equally the case with adversaries and admirers. Among the persons who it might be taken for granted were thoroughly acquainted with it, Mr Senior would certainly have been one. Yet
Mr Senior gives a very different account of the matter in the
letters addressed by him to Mr Malthus, and appended to his
two lectures on Population. He there observes that he had been
misled in the representation he had given of Mr Malthus's opinions in his lectures by the way in which Mr Malthus had used
the word ' tendency:' and adds, ' I believe that I was led into

' this error principally by the conduct of all those writers who,
' since the appearance of your work, have written on population.
' The multitudes who have followed, and the few who have en-
' deavoured to oppose you, have all assumed this to be your opi-
' nion. And yet when I recur to your writings, I see how in-
' consistent it is with your uniform statement, that the pressure
' of population upon subsistence is almost always the most severe
' in the rudest states of society, where the population is the least
' dense, and the means of procuring subsistence, supposing they
' were employed, would be the greatest in proportion to that
' population.' Mr Senior has elsewhere stated that ' Mr Mal-
' thus's opinions appear to have been considerably modified during
' the course of his long and brilliant philosophical career.' We
have not been able to find in Mr Malthus's writings any evidence
for this assertion beyond the extent which we have already noticed. Mr Malthus considered the quarto edition of 1803 as
only nominally a second edition. It was in substance, as he
says in the preface, a new work—the first in which (beyond a
few words on Mr Pitt's Poor Bill) he carried the application of
principles to public measures—the first in which he examined
the subject in its details : and the first which he thought worthy
of his name. Nothing is easier than to ascertain the subsequent
alterations which Mr Malthus introduced. In the preface to the
third edition he almost enumerates the single paragraphs which he
had changed. Mr Senior proceeds, 'But when the opposite doctrine,
' namely, that, in the absence of disturbing causes, subsistence
' is likely to increase more rapidly than population, was brought
' before him by Mr Senior, he appears to have disavowed, we
' will not say his former expressions, but the inferences to which
' they lead.' Mr Malthus's letter, as we read it, is so far from
being a disavowal of any expressions or inferences to be found
in his writings, that it appears to us to be a re-affirmance of
them all. The constant pressure of population, he repeats, is
the essence of the principle of his work. This pressure, therefore, must be felt in all stages of society ; the only difference
between an unimproved and an improved state of society will be
the nature of the check employed—in the one case misery and
vices of an atrocious kind ; in the other, moral restraint, together with mitigated misery and vicious habits of a more humane
and polished character. There will be still existing, therefore,
not merely a tendency to press, but an absolute pressure ; the
difference being only this — that the pressure is not now so
visible and shocking as at former times. In the further progress
of civilisation it may be in some countries less severe than it is
at present in England, and of a less immoral or violent descrip-

tion; yet, unless human nature changes, the advantages to be looked for in this direction, however indefinite, are not unlimited. The failures, we apprehend, must, in that case, continue to be so numerous, that population will after all be still ' kept principally ' back by vice and misery,' and the deduction to be made on this account from the ' permanent welfare of the mass of mankind' will still remain much more than can be made consistent with any scheme of a complete command over the means of comfortable subsistence by every body upon earth.   We know of our own knowledge that Mr Malthus did not mean to retract, nor did he consider that he was understood to have retracted in this correspondence a single syllable of the opinions which he had previously published.   He observes in his letter that he prefers his own words and meaning to what Mr Senior proposed to substitute.   Some time afterwards, on alluding to the above discussion, he remarked, that it was among the disadvantages of public lectures, that the lecturer sometimes thought he was called upon to say something new, where nothing new was to be said.   In case Mr Malthus had been convinced of the reasonableness of the objection taken to the language in which he had expressed himself, he would not have hesitated a moment to give it up.   He was fully aware of the risk to which he had been exposed.   In consequence, he observes, in the additions made to the Essay in 1817; ' It is probable, that having found the bow ' bent too much one way, I was induced to bend it too much the ' other, in order to make it straight.   But I shall always be quite ' ready to blot out any part of the work which is considered by ' a competent tribunal as having a tendency to prevent the bow ' from becoming finally straight, and to impede the progress of ' truth.'   The supposed deflection is so slight, that, after much careful looking for it, we have been unable to perceive it.   The friends of truth need wish for nothing more than that the bow may be always kept in equally prudent hands.

Mr Senior is among the most clear and judicious expounders of Political Economy.   He closes his notice of this little controversy with bearing his admiring testimony to the services which Mr Malthus had conferred upon the science to which he himself so honourably belongs.

' Although Mr Malthus himself, in his earlier publications, has, perhaps, fallen sometimes into the exaggeration which is natural to a discoverer, the error, if he has committed one, does not affect the practical conclusions which place him, as a benefactor to mankind, on a level with Adam Smith.   Whether, in the absence of disturbing causes, it be the tendency of subsistence or of population to advance with greater rapidity, is a question of slight importance, if it be acknowledged that human happiness or misery depend principally on their relative advance, and that there are causes, and causes within human control, by which that advance can be regulated. These are propositions which Mr Malthus has established by facts and reasoning, which, opposed as they were to long-rooted prejudice, and assailed by every species of sophistry and clamour, are now admitted by the majority of reasoners, and even by a large majority of those who take their opinions upon trust.'

Mr Ricardo's estimate of the merits of the Essay on Population is as strongly expressed in one of his letters. What is here called the first edition is evidently the edition of 1803.

' The edition which I have of your work is the first, and it is many years since I read it. The general impression which I retain of the book is excellent. The doctrines appeared so clear and so satisfactorily laid down that they excited an interest in me inferior only to that produced by Adam Smith's celebrated work. I remember mentioning to you, and I believe you told me that you had altered it in the following edition, that I thought you argued in some places as if the poor rates had no effect in increasing the quantity of food to be distributed—that I thought you were bound to admit that the poor laws would increase the demand, and consequently the supply. This admission does not weaken the grand point to be proved.'—(January 1816.)

On the publication of the fifth edition, Mr Ricardo wrote as follows:—

' I thought I had written to you about the additional matter in your excellent work, although I had not given it all the examination I intended. I read it as I was travelling, and noticed the pages wherever I saw the shadow of a difference between us, that I might look at the passages again when I got home, and give them my best consideration. I have it now here, and have been reading all the new matter again, and am surprised at the little that I can discover with the utmost ingenuity to differ from. In every part you are exceedingly clear, and time only is wanted to carry conviction to every mind.'—(Oct. 1817.)

Mr Malthus's Essay on Rent was a masterly performance, of which Mr Ricardo always spoke in the highest terms. The near approach which preceding writers, for instance Dr Anderson in the Bee, may have made to the correct principles, detracts little from its merits. While the independent but simultaneous publication by the late Sir E. West only shows that the science upon this subject had reached the point where accident or industry will determine to which of the leading minds the discovery shall fall. The substance of this Essay has been transferred to the Principles of Political Economy. This is not the case with Mr Malthus's other minor writings. A collection of them would form a very interesting volume. We wish some bookseller would undertake it. They are excellent examples of clear reasoning, comprehensive views, and, above all, of incomparable fairness. A list of them is given at the 42d page of the Memoir.

To which may be added two papers published in the Transactions of the Royal Society of Literature : several papers, in this Journal: and an article in the Quarterly Review, on the main differences by which the new school of Political Economy is distinguished from the school of Adam Smith and Mr Malthus. This last article he considered one of the best things which he had ever done in Political Economy.

Mr Malthus was not fond of storms, as the petrel is said to be, for their own sake.   But it will be seen, on looking at the date and nature of his pamphlets, that he usually turned out in one. At these times, the opportunity of being useful was excitement enough: and his spirits rose with the occasion.   The exuberant chivalrousness of his youth had sobered down with years into a quiet civil courage, of which you were always sure.   For it was grounded upon a just confidence in the purity of his intentions and the goodness of his cause.   'He feared no danger, ' for he knew no sin.'   His ' investigation of the cause of the ' present high price of provisions' in 1800 was a good beginning. An ignorance of the real cause of the extreme highness of the price in proportion to the scarcity, as well as of the remedial proceedings which a scarcity required, was endangering the public peace.   It was a novel thing for a young clergyman to be seen protecting middle-men and corn-factors against mobs and magistrates, and warning the ignorant of all classes to take heed of the perilous consequences of their selfish passion.   He recommended the abolition of the assize of bread, and told the people that the ' popular clamour, headed by the Lord Chief Justice, and enforced ' throughout the country by the instructions of the Grand Juries, ' must make every reflecting mind tremble for the future supply ' of our markets.'

Another instance, although somewhat in a different way, is his pamphlets of 1814 and 1815 on the effect of Corn Laws.   He was quite aware of the risk which his reputation was running by the course of argument he pursued on that occasion.   He said that he well knew that nothing he had ever written had injured it so much. On the whole, too (to use his favourite summing up), he was not on this occasion as sure as usual of the soundness of the judgment which he had pronounced.   He continued to think that the friends of truth and of fair-dealing had received considerable provocation by the one-sided manner, as well as by the insolence of personal imputations with which the discussion had been conducted against the landlords.   He deemed it highly useful that inflammatory declamation should be met by cool argument—that both sides of the question should be heard with patience, and unreasonable expectations, one by one, exposed.   There are invidious duties which it demands a certain spirit to discharge.   Of these, he felt it to be one, to put people upon their guard—that they were not to expect from the repeal of Corn Laws, advantages of a kind which no repeal of measures of this nature could possibly confer. This duty he never regretted that he had performed.   But his general principles in favour of freedom of trade were so absolute, that, at times, doubts came over him, whether any exception ought to be admitted.   It follows, that he was far from continuing always equally satisfied that the necessity of the particular exception, which he had argued, in behalf of restrictions upon the importation of corn was sufficiently made out.   It may be useful to those people who believe that they have only to know what is a person's interest, in order to be enabled infallibly to infer what will be his opinions, to attend to what Mr Malthus has said in this respect, with regard to the doctrines held on Corn Laws and on Rent by Mr Ricardo and himself.   ' It is somewhat singular that Mr Ricardo, a con- ' siderable receiver of rents, should have so much underrated their ' national importance, while I, who never received nor expect ' to receive any, should probably be accused of overrating their ' importance.   Our different opinions, under these circumstances, ' may serve at least to show our mutual sincerity, and afford a ' strong presumption, that to whatever bias our minds may ' have been subjected in the doctrines we have laid down, it ' has not been that, against which perhaps it is most difficult to ' guard, the insensible bias of situation and interest.'

A universal distrust of mankind will not only often lead to personal injustice—it must be also often injurious to the public service.   To substitute general suspicion for a knowledge of cha- racter is a poor way of governing.   On two occasions Mr Mal- thus replied in print to charges made against the East India College, where he held the office of Professor of Political Eco- nomy.   Mr Ricardo once remonstrated with Mr Douglas Kin- naird, for treating the authority and the testimony of Mr Malthus with so little ceremony, in one of his speeches against the Col- lege at the Court of Proprietors.   Mr Kinnaird thought it a sufficient answer to observe that Mr Malthus was an interested witness.   Now, the only advantageous way in which the English public can interpose on behalf of the people of India, is to secure at home as far as possible the moral and intellectual qualifica- tions of the civil servants: that is, to raise and verify the capa- bilities of the young men who are periodically sent from England to be the real governors of that distant empire.   We suppose that a similar scepticism on the possibility of disinterested answers is more widely spread.   It seems otherwise scarcely possible, that on the different occasions when the most effectual means of improving that important service have been under discussion, the public should take so little interest in learning from the only people who can really tell them how much, in this respect, the East India College has done—wherefore it has done no more up to the present moment—and what it is, which it may be made capable of doing. This principle of universal scepticism is of late constantly interposed in the way of truth and reason. For instance, no Irish country gentleman is to be allowed, at the peril of his character, to have an opinion on Irish poor laws, save upon one side : and that not the side maintained by Malthus. Push the principle a little farther: and all appropriate knowledge will be excluded upon almost every subject. No Irishman must speak at all for or concerning Ireland. And only fools and knaves will have the monopoly of being heard as the only impartial witnesses, wherever sense or virtue are concerned.

We have already given from their correspondence some of Mr Ricardo's criticisms on Mr Malthus's writings. The correspondence is equally honourable to them both. Mr Ricardo expresses more than once his wish that the public might have the benefit of their discussions. We doubt whether they could ever have their discussions in a more instructive,—we are sure they never could in a more delightful form.

' I should be very glad if we could fairly submit our different views to the public, that we might have some able heads engaged in considering them.' (October, 1816.) ' Your excuse for not going on with the discussion which you commenced is ingenious, and I ought to be satisfied with it, as it is accompanied with a pretty compliment to me—indeed as pretty a one as could well be paid to a person who is so uniformly your adversary. I, however, agree with you ;—we know each other's sentiments so well, that we are not likely to do each other much good by private discussion. If I could manage my pen as well as you do yours, I think we might do some good by a public discussion.'—(November, 1821.)

Mr Ricardo took a pleasure in stimulating his friend's exertions where they differed. When they agreed, he felt a still more generous triumph in his success.

' I am pleased to learn that you are busy writing, with a view to immediate publication. The public pay a most flattering attention to any thing from your pen, and you are not fulfilling your duty to society, if you do not avail yourself of this disposition to endeavour to remove the cloud of ignorance and prejudice which every where exists on the subjects which have particularly engaged your time and reflection.'—(January 13th, 1815.) ' We have a right to look to you for the correction of some difficulties and contradictions with which political economy is encumbered.'—(May, 1816).

260

It is not often that criticism is invited with the ingenuous sincerity contained in the following challenge :—

'With regard to any remarks on my opinions, you must be governed by your own discretion. If those opinions are wrong, I should like to see them refuted, but, thinking as I do, that they are, in all essential points, founded on correct principles, I ask for no mercy. I do not care how severely they are attacked ; there is nothing you could say of them which would hurt me, if what you said did not express contempt, and that I know you do not feel for me. ·Act, therefore, towards me as if I were a perfect stranger, and notice me or not as you think best.'—(March, 1815.) 'When I say mine is the true faith, I mean to express only my strong conviction that I am right. I hope you do not attach any thing like arrogance to the expression. I am in the habit of asserting my opinion strongly to you, and I am sure you would not wish me to do otherwise. I am satisfied that you should do the same by yours, and I dare say you will agree with me that you are not more inclined to mere authority without being convinced than I am.'—(October, 1820).

How true is it that the greatest minds have the least affectation and conceit ! Mr Ricardo's confidence, as above expressed, was graced by the most unfeigned humility. He thus acknowledges a compliment, which Mr Malthus had paid him in the first edition of his political economy.

'The compliment you pay me in one of your notes is most flattering. I am pleased at knowing that you entertain a favourable opinion of me, but I fear that the world will think as I think, that your kind partiality has blinded you in this instance.'—(4th May, 1820).

The last sentence in what we believe was the last letter which Mr Ricardo wrote to Mr Malthus before his death, is a fit conclusion to this remarkable correspondence.

'And now, my dear Malthus, I have done. Like other disputants, after much discussion, we each retain our own opinions. These discussions, however, never influence our friendship; I should not like you more than I do if you agreed in opinion with me.'—(31st August, 1823).

It is not to be wondered at, after this tender and almost prophetic parting, if the only time that we ever saw an approach to anger on the countenance of Mr Malthus, was, when he once mentioned attempts which had been made to cause or represent a jealousy between them. He added, ' I never loved any body ' out of my own family so much. Our interchange of opinions ' was so unreserved, and the object after which we were both en- ' quiring was so entirely the truth, and nothing else, that I can- ' not but think we sooner or later must have agreed.'

The world knows nothing of Mr Malthus but as a political economist. He was also an excellent judge of human life in all its bearings, and not the less so, from his disposition to look at every thing on its brightest side. His particular opinions have been called melancholy. But he neither thought them so, nor found them so. The result of his general observation on mankind was even more favourable than that of Paley, who has always been considered (and justly) a very cheerful moralist. Paley rose up so embarrassed and subdued from a view of this life only, that he refuses, in his Natural Theology, to argue the case of the Divine benevolence, except on the supposition of a future state. On the contrary, life, in the eyes of Mr Malthus, 'independently ' of a future state, was, generally speaking, a blessing :' its partial pains were ' dust in the balance ;' and, ' we have every reason' (he says) ' to think, that there is no more evil in the world than ' what is absolutely necessary as one of the ingredients ' in the mighty process.' His views respecting the specific object of the mighty process carrying on in this life were of a sort that are useless to the great body of mankind ; and as they were unsatisfactory to some of his private friends, he left them to their fate, to perish with his reply to the perishable theories of Condorcet and Godwin. They contain, however, the principle of the answer which he continued to give, as often as he was applied to for a philosophical solution of the problem of human life.

' It is an idea that will be found consistent equally with the natural phenomena around us, with the various events of human life, and with the successive revelations of God to man, to suppose that the world is a mighty process for the creation and formation of mind. Many vessels will necessarily come out of this great furnace in wrong shapes. These will be broken and thrown aside as useless ; while those vessels whose forms are full of truth, grace, and loveliness, will be wafted into happier situations, nearer the presence of the Mighty Maker.'

But Mr Malthus was not, what we sometimes see, a philosopher on paper only : able to legislate for society—unable to judge wisely, to will resolutely, and to act consistently at home. He knew himself and the degrees according to which different things were either suitable to or desirable for him. If he had judged of mankind by his own standard, he must have admitted as a truth that which he was constantly reproving as an error— the supposition, that all people were endowed with the requisite sagacity for discovering their true interest, and with the requisite strength of character to steadily abide by it. This power seemed in his own case to be so thoroughly innate, that we have often wondered whether it always was so, or what were the sort of difficulties which he had to overcome. There was nothing of the schools about him ; no constraint which suggested the thought of bygone efforts ; none of those pedantic rules, which are the common props and outworks of artificial virtue or hollow reputation. Every thing in him was accessible and easy. While he had no fear of the masters of the earth getting in the way of his sunshine, he was sensible of the advantages of money and station up to a certain point. On the other hand, he saw that the point was reached, and that the turn at which the disadvantages begin to preponderate, takes-place much sooner than many, who are yet neither misers nor spendthrifts, are in the least aware. The pleasures of the affections and of the understanding had long flowed in so freely and uninterruptedly upon him, that we are certain he would have regarded with apprehension any change in his position which would have encroached upon these enjoyments, and substituted more brilliant engagements in their room. At the same time, the disposers of preferment, whose favour he courted only by deserving it, have on this account nothing to plead in their excuse. It did not lie in the path which they are treading to ask what were the wants, the wishes, or the claims of the first Political Economist of his age. In saying ' Malthus alone escaped their judging eye,' there is no exception to be made in respect of any bishop that we ever heard of. With regard to great men and governments : Lord Liverpool had an aversion for political-economy-clergymen. We should like to know, notwithstanding, to what class of men on the face of the earth a knowledge of political economy can be more necessary than to the men who by their office are the most usual distributors of public charity, and the appointed teachers of the poor. Lord Lansdowne and Lord Holland, we believe, did every thing in their power. But the fact is not the less painful. To the discouragement of great abilities, virtuously employed, and to the discredit of his country, Mr Malthus, at the age of seventy, died, having never held any thing in the Church, except some small family preferment. Were it not that it would seem to contradict its serene expression, we have often thought of writing under Linnell's admirable portrait of him, " Ingrata Patria." When we look at the nature of the pretensions in favour of which claims like those of Mr Malthus were, in point of fact, postponed, what are we to think of the destiny which overhangs the Church, and of the effrontery which continues to contend, that cathedral stalls and unequal livings must be kept up as the rewards of literary merit ? The abuse of patronage has destroyed cathedral chapters. If it is persevered in, it must hasten the reformation of the remaining inequalities in the distribution of church property. An abuse of this nature is an evil which they that run can read : it is therefore the specific kind of evil which brings establishments to an untimely end. Paley put a question concerning Church

property fifty years ago. ' To those who have the manage-
' ment of such matters I submit this question ; whether the impo-
' verishment of the fund, by converting the best share of it into *an-*
' *nuities* for the gay and illiterate youth of great families, threatens
' not to starve and stifle the little clerical merit that is left amongst
' us ?' (Moral Philosophy.) Paley asked the question. How was
he answered? By neglect. The Church of England must be supposed to be either indifferent to clerical merit, or to be well assured that the clerical merit which it has is of a kind that can
neither be starved nor stifled by human means. Otherwise it
never could have expected it to survive the last half century of
Suttons and Tomlines, Sparkes and Fishers. We are speaking
much more in behalf of the public than in either anger or
sorrow, on the personal account of Mr Malthus. With him,
' Goodness and greatness were not means but ends.' Im-
passive to abuse, almost unconscious of neglect, he was nevertheless peculiarly susceptible to praise. He often spoke of
it as the thing which more than any other affected him to
tears. Few things could have touched him more sensibly than
any mark of public gratitude and private sympathy from the
members of a government in whose political creed he perfectly
agreed. If the poor law amendment bill has been difficult to
carry, even under existing circumstances—it would have been
absolutely impossible, unless Mr Malthus had stood in the gap
for so many years, bearing the brunt of argument and obloquy,
fearless of danger, regardless of every interest but the interests
of truth.

The faculties and qualities of Mr Malthus appeared not simply to be in harmony with, but to be supported by each other.
The keeping was so complete, that you could not imagine them
apart; nor conceive that his moral or intellectual nature would
have been either of them what they were, unless they had met,
and acted, and grown up together. They had this, too, in common. The strength of both equally lay in the exquisite proportion of their respective parts. There was, in both cases, an
irresistible, though imperceptible superintendence, which kept
every thing in its proper place, and gave consistency and unity to
the whole. The consequence was, that the whole produced an effect much beyond what might have been expected from a separate examination of the parts of which it was composed. Instead of the waste of intellectual power, or the wear and tear of
moral struggles, in which so much of ordinary existences is consumed, he had always the clear mastery and possession of himself. The law of his nature fulfilled its onward course, free from
disturbing causes. A smooth and winning calmness was thus

spread over all his motions, and diffused through his inmost being, making his life a mirror of clear and flowing waters, which it was beautiful to behold. But in order that a stranger may adequately appreciate an excellence of this order, it is necessary that he should become well acquainted with it. He must have time to see and take in the whole. For it is not in buildings only that one of the first effects of perfect proportion is to diminish apparent size, and that some degree of taste and experience is wanted to understand the nature and extent of the advantages which it confers. Mr Malthus in this manner combined and reconciled opposite natures in his own. He was upright without severity, blameless without insipidity, amiable without weakness. There was no counterbalancing of great virtues by great faults; no purchasing of an exemption from faults by the absence of virtues. It seemed almost as though he could not have had more of any virtue than he had without introducing some defect; so that, although a more brilliant exterior might easily be imagined to have been thus produced, the alteration nevertheless would probably have injured the proportion of the whole, and rendered it less powerful and less complete.

But more than this. The endowments of head and heart which were most characteristic of Mr Malthus, were precisely those which are more captivating than striking. They did not break out in sparkles, or come up in bubbles on the surface at a moment's notice; but were in their nature so calm and deep, that a superficial looker-on might pass them over altogether. He was eminently wise and good. Now, wisdom and goodness are not things to be judged of at first sight. We can easily understand that persons may have been thrown into his company, at a dinner party, or even at the Political Economy club, and have gone away with a certain feeling of disappointment. It is not ladies and gentlemen out of the country only, who require from the tongue of every distinguished man—no matter what may be the nature of his reputation—the successive sallies of a professional diner-out. Mr Malthus was so wanting in all the conditions necessary to display, that a Boswell would have lost his time with him. There was nothing about him of the flights of Burke. He would never have astonished the companion of five minutes caught with him in a shower under Temple Bar. He had, if possible, still less of the coarse antagonistic propensity which made so much of the conversational fame of Johnson. Instead of treating every company he fell in with as an enemy's party, whom he had to attack, expose, and rout, Mr Malthus felt it a duty and delight to accommodate himself to his company, and to put every body at their ease. He had no taste or talent for striking out sudden incongruous resemblances ; but he excelled in tracing the simpler associations of thought, which are the very links of truth, and (as far as they depend on cause and effect) the elements of all useful knowledge. His playfulness, like that of almost all men eminent also for their judgment, took more the form of humour, than of wit. The humour which had distinguished him at school and college gradually subsided into an enjoyment of it in others rather than the exercise of it in himself. His early essay of 1798 had had in it much of the freshness of style, the various allusions and pleasant tone of Tucker. The disingenuous manner in which a portion of its figurative language was afterwards turned against him, naturally tended to confine him for the future, when addressing the public, to the course of his argument. He had been taught the danger of playing with this species of edge-tools. The scientific character of his later writings, and the unremitted thought which he of necessity bestowed on them, must also have powerfully contributed to the same effect. Accordingly an afternoon might only exhibit a character of this kind in the light of a very sensible and well-bred person. This never could be otherwise. For, from the sole of his foot to the crown of his head, Mr Malthus was a perfect gentleman, at all times and under all circumstances. But it was by degrees— seeing him day after day—that the extent and beauty of his nature unfolded itself to your view. His tastes and habits were, in truth, so simple and unassuming, that you were left to yourself, as occasion might occur, to discover his superiority. The discovery, when made, was so much the more delightful.

Mr Malthus had also this great advantage—whatever was his understanding, he always gave himself the full use of it. Its light was dry light, there was nothing of temper to discolour it, or of obliquity to turn it. The rectitude of his judgment was not simply left undisturbed; it was invariably aided by the rectitude of his purpose. In estimating the relative importance of different subjects he had no criterion but their tendency to promote or to retard the happiness of mankind. In investigating the particular subject on which he might happen at any time to be engaged, he seemed to have no conception of the possibility of any other object than the discovery of truth. The combination of these two characteristics made him in all private relations, however serious or however trifling, always the same, strictly equitable and considerately indulgent. We have seen his sense of equity severely tried. As soon as he saw his way, there was not a moment's pause. The ease with which he rose, as it were, upon the wing and bore away into a purer region, was morally sublime. He was far from being indifferent to fame. But his devotion to

truth was so intense that he seemed physically incapable of ar-
guing for victory. He was by no means unconscious of the value
of his philosophical services.   But there was an utter absence of
all personal consideration in the main satisfaction which he derived from the survey of them ; and he cared little in comparison
who it was that had been right, provided only that the right prevailed. We are confident, in case, on farther discussion, his theory
of population had been overthrown, that all sense of mortification
would have been lost in the tranquil exultation that man had
made good another step towards the vantage ground of truth.
As is observed in the present *Memoir*, his love of excellence was
quite distinct from the love of excelling.   It is difficult to say
how much of this is to be attributed to the fact that in the
mode in which his education had been conducted, the motive of
emulation had been left comparatively quiet. Not a trace of any
consciousness of personal superiority ever appeared in his habits
or demeanour.   It is one of the blessings of well-ordered natures
to be always comparatively at leisure and unconstrained.   While
he was most deeply engaged in his philosophical speculations, he
could pass at once from his study to his drawingroom with an
elastic step and placid countenance, to animate and share the
cheerfulness around him. By a happy use of them, he made every
day the best kind of holiday.   But in later years, the days which
he seemed to set apart particularly to enjoy as such, were the periodical visits of Mr Whishaw and Mr Smyth, two of the oldest
of his friends.   At the time that he was celebrated all over Europe, he continued, at an advanced age, to discharge with exem-
plary punctuality the most minute routine duties of the College
at Hayleybury, of which he was so great an ornament. He presumed on nothing from his reputation ; he sought to be excused
from nothing on account of his standing and his years.   His
discretion and urbanity, his authority and attraction, made him
the most enviable colleague that the members of a public body
could ever wish to act with ; and his union of the severe and
gentle virtues was so rare and so complete, that he was equally
the object of their admiration and their love.

    The Bishop of Chichester, speaking of the character of Mr
Malthus in a social and domestic point of view, says truly—' It is
' difficult to speak of it in terms which would be thought extrava-
' gant by those who knew him intimately, and who, after all, are
' the only judges of it.'   He adds, ' His temper was so mild and
' placid, his allowances for others so large and so considerate, his
' desires so moderate, and his command over his own passions
' so complete, that the writer of this article, who has known him
' intimately for nearly fifty years, scarcely ever saw him ruffled,

' never angry, never above measure elated or depressed.' (*Memoir*, p. 49.) In what we have ourselves been saying on this point we have spoken only that which we had the happiness of seeing; and we know our testimony is true. His mild and benevolent form is often before us. God forbid that we should forfeit the privilege of calling up into our chambers of imagery that so benignant presence! Yet, undoubtedly, we should feel that all honourable recollection of his friendship was inconsistent with the consciousness of having trespassed in his praise a syllable beyond—what he valued above all things—the modest and simple truth. Taking him all in all, he was the best man and truest philosopher we ever were acquainted with. It is some consolation on the loss of him, that we did not wait for his death to canonize his virtues. Looking back upon them, we can only repeat for ourselves what Bishop Burnet says of himself and of his free and frequent conversation with Archbishop Leighton. ' For ' that pattern which I saw in him, and for that conversation which ' I had with him, I know how much I have to answer to God.'

APPENDIX

From *Edinburgh Review,*

August 1810

For the doubtful authorship of this article, see Semmel's article pp. 15-16 *supra*. (*Publisher*).

Art. XI. *Disquisitions on Population.* By Robert Acklom Ingram, B. D. 1809.

Reply to the Essay on Population by the Rev. T R. Malthus: *In a Series of Letters.* 8vo. London, 1808.

W E should scarcely have thought it worth while to take any notice of these disquisitions, which consist, in a great degree, of strange misapprehensions and misrepresentations of the doctrines they profess to discuss, if we had not observed, among many persons, besides Mr Ingram and his anonymous coadjutor, an ignorance of the principles of population, which seems to us nearly unaccountable, considering the careful and detailed manner in which the subject has been lately explained. The excellent work of Mr Malthus, though it has certainly produced a great and salutary impression on the public mind, appears to us to have been much more generally talked of than read, and more generally read than understood. To those who have gone over it with attention, without being able to understand it, we cannot flatter ourselves, that the few observations which we are about to make will be of much use ; but there is a class of readers for whom we cannot help feeling considerable affection, who are tempted, we believe, occasionally to turn over our transitory pages, when they would shrink from the perusal of a bound quarto, or two massive octavos. That these judicious persons are in nowise deterred from discussing the merits of the said quartos and octavos merely because they have not read them, every day's experience sufficiently proves ; and, indeed, it would be a cruel preventive check on conversation, to insist upon such previous drudgery ; but still, if we may judge of the feelings of others from our own under similar circumstances, it is, upon the whole, an advantage to a man to understand something about the subject on which he is going to deliver his opinion. It is a great gratification to us to think, that we have afforded this advantage to our friends, on many important subjects, in morals, politics, and the various branches of science ; and we would fain hope, that we may now render them a small service of the same kind, on the no less important subject of population. At all events, we can promise them, that what we are going to say will, in one respect at least, have a much stronger claim on their attention than the work of Mr Malthus,—that of brevity.

This celebrated work may be said to consist of two separate parts. In the first place, of some very important statements in point of *fact*, the truth of which neither is nor can be denied, though the different parts of the statement had never before been brought together, nor the nature of their connexion pointed out : and, in the second place, of certain *reasonings* and practical inferences deduced from these facts. Now, the first part, or the mere statement of indisputable facts, forms by far the largest and the most important part of the work ; and, strange as it must appear to every one who is capable of forming an opinion on the subject, it is to this part that the most violent objections have been made. It is for having stated, with inimitable caution and accuracy, facts which cannot possibly be called in question, that Mr Malthus has been assailed with such clamorous reproaches, —that he has been accused of sophistry, of presumption, of blasphemy, inhumanity, and love of vice and corruption. Against such charges, we know that he would disdain to be defended; nor would our compassion for those who have advanced them have been quite strong enough to make us undertake the hopeful task of undeceiving them, if their errors did not appear to originate in a few fundamental mistakes, which may probably obstruct the reception of important truths in more dispassionate minds.

The radical proposition, then, which we wish to impress upon our readers is, that throughout the greater part of his invaluable work, Mr Malthus is occupied merely with the statement, detail and illustration, of a few very important and radical *facts*, the truth and certainty of which, none of his detractors have been bold enough to call in question; and that, disclaiming all pretensions to discovery, he has aimed only at fixing the attention of mankind on the true character of certain phenomena that have always been before their eyes. To satisfy the most suspicious of our readers, how very innocent, and, at the same time, how very important this task was, we shall now endeavour to give such a short abstract of the fundamental principles of the work, as, we flatter ourselves, will occasion no perplexity to persons of the most slender capacity.

In the first book of the *Wealth of Nations*, Dr Smith, when explaining the causes which proportion the reward of labour to the extent of the funds for its support, justly observes, ' It is in ' this manner that the demand for *men*, like that for any other com- ' modity, necessarily regulates the production of men ;—quickens ' it, when it goes on too slowly ; and stops it, when it advances too ' fast. It is this demand which regulates and determines the state ' of population in all the different countries of the world—in North ' America, in Europe and in China ; which renders it rapidly pro- ' gressive in the first, slow and gradual in the second, and altoge- ' ther stationary in the last. ' This passage of Dr Smith, which we think we have heard first suggested to Mr Malthus the idea of his essay, is illustrated and confirmed by a crowd of indisputable facts, to whatever country on the globe our view may be directed.

In taking a survey of this kind, it will speedily be discovered to be a fact that admits of no dispute, that the rate of population is by no means the same in all the countries of the world,—and that there is a notable difference in its progress, not only in North America, for instance, compared with Europe or Asia in general, but a similar difference in the different states of Europe, at the same pe-

271

riod of time, and in the same state at different periods. As men cannot live without food, it will also be readily admitted to be a fact, that those variations in the rate of population must have been universally preceded and accompanied by variations in the means of maintaining labourers ; on which, indeed, the demand before mentioned must necessarily depend. Where these funds are rapidly increasing as in North America, the demand for an increasing number of labourers, makes it easy to provide an ample subsistence for each ; and the population of the country is observed to make rapid advances. Where these funds increase only at a moderate rate, as in most of the countries of Europe, there the demand for labourers is moderate ; the command of the labourer over the means of subsistence is consequently much diminished ; and the population is observed to proceed with a moderate pace, varying in each country, as nearly as may be, according to the variations in the funds for its support. Where these funds are stationary, as we are taught to believe is the case in China, and as has certainly been the case in Spain, Italy, and probably most of the countries of Europe, during certain periods of their history, there the demand for labour being stationary, the command of the labourer over the means of subsistence, is comparatively very scanty, and population is observed to make no perceptible progress, and sometimes to be even diminished.

In the second place, it is a fact equally notorious, that the actual increase of the funds for the maintenance of labour does not depend simply upon the physical capacity of any particular country to produce food and other necessaries, but upon the degree of industry, intelligence and activity, with which these powers are at any particular time called forth. We observe countries, possessing every requisite for producing the necessaries and conveniences of life in abundance, sunk in a state of ignorance and indolence, from the vices of their governments, or the unfortunate constitution of their society,—and slumbering on for ages with scarcely any increase in the means of subsistence, till some fortunate event introduces a better order of things ; and then, the industry of the nation being roused, and allowed to exert itself with more freedom, more ample funds for the maintenance of labour are immediately provided, and population is observed to make a sudden start forwards, at a rate quite different from that at which it had before proceeded.

This seems to have been the case with many of the countries of Europe, during some periods of their history ; but is more particularly remarkable in Russia, the population of which, though very early inhabited, was so extremely low before the beginning of.the last century, and has proceeded with such rapid steps since, particularly since the reign of Catherine II.

It is also a fact that has often attracted observation in a review of the history of different nations, that the waste of people occasioned by the great plagues, famines and other devastations, to which the human race has been occasionally subject, has been repaired in a much shorter time than it would have been, if the population, after these devastations, had only proceeded at the same rate as before. From which it is apparent, that, after the void thus occasioned, it must have increased much faster than usual ; and the greater abundance of the funds for the maintenance of labour, which would be left to the survivors under such circumstances, indicates again the usual conjunction of a rapid increase of population with a rapid increase of the funds for its maintenance. Just after the great pestilence in the time of Edward III., a day's labour would purchase a bushel of wheat; while, immediately before, it would hardly have purchased a peck.

With regard to the minor variations in the different countries of Europe, it is an old and familiar observation, that, wherever any new channels of industry, and new sources of wealth, are opened, so as to provide the means of supporting an additional number of labourers, there, almost immediately, a stimulus is given to the population ; and it proceeds, for a time, with a vigour and celerity proportionate to the greatness and duration of the funds on which alone it can subsist.

In the third place, it is no less certain and visible, that, in a few countries where the funds for the maintenance of labour are in great abundance, the rate at which population increases is so rapid, that, if it were to continue unabated, the largest and richest territory, nay, the whole globe of the earth, would, in a few centuries, be completely possessed ; but, as the great abundance of these funds appears absolutely to depend upon the circumstance of there being an abundance of good land to be had at a very low price, it is quite clear that this state of things cannot possibly continue ; and that the funds for the maintenance of labour must, in the progress of cultivation and population, cease to increase with the same rapidity very long before they come to a stop, or before the country can be considered as fully peopled. The impossibility of the continued increase of these funds at the same rate, will be still more evident when applied to the peopled states of Europe and Asia, under any imaginable system of government : and, in reference to the peopling of the whole earth, it involves a manifest absurdity, to suppose, that a certain abundance of the funds for the maintenance of labour, which, wherever it has been found to exist, depends upon the land bearing a very great proportion to the people, should experience no change, while this proportion was gradually altering, so as ultimately to become the opposite of what it was at first.

From this slight survey of what has certainly taken place, and is actually taking place, with respect to the funds for the maintenance of labour in different countries, we conceive that the three following propositions may be stated as among the *facts* least capable of being controverted.

1. That man, like all other animals, multiplies in proportion to the means of subsistence which, under the actual circumsances in which he lives, are placed within his reach.

2 That there is a power of increase in the human race, much greater than is generally exercised, always ready to exert itself as soon as it finds an opening ; and appearing continually in sudden starts of population, whenever the funds for the maintenance of labour have experienced an increase, in whatever way this may have been occasioned.

3. That this power of increase is so great, and, in its nature, necessarily so different from any increase which can result from adding together different portions of a limited quantity of land, or gradually improving the cultivation of the whole, that the funds for the maintenance of labour cannot, under any sytsem the most favourable to human industry, be made permanently to keep pace with such an increase of population as has been observed to take place for short periods in particular countries ; and consequently, as man cannot live without food, that the superior power of population cannot be kept on a level with the funds which are to support it, without the almost constant operation of considerable *checks*, of some kind or other.

What these checks are, is the next important question ; and, keeping in mind, that it is strictly and purely a question of mere *fact*, and not of reasoning or hypothesis, let us first hear Dr Smith. In speaking of the dependence of man, like other animals, on the means of subsistence, and of the impossibility of his increasing beyond them, he observes, ' But, in civilized soci-
' ety, it is only among the inferior ranks of people, that the
' scantiness of subsistence can set limits to the further multipli-
' cation of the species ; and it can do so in no other way, than
' by destroying a great part of the children which their fruitful
' marriages produce. '

As the poverty and misery which would destroy a considerable portion of children, must necessarily be most severely felt, not only by the human beings thus suffering, but by their parents and survivors, it must be acknowledged, that such a premature mor-

274

tality is a very harsh leveller ; and it is fortunate for the human race, that there are other ways besides this, by which population may proportion itself to the means of subsistence. Mr Malthus shows clearly, that the effects of the difficulty of providing for a family, do not appear merely in premature mortality, but in the delay of engaging in a connexion which is likely to be attended with such a consequence. And this view of the subject not only accords better with our ideas of a being who possesses the distinctive faculty of reason, but is completely confirmed by what is taking place in all the countries with which we are acquainted, where we find, that when the funds for the maintenance of labour become comparatively scanty, the marriages generally become later and less frequent.

It appears, then, without entering into any argument or detail, that the checks to population may be divided into two general classes—those which operate in *preventing the birth* of a population which cannot be supported, and those which *destroy it* after it has been brought into being ; or, as Mr Malthus has called them, the *preventive* checks and the *positive* checks.

The necessary and constant operation of some checks to population, in almost all the societies with which we are acquainted, being fully established, and these checks being most clearly divisible into the two before mentioned classes, we can scarcely hesitate in determining which of them we should wish to see put in operation.

It is observed, in most countries, that in years of scarcity and dearness, the marriages are fewer than usual ; and if, under all the great variations to which the increase of the means of subsistence is necessarily exposed from a variety of causes ; from a plenty or scarcity of land ; from a good or a bad government ; from the general prevalence of intelligence and industry, or of ignorance and indolence ; from the opening of new channels of commerce, or the closing of old ones, &c. &c., the population were proportioned to the actual means of subsistence, more by the prudence of the labouring classes in delaying marriage, than by the misery which produces premature mortality among their children,—it can hardly be doubted that the happiness of the mass of mankind would be decidedly improved.

It is further certain, that, under a given increase of the funds for the maintenance of labour, it is physically impossible to give to each labourer a larger share of these funds, or materially to improve his condition, without some increase of the preventive check ; and consequently, that all efforts to improve the condition of the poor, that have no tendency to produce a more favourable proportion between the means of subsistence and the popu-

lation which is to confume them, can only be partial or temporary, and muft ultimately defeat their own objeçt.

It follows, therefore, as a natural and neceſſary cónclufion; that
in order to improve the condition of the lower claſſes of fociety,
to make them fuffer lefs under any diminution of the funds for
the maintenance of labour, and enjoy raore under any actual
ftate of thefe funds, it fhould be the great bufinefs to difcourage helplefs and improvident habits, and to raife them as much
as poffible to the condition of beings who ' look before and
after.' The caufes which principally tend to fofter helplefs, indolent and improvident habits among the lower claſſes of fociety, feem to be defpotifm and ignorance, and every plañ of con-
duçt towards them which increafes their dependence, and weak-
ens the motives to perfonal exertion. The caufes, again, which
principally tend to promote habits of induſtry and prudence, feem
to be, good government and good education, and every circumftance which tends to increafe their independence and refpeçtability. Wherever the regifters of a country, under no particular dif-
advantages of fituation, indicate a great mortality, and the general prevalence of the check arifing from difeafe and death, over
the check arifing from prudential habits, there we almoſt invariably find the people debafed by oppreffion, and funk in ignorance
and indolence. · Wherever, on the contrary, in a country without
peculiar advantages of fituation, or peculiar capability of increafe,
the regifters indicate a fmall mortality, and the prevalence of the
check from prudential habits above that from premature mortality ;
there, we as conftantly find fecurity of property eſtabliſhed, and
fome degree of intelligence and knowledge, with a taſte for clean-
linefs and comforts, pretty generally diffufed.

Nor does experience feem to juftify the fears of thofe who
think, that one vice at leaſt will increafe in proportion to the increafe of the preventive check to population. Norway, Switzerland, England and Scotland, which are moft diftinguiſhed for the
fmallnefs of their mortality, and the operation of the prudential
reftraint on marriage, may be compared to advantage with other
countries, not only with regard to the general moral worth and
refpeçtability of their inhabitants, but with regard to the virtues
which relate to the intercourfe of the fexes. We cannot, as Mr
Malthus obferves, eftimate with tolerable accuracy the degree in
which chaftity in the fingle ftate prevails. Our general conclufions muft be founded on general refults ; and thefe are clearly
in our favour.

We appear, therefore, to be all along borne out by experience
and obfervation, both in our premifes and conclufions. From
what we fee and know, indeed, we cannot rationally expeçt that

the paffions of man will ever be fo completely fubjected to his reafon, as to enable him to avoid all the moral and phyfical evils which depend upon his own conduct. But this is merely faying, that perfect virtue is not to be expected on earth ; an affertion by no means new, or peculiarly applicable to the prefent difcuffion. The differences obfervable in different nations, in the preffure of the evils refulting from the tendency of the human race to increafe fafter than the means of fubfiftence, entitle us fairly to con-clude, that thofe which are in the beft ftate are ftill fufceptible of confiderable improvement ; and that the worft may at leaft be made equal to the beft. This is furely fufficient both to animate and to direct our exertions in the caufe of human happinefs ; and the direction which our efforts will receive, from thus turning our attention to the laws that relate to the increafe and decreafe of mankind, and feeing their effects exemplified in the ftate of the different nations around us, will not be into any new and fufpi-cious path, but into the plain, beaten track of morality. It will be our duty to exert ourfelves to procure the eftablifhment of juft and equal laws, which protect and give refpectability to the low-eft fubject, and fecure to each member of the community the fruits of his induftry ; to extend the benefits of education as widely as poffible, that, to the long lift of errors from paffion, may not be added the ftill longer lift of errors from ignorance ; and, in general, to difcourage indolence, improvidence, and a blind indulgence of appetite, without regard to confequences ; and to encourage induftry, prudence, and the fubjection of the paffions to the dictates of reafon. The only change, if change it can be called, which the ftudy of the laws of population can make in our duties, is, that it will lead as to apply, more fteadily than we have hitherto done, the great rules of morality to the cafe of marriage, and the direction of our charity ; but the rules themfelves, and the foundations on which they reft, of courfe remain exactly where they were before.

This appears to us to be the substance of what Mr Malthus has said. Yet this theory, and these conclusions, simple and con-sistent as they appear to be, and resting, as they do all along, up-on the most obvious and undeniable facts, are rejected by a pret-ty large class of religious and respectable people, because they think, that the acknowledgement of a law of increase in the hu-man race greater than any possible increase of the means of sub-sistence, is an impeachment of the power or benevolence of the Deity. Mr Ingram says, ' that upon the first perusal of the senti-ments contained in the Essay, the religious mind revolts at the apparent want of intelligence and contrivance in the Author of the creation, in infusing a principle into the nature of man, which it required the utmost exertion of human prudence and ingenuity to counteract. '

In answer to this, and to all similar objections, we should observe, first, that we are not permitted to reject truths, of which our senses and experience give us the firmest assurance, because they do not accord with our preconceived notions respecting the attributes of the Deity. All our evidence for the prevailing benevolence of the works of creation—all our evidence of the power of the Creator—is derived from these sources. This evidence we must not, and cannot refuse to hear, in the first instance; and it is an after concern, to reconcile the undeniable state of the fact to the attributes which we assign to the Divinity.

But to such persons as Mr Ingram, and the class who often urge this objection, we have a further answer. We should observe, that from those who do not believe in revelation, we might expect such an objection; but that it appears to come with peculiar inconsistency from Christians. We do not pretend to be deep theologians; but we have always understood that the highest authorities, both in the English and Scotish church, have uniformly represented this world as a state of discipline and preparation for another; and indeed, that this doctrine is almost universally considered as the characteristic doctrine of the New Testament.

Now, we will venture to say, that, in the whole compass of the laws of nature, not one can be pointed out, which, in so peculiar and marked a manner, accords with this view of the state of man on earth. The purpose of the earthquake, the hurricane, or the drought, by which thousands and even millions of the human race are at once overwhelmed, or left to perish in lingering want— it must be owned, is inscrutable; particularly as we have been expressly cautioned, in scripture, not to be too ready to consider such events in the light of judgments for the offences of the persons thus suffering. Yet that these events, which are of obvious and acknowledged recurrence, should be passed over without difficulty by the Christian, and that he should be staggered by a law of nature, which eminently illustrates and confirms one of the main doctrines of his religion, is, we own, to us, quite unaccountable; and affords a very curious instance of the inconsistency of human reason. If it be really true, as we believe it is, that this life is a state of discipline and preparation for another, is it possible that we should find any difficulty in believing that a law of nature exists peculiarly calculated to rouse the faculties, and direct the exertions of the human race, which, by its varying pressure, and the various difficulties to which it gives rise, exercises and enlarges the powers of the mind, and calls into action all the great moral virtues which dignify and adorn human nature, as necessary to human happiness; which, above all, is constantly inculcating the necessity of the subjection of the passions to the dictates of reason and religion, and which, even if vice and misery were almost banished from the earth by the efforts of human virtue, would occasion the necessity of constant watchfulness and attention to maintain and secure the happiness which had been obtained?

On the other hand, if this law does exist, as we cannot for a moment doubt, from the evidence of incontestable facts, it merely affords a striking illustration and confirmation of that view of human life which is held out to us in the Scriptures; and, instead of being objected to by the Christian, it ought to be hailed as a powerful ally; as, to us at least, it appears to be one of those natural laws discovered by human experience, which may be urged with considerable force in favour of revealed religion.

The next class of objectors consists of worldly statesmen and politicians, who, at the slightest mention of checks to population, immediately conceive that our armies will want soldiers, and our manufactures hands. To such persons, it would of course be in vain to urge, that defence is better than conquest, and that the happiness of a society is a consideration paramount to the extent of its exports. If we had no other arguments than these, we know full well that it would be useless to urge them against such objectors. But, even these persons, we think, must allow, that the power of a country, both in war and in commerce, must depend upon that part of its population which is active and efficient, not upon that which is helpless and inefficient. If it has been found by experience that one country, which has, we will say, 200,000 births in each year, does not rear so many to puberty as another country which has only 160,000, must it not be allowed, that the first is the weaker of the two? And if, in addition to the question of numerical force, we take into consideration the state of misery and depression in the first country, which must have occasioned the premature mortality, we cannot doubt that the second would be infinitely superior in the industry and energy, as well as the happiness of its inhabitants. Not only would a country, where the checks to population arise from the prudential habits of the lower classes, rather than from premature mortality, possess a greater military and manufacturing population, with the same means of subsistence, but, from the very circumstance of the country's containing this larger proportion of persons in the active periods of life, the means of subsistence would stand a much fairer chance of being increased with rapidity. This is, in fact, confirmed by experience. England, Scotland, Switzerland and Norway, where the premature checks to population are obferved to prevail with the greateft force, increafe fafter in the funds for the maintenance of labour and, of courfe, in the population fupported by them, than moft of the countries of Europe that have a larger proportion of births.

So far, therefore, is it from being true, that the increafed prudence of the poor, with regard to marriage, would be attended with a falling off in the military and commercial population of a country, or by any obftru[] to its further increafe, as far as our experience has hitherto gone, it muft be acknowledged that its effe[]s have been juft the reverfe.

We have heard it, however, afked, whether, if the advice which inculcates an increafed prudence with regard to marriage, were really attended to, it might not be carried too far, and materially diminifh the population of a country, or prevent its increafe? In anfwer to this, we fhould readily allow, that the event, however improbable, was within the range of poffibility; but fhould add, that if fuch poffibilities were to preclude fimilar precepts, the range of moral inftru[]ion would be limited indeed. It will hardly be admitted, that we fhould be deterred from enforcing, with all our power, the precepts of benevolence in oppofition to felfifhnefs, becaufe, if we really made men quite regardlefs of their own interefts, we fhould do much more harm than good. There is, in fuch cafes, a mean point of perfe[]ion, which it is our duty to be conftantly aiming at; and the circumftance of this point being furrounded on all fides with dangers, is only according to the analogy of all ethical experience. The fa[] undoubtedly is, that, in the paft hiftory of the world, and in its a[]ual condition, we fee countlefs examples of the mifery produced by the negle[] of this prudential abftinence; and no inftance, even of the flighteft inconvenience, from its exceffive influence. As there is, in reality, no danger of ever making the mafs of mankind too generous or too compaffionate, fo there is juft as little of our depopulating the world by making them too much the creatures of reafon, and giving prudence too great a maftery over the natural paffions and affe[]ions. The prevailing error in the game of life is, not that we mifs the prizes through excefs of timidity, but that we overlook the true ftate of the chances in our eager and fanguine expe[]ations of winning them. Of all the obje[]ions that ever were made to a moralift who offered to arm men againft the paffions that are everywhere feducing them into mifery, the moft flattering, but, undoubtedly, the moft chimerical, is, that his reafons are fo ftrong, that if he were allowed to diffufe them, paffion would be extinguifhed altogether, and the activity, as well as the enjoyments of man, annihilated along with his vices.

What we have now ſtated is as much, we ſuppoſe, as the indolent ſtudents, for whoſe benefit it is chiefly intended, will be
well able to digeſt at a meal.　We ſhall ſtop here, therefore, for
the preſent ; and, if any of them are induced, by what we have
ſaid, to venture on the peruſal of Mr Malthus's entire book, we
engage, for their encouragement, to help them over the ſtartling
paſſages of it, by a ſhort examination of the other objections which
have been urged againſt it.